Serving Our Country

Serving
Our Country

*Japanese American Women
in the Military during
World War II*

BRENDA L. MOORE

RUTGERS UNIVERSITY PRESS
New Brunswick, New Jersey, and London

Library of Congress Cataloging-in-Publication Data

Moore, Brenda L., 1950–
   Serving our country : Japanese American women in the military during
World War II / Brenda L. Moore.
     p. cm.
Includes bibliographical references and index.
   ISBN 0–8135–3277–9 (cloth : alk. paper) — ISBN 0–8135–3278–7
(pbk. : alk. paper)
  1. United States. Army Women's Army Corps—History. 2. World War,
1939–1945—Participation, Japanese American. 3. Japanese-American
women—History. 4. Women soldiers—United States. 5. United States—
Ethnic relations. I. Title.
  UA565.W6 M66 2003
  940.54′04—dc21

                                      2002015875

British Cataloging-in-Publication information is available from the British Library.

Manufactured in the United States of America

This book is dedicated to the memory of my parents,
Hester W. Moore, December 12, 1929–February 9, 2002
Albert Moore, October 12, 1926–December 10, 1968

Contents

List of Tables   ix
Preface and Acknowledgments   xi

Chapter 1   Introduction   1

Chapter 2   Before the War   31

Chapter 3   Contradictions and Paradoxes   60

Chapter 4   Women's Army Corps Recruitment of Nisei Women   88

Chapter 5   Service in the Women's Army Corps   106

Chapter 6   Commissions in the Army Medical Corps   135

Chapter 7   The Postwar Years   148

Appendix: Wacs Who Entered the Army from
Hawaii, December 1944   167

Notes   169
Glossary   191
Bibliography   195
Index   203

Tables

1. Occupations of Nisei Women, 1943   18
2. Specified Quotas for the Enrollment of Nisei Women into the WAC by Service Command   19
3. War Relocation Authority Internment Camps   73
4. Military Intelligence Service Language School Courses   120

Preface and Acknowledgments

Y EARS OF STRAINED RELATIONS between the United States and Japan reached a climax on the morning of December 7, 1941, when Japan launched a successful air attack on Pearl Harbor and other nearby military installations in Hawaii, including Ewa, Kaneohe Bay, and Bellows, Hickam, and Wheeler Fields.[1] This attack left the American government in a state of shock: four U.S. battleships, three destroyers, and four small ships were obliterated. Some 288 American aircraft were damaged, and more than twenty-four hundred American lives were lost. By contrast, only the crew members of twenty-nine Japanese planes suffered casualties.[2]

On December 8, U.S. President Franklin D. Roosevelt went before a joint session of Congress and called for a declaration of war against Japan. Radio stations throughout the country broadcast the stirring words of the American president as he called December 7 "a day that would live in infamy." For Americans, the war was defined as a struggle against the governments of Axis nations—a battle against fascism, Nazism, and totalitarianism. But the war was also an event that would expose the paradox of American democracy and the injustices of American racism, and thereby lead to social change.

Virtually all Americans held the ideal of democracy in high esteem. Therefore it is not surprising that, as the United States prepared for combat, men and women of all racial and ethnic backgrounds answered the War Department's call to military service. Ironically, some of the people who supported the nation's war efforts were denied the very rights they were willing to fight and die for. Nonetheless, they contributed to the nation's war effort, in the hope of removing barriers to inclusion.

Today the World War II service of racial minorities and of women in the U.S. military has almost been forgotten. A number of scholarly works in recent years recall the contributions made by African American men and women to the U.S. war effort. Scholarly books, articles, and documentaries about the Tuskegee Airmen, the 6888th Central Postal Battalion, the Triple Nickles, and the Buffalo Soldiers were released as recently as the late 1980s and the1990s,[3] telling of these service members who struggled for a "double V"—victory abroad as well as victory over racism at home. Still, these studies are too few.

Similarly, not until recently have we begun to hear about the brave Japanese American men who participated in the war effort as members of Military Service Intelligence. These men engaged in battlefield intelligence, translated strategic documents, and interrogated the "enemy" in the Pacific Theater. Six thousand Nisei (children of Japanese immigrants, born in the United States) reportedly trained to serve with the Allied Forces in the Pacific; 3,700 served in combat areas.[4] In addition, the 100th Infantry Battalion, later united with the 442nd Regimental Combat Team (RCT), fought gallantly in Italy and in France.[5] History reveals that Japanese Americans sacrificed their lives in comparatively large numbers during the war.[6] Perhaps the greatest number of casualties occurred in October 1944, when the 442nd was sent on a mission to rescue the 36th Division's 141st Infantry Regiment, more commonly known as "the Lost Battalion." A reported 800 members of the 442nd RCT were either killed or wounded in the Vosges Mountains while rescuing 220 members of the Lost Battalion.[7]

Far less is known about the Nisei women who served in the United States military, most as members of the Women's Army Corps but some as nurses and doctors in the Army Medical Corps. The purpose of this book is to document the stories of Nisei women who served in the military during World War II, and to analyze the events that helped to shape their lives. What were their lives like before they entered the military? What motivated them to join the active armed services? What effect did military service have on their lives in subsequent years? These and other questions are explored.

Although the Women's Army Auxiliary Corps (the precursor to the Women's Army Corps) had been in existence since July 1942, Nisei women initially were denied entry.[8] The first Nisei woman was not inducted until November 1943. By December, five Nisei women had completed basic training at Fort Des Moines, Iowa. The Army Medical Corps, which included the Army Nurse Corps, opened to Nisei women in February 1943. Mary Yamada, a former member of the ANC, was among the women interviewed for this study; Yamada speaks about her experiences in applying for, and eventually serving in, the ANC.

The analysis presented here relies on both primary and secondary sources. I located and interviewed some of the Japanese American women who served in either the Women's Army Corps or the Army Nurse Corps (ANC). Of the fourteen Nisei women I contacted, twelve had served in the WAC and two had been ANC nurses. Nine agreed to participate in this study; five declined.

Eight of my nine informants had been Wacs, and one a member of the ANC. Four of these participants had been inducted into the service from the U.S. mainland; five had entered the military from Hawaii. Also included are excerpts from two interviews conducted by the National Japanese American Historical Society (NJAHS), the first with Cherry Shiozawa, a former Wac, and the other with Yoshiye Togasaki, a medical doctor. Togasaki joined the United Nations Rehabilitation and Relief Association (UNRRA) in 1945 to administer medical services at refugee camps in Europe; while applying, she learned that, because she would be serving in a war zone, she was required to become a commissioned officer in the U.S. Army. She revealed this experience in an oral history interview conducted by the NJAHS; with the permission of the NJAHS, excerpts from that interview are cited.

All names in this study are real except those of the four Nisei women who entered the military from the mainland; at their request, I refer to them throughout by pseudonyms. Using a life course perspective, I include firsthand accounts of these women's lives before and during military service. I also discuss at length the effect of military service on the women's later lives.

In addition, I examined thousands of pages of archival documents, as well as War Department and other government papers, on the sociopolitical status of Japanese Americans during World War II. I obtained these official records from sources including the National Archives in Washington, D.C., and in Suitland and College Park, Maryland; the Japanese American Historical Society in San Francisco and in Chicago; the National Japanese American Museum in Los Angeles; the Kroch Collection at Cornell University, Ithaca, N.Y.; the Department of Defense Language School in Monterey, California; the Romanzo Adams Social Research Laboratory at the University of Hawaii, Honolulu; and the U.S. Army Museum of Hawaii at Fort Shafter, Hawaii. Holdings at each facility revealed a different aspect of the lives of Japanese American women in general, and of Nisei military women in particular.

The voices of the nine women I interviewed are supplemented by those of the many Nisei servicewomen cited in newspapers during the war. In addition, they are supplemented by information found in nontechnical literature such as personal diaries and biographies.

Some of the photographs and military documents used here were provided by the estate of former Wac Florence Kanashiro Kahapea.

A former Nisei Wac stated in a letter to me, "You would need to do considerable research to reach even a partial understanding of the trauma suffered by the Nisei incarcerated without due process and the soul-searching motivation that led to our volunteering [for military service]." I hope that *Serving Our Country* will illuminate not only the military experiences of the Nisei women who volunteered, but also the historical, social, economic, and political factors that surrounded their lives during a period of mass upheaval. Documenting these women's military experiences as seen through their own eyes contributes greatly to our understanding of the role played by Japanese American women in national defense, and of their contribution to the country's progress toward the ideal of democracy.

This book has been the destination of a long, interesting journey. Many persons and organizations have given help along the way. I received grant support from the Ford Foundation, the State University of New York (SUNY) at Buffalo School of Law (Baldy Center), and SUNY at Buffalo College of Arts and Sciences Publication Subvention Fund. I am grateful to colleagues, anonymous reviewers, and the editorial staff at Rutgers University Press for their helpful comments on earlier drafts of this manuscript. I owe a debt of gratitude to the many archivists who assisted me in locating archival documents. I am thankful to the women who were kind enough to share their stories with me. Finally, I am deeply indebted to my family members and friends for their unyielding support.

Serving Our Country

Chapter 1

Introduction

*We have lived long enough in America to appreciate
liberty and justice. We cannot tolerate the attempt of a
few to dominate the world. We have faith in free
institutions, of individual freedom, and we have courage
of our convictions to back up our words with deeds of
loyalty to the United States government! . . . Fellow
Americans, give us a chance to do our share to make this
world a better place to live in.*

—Editorial published in
Japanese American newspaper[1]

SINCE THE AMERICAN REVOLUTION, the concept of the citizen soldier has existed in the United States. Historically, racial and ethnic minorities were afforded no more rights than noncitizens; many served in the armed services
with the expectation of attaining the citizenship rights denied them. Participation in the American armed services has always been viewed as an obligation of male citizens—free, white men. In the words of the late sociologist
Morris Janowitz, "Military service emerged as the hallmark of citizenship and
citizenship as the hallmark of a political democracy."[2] For minorities, military service was viewed as an avenue of upward mobility.[3]

Although U.S. citizenship initially was reserved for native-born white
males, the shortage of white manpower during wars often led to the recruitment of racial minorities, particularly African Americans but also Americans
of Hispanic and Native (American Indian) descent. In addition, European
and Asian immigrants were recruited. The U.S. government offered citizenship rights to men of racial minority (citizens) and immigrant groups (aliens)
in exchange for military service, yet the European male immigrants usually

indeed received citizenship in return for their service, the military achievements of racial minorities were quickly forgotten after the war.

The African American male soldier is a case in point. After World War I, African Americans were still denied civil liberties even though more than fifty thousand black men had served in Europe as stevedores, engineers, and laborers, as well as infantrymen in the acclaimed 369th, 370th, 371st, and 372nd all-black infantry units. Less than a year after World War I, seventy African American men were lynched in the United States; ten were soldiers in uniform.[4] These men died at the hands of angry mobs, for alleged crimes, without the court trial guaranteed by the U.S. Constitution. Moreover, in most southern states, African Americans were denied the right to vote, to hold jobs commensurate with their education and skills, or to purchase homes outside black neighborhoods.

These conditions would begin to change in the years following World War II, when the United States began addressing structural inequality against blacks. The contradiction between the American creed of democracy and the practice of racial discrimination directed against nonwhites came under severe attack during World War II; at its close, male military veterans of all racial backgrounds would begin reaping some of the benefits provided their white male counterparts. With the passage of the GI Bill (the Servicemen's Readjustment Act of 1944), military service enhanced opportunities for minority males to obtain higher education after the war and eventually compete more effectively for higher paying jobs.[5]

To encourage women to serve, the U.S. government emphasized the need to relieve men in support positions to take part in direct combat. American women had always been employed by the army as civilian nurses, clerks, laundresses, and telephone operators. Unlike white male immigrants, however, women were not offered citizenship rights in exchange. Moreover, they were not eligible to use military facilities, to receive government life insurance, or to be awarded military burial if killed while performing military service. This situation would also change during World War II, when servicewomen began to receive the same military benefits as men.

The social, political, and economic statuses of *Nisei* women who served in the military during World War II changed as well. Their lives are the subject of this book. Until now, the military contribution of Nisei women has received little or no attention in scholarly writings. With the exception of Stacey Hirose's M.A. thesis, "Japanese American Women and the Women's Army Corps, 1935–1950," and two chapters written on the topic, no study has been published about the contributions made to America's war efforts by Nisei military women.[6] This study documents the broad contributions made by Nisei women on active duty during World War II. In addition, I analyze the effects of military service on the women's subsequent lives. Historical facts, as well as the perceptions of Nisei women about their lives before, during, and after the war, are illuminated. Both macro and micro perspectives are employed as I explore how changes in the society in general, and in military service in particular, helped to shape the lives of these women.

In this chapter, I provide an overview of the issues to be discussed. I examine when Nisei women were inducted into the military and some of the circumstances that led the War Department to accept them, as well as the factors that motivated Nisei women to join the military. Finally, I examine the degree to which the family and friends of these women were supportive of their decision to put on the uniform.

Before World War II, women's service in the U.S. military was limited to the Army Nurse Corps (ANC). There is no record of Japanese American women serving in the ANC at that time. On the other hand, historical documents reveal that an estimated five thousand Nisei men were on active duty before the United States declared war on Japan.[7] To understand the social and political circumstances leading to military enrollment of Nisei women during World War II, we must first examine military policies governing the assignment of white women, as well as directives on how Japanese American men were to be utilized. At this intersection of race and gender, the story of Nisei women in the U.S. military begins to unfold.

Policies of Racial Exclusion

In the United States, race has been constructed on an axis between the two poles, black and white. The former represents racial oppression and exclusion, the latter symbolizes power and privilege. Historically, scholars have placed Japanese Americans somewhere between black and white in the racial hierarchy. At times Japanese Americans have been classified as being "near whites"; at other times they have been viewed as "just like blacks." [8] However, in recent years scholars have argued that the black/white paradigm falls short in identifying issues specific to non-white and non-black racial groups.[9] As argued by Angelo Ancheta:

> The racial experiences of Asian Americans . . . diverge fundamentally from the experiences of blacks. Subordination falls along a separate axis. . . . The axis is not white versus black, but American versus foreigner. . . . [T]he color dichotomy that operates to cast blacks as inferior to whites differs from the citizenship dichotomy that operates to cast all Asian Americans . . . as foreign-born outsiders.[10]

At no time in American history has this divergence been more apparent than during World War II. Japanese Americans occupied an ambiguous position in the racial landscape, neither black nor white. This racially obscure position made it difficult for the U.S. War Department to classify Japanese American soldiers. Prior to the bombing of Pearl Harbor, the War Department assigned Japanese American men to white units. These men were drafted to serve in the United States military under the Selective Service and Training Act of 1940, which stipulated that draftees and volunteers for military service would not be discriminated against because of race or color; they served in units with white soldiers, such as the 298th and 299th Infantry Regiments and the 7th Infantry Division, 6th Army. African American men, by contrast, were restricted by a seven-point policy implemented by the War Department: specifying, among other things, that they would serve exclusively in racially segregated (all-black) units.[11] (At this time, the active armed services were closed to women.)

The status of the Nisei soldier changed abruptly following the Japanese attack on Pearl Harbor. Shortly after the United States declared war on Japan, Nisei soldiers were discharged from their military units, and the induction of Japanese American men into the U.S. military was discontinued by an informal agreement between the War Department and the Selective Service System.[12] Ken Tagami, a Nisei soldier, was drafted into the U.S. Army in February 1941 and assigned to the 7th Infantry Division, 6th Army, under the command of General Joseph Stilwell. In a published interview, Tagami recalled that most Nisei in the 6th Army were eventually shipped out to Camp Crowder, a military installation in Missouri.[13] Tagami was ordered to surrender his weapon in February 1942, and subsequently was reassigned to the Military Intelligence Service Language School (MISLS), composed mostly of Japanese Americans.

Treated as foreigners, many Nisei soldiers were stripped of their weapons after Japan bombed Pearl Harbor. In their publication on Japanese Americans serving in the military intelligence, Clifford Uyeda and Barry Saiki revealed that some Nisei were even forced into prison compounds surrounded by machine guns. According to one study, these soldiers were discharged from the military and eventually were reclassified as "enemy aliens," undesirable for service:

> Many Nisei, inducted before Pearl Harbor, had been given honorable discharges, after the war began, with no specification of cause of dismissal. In March, 1942, potential Nisei inductees were arbitrarily assigned to IV-F, the category previously reserved for persons ineligible for service because of physical defects; and on September 1, 1942, this

classification had been changed to IV-C, the category ordinarily used for enemy alien. [14]

Allan Beekman reported that, in Hawaii, "[t]he draft status of the Nikkei (American of Japanese descent) was changed to 4-C, enemy alien, making them undraftable and unacceptable. At Schofield Barracks, 1,564 Nikkei soldiers were stripped of their weapons and demoted to work detail. On January 19, 1942, the Territorial Guard of Hawaii would brusquely dismiss its Nikkei members."[15]

An exception was made for Nisei men assigned to the MISLS, as well as those assigned to the 100th Battalion (a unit that evolved from the Hawaii National Guard). During the fall of 1942 the army policy was modified, permitting Nisei men skilled in the Japanese language to serve as teachers at MISLS. Some Nisei soldiers, such as Ken Tagami, were reassigned to MISLS after being discharged from their former units. Without the knowledge of the American public, several of these Nisei soldiers served as military translators, interrogators, and spies in the early phase of American involvement in the war. A few thousand, it is reported, served actively in the Pacific Theater of Operation, translating captured documents and monitoring radio traffic.[16] Some served in headquarters units, others with combat units. Members of the 100th Battalion were sent to Camp McCoy, Wisconsin, in June 1942, and later were assigned to Camp Shelby, Mississippi, before deployment to North Africa.

Most Japanese American men, however, were temporarily denied citizenship rights and the duty to serve in the military, until February 1, 1943. The suspension of Japanese Americans from military service was partly attributable to wartime exacerbation of the fear, hysteria, and discrimination so often present in societies intolerant of racial and ethnic differences. Although Japanese Americans were neither black nor white, before December 7, 1941, they were more closely aligned in the social landscape with whites than with blacks. They occupied the position of a middleman minority: relatively small-scale business people serving both the dominant white class and subordinate groups in the society.[17] When the United States declared war on Japan, the position of Japanese Americans changed, and it may appear, because of the extreme form of racial oppression they were subjected to, as though this position shifted toward that of blacks. Upon close inspection, however, it becomes evident that Japanese Americans became racialized during World War II, occupying a racial identity separate from that of whites or blacks. (I return to this subject in chapter 3.)

Surely anti-Japanese sentiments existed in the United States before World War II. Historian Roger Daniels asserts that the anti-Japanese movement in

California dates back to the late nineteenth century, when middle-class politicians and the National American Federation of Labor (NAFL) took a stand against all Asian immigration. Daniels identifies labor leaders such as Dennis Kearney, and politicians who fancied themselves progressive, as the leaders of this early anti-Japanese crusade. Still, although Japanese Americans suffered the effects of racial stereotyping before World War II, they experienced more severe forms of discrimination after Japan attacked Pearl Harbor.[18]

Some Nisei servicewomen remembered vividly growing up in an America that treated Japanese Americans differently than whites. Mary Yamada, a former member of the Army Nurse Corps, recalled a great deal of discrimination against Japanese Americans living in Los Angeles before the war. She described the situation of the Los Angeles Nisei during the Great Depression:

> I always knew that the Japanese were being discriminated against for
> one reason or another. I remember as a child, when I was working in
> our store, we used to have telephone poles in those days, and I
> remember seeing placards [saying] . . . "Japs Get Out." . . . Of course
> there was a lot of discrimination in Los Angeles, and I guess that was
> why I decided I would become a doctor. . . . But that was during the
> depression years, when I was at the university and many of the [Nisei]
> men were working at a fruit market; apparently they couldn't get
> jobs. . . . They had their degrees, but they couldn't get jobs.

Differential and inferior treatment of Japanese Americans was exacerbated after the bombing of Pearl Harbor. Irene Nishikaichi (a pseudonym), a former Nisei Wac, recalled that severe restrictions were imposed on Japanese Americans in California shortly after the Japanese air strikes: "Even before evacuation, I couldn't cross the street to go to school. This was around February whenever the presidential proclamation was issued. I could go up one side of the street, but I couldn't cross the street to go to school. So I had to drop out."

Japanese Americans became scapegoats for many Americans' desire for revenge on Japan. The hatred expressed against them was fueled by the fear and helplessness felt by non-Japanese Americans as they witnessed several military victories by Japan during this early phase of the war. In the words of tenBroek and Matson:

> Before they could recover from the initial shock, West Coast residents
> were confronted with more bad news. Coincident with the Pearl
> Harbor attack enemy forces had struck with disastrous effect at Hong
> Kong, Manila, Thailand, Singapore, Midway, Wake, and Guam.
> Japanese bombers had at a single blow destroyed the air defense of
> Hong Kong, and within a few days occupied Kowloon peninsula and

placed the British crown colony in jeopardy. On December 10 the "impregnable" British warships *Repulse* and *Prince of Wales* were sunk by Japanese planes, thus upsetting the balance of naval power in the far Pacific.[19]

Groundless talk of Japanese Americans aiding Japan by working as saboteurs spread throughout the United States. *Issei* farmers were accused of smuggling poison into vegetables bound for market and of growing flowers in a way that gave signals to enemy war planes.[20] Editors of a popular Japanese American newspaper published in Los Angeles responded in the following editorial:

> Rumors are always a nuisance to everyone. Loose talk, never substantiated, has resulted in untold grief, in great tragedies and irreparable damage. . . . Ever since the Japanese attack on Pearl Harbor, rumors were given out by responsible persons that a sabotage by resident Japanese was largely responsible for the success of Japan's initial attack. . . . Contrary to rumors, there was no sabotage in Honolulu on Dec. 7 when Japanese attacked Pearl Harbor, and there has been none since.[21]

As victims of racial antagonism, Japanese Americans living on the mainland (both Issei and Nisei) lost civil service jobs. In many cases, businesses were lost and professional careers were disrupted.[22] Grace Harada (a pseudonym), a former Nisei Wac, explained that her father lost his job and the family home in Idaho:

> My father worked for the railroad and when the war broke out, . . . because of his being of Oriental ancestry, they made him quit his job. . . . We didn't have to evacuate, but at the time [we] lived in a house the railroad owned because [my father] was a foreman, and [we] were entitled to live there. But then we had to vacate the house and move away.

Another former Nisei Wac, Ellen Fuchida (a pseudonym), described how her neighborhood in Utah changed after the Japanese air strikes at Pearl Harbor: "I had all these [Caucasian] friends I'd grown up with all my life and the only time we really felt different is when the war broke out. About three customers who had been purchasing things from my mother's grocery store for years and years stopped."

Distorted images of Japanese Americans were presented in the American press. These distortions were too often internalized by impressionable Americans, many of whom were either immigrants or offspring of immigrants themselves. Racist comments were made by some public officials, such as Lieutenant General John L. DeWitt, Commanding General of the Western Defense

Command. In public statements, DeWitt declared that the Japanese "race" was an enemy "race" and, even though second- and third-generation Japanese were born on United States soil, possessed U.S. citizenship, and had become "Americanized," the "racial strains" were undiluted.[23] Similarly, California's attorney general, Earl Warren, and California Governor Culbert L. Olson depicted American Japanese as a threat to U. S. security.[24]

Public statements such as these, along with erroneous stories printed in the news media, helped to ignite the distrust, fear, and hysteria directed against Japanese Americans. Similarly to the way African Americans had been victims of dehumanization since the institution of American slavery, the Nisei were now being socially constructed as belonging to another human species, incapable of being loyal citizens of the United States. In metropolitan areas of West Coast states, Federal Bureau of Investigation (FBI) officials began to round up Japanese nationals (Issei) thought to be a threat to the U.S. war effort. The country's borders were closed to all persons of Japanese ancestry; they were not permitted to leave or enter the country.

The anti-Japanese campaign was not confined to the West Coast; these negative sentiments were held nationwide. As one observer wrote:

> Life became terrifying for [Japanese-Americans] on the run. They found signs in barbershop windows reading JAPS SHAVED. NOT RESPONSIBLE FOR ACCIDENTS, or in restaurant windows, THIS MANAGEMENT POISONS BOTH RATS AND JAPS. Gas stations refused them gas. They couldn't get water, or even the use of public toilets. Five Nisei reached New Jersey and were hired by a farmer; a vigilante committee put the farmer's barn to torch and threatened to kill his youngest child. In Denver, where a Nisei girl found a job, she tried to attend church. The minister himself blocked the way. He asked, "Wouldn't you feel more at home in your own church?"[25]

Even so, expressions of anti-Japanese sentiment in the eastern United States, severe as they were, were comparatively isolated incidents. Most acts of overt discrimination against Japanese Americans during the war occurred on the West Coast, where the largest proportion lived.

The fact that Japanese Americans were able to relocate to the eastern and southwestern regions of the United States during the war suggests that racial antagonism against them was less severe in these areas than on the West Coast. Again, an analogy can be drawn between the experiences of African Americans and those of Japanese Americans. That is, the acts of racism experienced by Japanese Americans on the West Coast during the war are similar to the overt acts of violence perpetrated by whites against blacks in the southern United States before the civil rights movement. In addition, the treatment of Japanese Americans on the East Coast during the war resembled the covert (and somewhat more "benign") acts of discrimination that blacks in the North encountered during the same time. For each group, racism was practiced in its most severe form where large numbers of group members lived. Unlike African Americans, however, who were relegated to an inferior social position in the United States through Jim Crow laws and practices, Americans of Asian descent were commonly viewed as aliens—even the Nisei, who were American citizens by birth.

The bombing of Pearl Harbor was the catalyst for the incarceration of innocent people who had always been viewed as foreigners by mainstream America. On February 19, 1942, President Roosevelt issued Executive Order 9066, authorizing mass evacuation of Japanese Americans.[26] On the following day, Secretary of War Henry L. Stimson authorized Lieutenant General DeWitt to determine which areas on the West Coast would be off-limits to Japanese Americans. Initially, those living in geographical areas designated off-limits were given the opportunity to move voluntarily wherever they chose outside the prohibited zones. Many of these found refuge in the homes of relatives and friends.

Former Wac Miwako Rosenthal (a pseudonym) and her family were living in California during this time; they were among these volunteer-evacuees:

> I was born in California but we were moved to Texas when the war
> broke out; my brother was in practice there. He was a doctor . . . a
> practicing pediatrician. When the war broke out we were in
> California. . . . My father had big holdings in California; he owned a
> farm and a trucking business that took all the vegetables to the
> market. We weren't poor. My father and mother were both well-to-do.
> That was all vested in my brother because they couldn't own land
> because of the alien land law, so [my brother] was the owner.

Japanese Americans who did not leave the Western Region by March 29, 1942, were forced to leave their homes and move into assembly centers. Eventually these forced evacuees were assigned to one of ten detention camps, which were regulated by the War Relocation Authority (WRA). Yoshiye Togasaki, a physician in the army during World War II, is a case in point. She was born in San Francisco on January 3, 1904. After graduating from the University of California at Berkeley with a bachelor's degree in public health, she attended Johns Hopkins Medical School and graduated with a degree in medicine. Togasaki started a private practice in Los Angeles in 1941; a year later she was evacuated to Manzanar Relocation Camp.[27] Similarly, Nishikaichi was evacuated from her home in Los Angeles along with her parents; they were sent to Poston Relocation Center in west central Arizona. In the end, a reported 109,650 persons of Japanese descent were forcibly removed from California, Washington (state), Oregon, and Arizona. Approximately eighty thousand of these evacuees were born in the United States, either children (Nisei) or grandchildren (*Sansei*) of Japanese immigrants (Issei).[28] These events changed the lives of Nisei servicewomen, and were among the factors that most considered in making the decision to enter the military. (See chapter 3.)

From several studies, including the published works of Roger Daniels and *Personal Justice Denied*, the 1992 report of the Commission on Wartime Relocation and Internment of Civilians, we now know that Japanese Americans posed virtually no threat to national security during the war. According to Daniels, Naval Intelligence Officer Kenneth D. Ringle reported in 1941 that more than 90 percent of the Nisei and 75 percent of the Issei were completely loyal to the United States. Daniels cited the following statement by Ringle in 1941: "[A]fter careful investigations on both the west coast and Hawaii, there was never a shred of evidence found of sabotage, subversive acts, spying, or fifth column activity on the part of the Nisei or long-time local residents."[29]

Fifty-one years after Ringle's report, the Commission on Wartime Relocation and Internment of Civilians reported similar findings exonerating Japanese Americans in the aggregate from the large-scale acts of treason they allegedly had committed. Part of the report reads as follows:

> It was common wisdom that the Nazi invasions of Norway and Western Europe had been aided by agents and sympathizers within the country under attack—the so called fifth column—and the same approach should be anticipated from Japan. . . . For this reason intelligence was developed on Axis saboteurs and potential fifth columnists as well as espionage agents. This work had been assigned to the Federal Bureau of Investigation and the Navy Department but not to the War Department. The President had developed his own informal intelligence system through John Franklin Carter, a journalist, who helped Roosevelt obtain information and estimates by exploiting sources outside the government. . . . Each of these sources saw only a very limited security risk from ethnic Japanese; none recommended a mass exclusion or detention of all people of Japanese ancestry.[30]

Policies of Gender Inclusion

For Nisei women, the right to serve in the military was contingent on laws governing the enlistment of white women. Previous studies have shown that war affects gender relations by changing the role of women.[31] Such was the case during World War II. With the United States actively involved in the war, discussions about the need for a women's corps to serve with the army became part of the political agenda. Stereotypes of women were perhaps the greatest obstacle to be overcome for women to be permitted to take a place in the war effort. The ideology of paternalism, which prevailed in the United States, defined women as less capable than men and in need of protection. Feminists advocated women's participation in the war effort, viewing it as a right of citizenship; as early as 1940, the War Department received pressure from organized women's groups to enroll women in the army. Interest in a women's corps accelerated after the United States declared war on Japan. Among the organizations lobbying for such a corps were the Women's League of Defense in Chicago, the Women's Ambulance and Defense Corps of Los Angeles, and the Toledo unit of the Willys-Overland Women's Motor Defense Corps, which proposed to train women for military service.

The subject of women in the armed services generated heated political debate, even though women had participated in previous years. Women served in an all-female nurse corps that Congress had established in 1901; in later years they received various entitlements, such as relative rank and retirement pensions. During World War I, the Navy enlisted thirteen thousand women as "yeomanettes" to serve as clerks, and the War Department also hired women telephone operators and clerks as civilian workers with the American Expeditionary Forces in France. Still, the idea of women serving in the army during World War II met strong opposition, particularly in Congress. As recorded in the official history of the Women's Army Corps, "Opposition was felt more on the floor of the House, and in the cloakrooms, than in the Committees on Military Affairs."[32] At least part of the explanation for the services' support is that military officials had witnessed competent performance by women, not only in the U.S. military during World War I, but also in the British and Canadian forces.

General George C. Marshall, Chief of Staff to the Secretary of War, argued strongly for the establishment of a women's corps. Marshall realized that women would be needed in the military if the War Department experienced personnel shortages. In 1941 he stated: "While the United States is not faced with an acute shortage of manpower such as has forced England to make such an extensive use of its women, it is realized that we must plan for every possible contingency, and certainly must provide some outlet for the patriotic desires of our women."[33] General Marshall knew that with the greater application of technology, a second world war would rely heavily on administrative and technical support. He also believed that women were more adept than men at clerical and administrative work. In a published interview, his successor, Colonel John H. Hildring, recalled, "General Marshall asked me why we should try to train men in a specialty such as typing or telephone work which in civilian life has been taken over completely by women; this he felt was uneconomical and a waste of time which we didn't have."[34]

Additional pressure to include women in the military surfaced in May 1941, when Congresswoman Edith Nourse Rogers introduced a bill for a Women's Army Auxiliary Corps. The possibility of establishing a women's corps raised a number of questions in Congress: What would the women's status be? What type of military jobs would women fill? Should women be granted disability pensions and veterans' benefits? Some members of Congress objected strongly to women serving in the military, viewing such service as men's duty. Others, although not totally against the idea, were opposed to authorizing military benefits for women.[35]

After long and arduous debate, the bill passed Congress. On May 15, 1942, President Roosevelt signed Public Law 77–554, establishing a Women's Army Auxiliary Corps (WAAC) for service with the U.S. Army.[36] The primary reason for the establishment of the WAAC was to release servicemen from clerical positions to serve in combat. The army was authorized to enroll up to 150 thousand women to serve as noncombatants at both the officer and the enlisted levels. The ranking of Waacs (members of the WAAC) differed from that of their male counterparts, as illustrated by military historian Bettie Morden:

> Women officers received appointments in the Women's Army
> Auxiliary Corps in the created grades of third officer, second officer,
> first officer, field director, assistant director, and director—comparable
> to the army's grades of second lieutenant through colonel. Enlisted
> women held the grades of auxiliary, junior leader, leader, staff leader,
> technical leader, first leader, and chief leader—comparable to the
> army's enlisted grades of private through master sergeant.[37]

Oveta Culp Hobby, a former member of the Texas legislature, newspaper and radio executive, publisher, lawyer, writer, president of the Texas League of Women Voters, civic worker, and the wife of former Governor William Hobby of Texas, was appointed as the WAAC director, and later was given the rank of colonel. Initially, African American activists protested Hobby's appointment, fearing that her southern background would cause her to discriminate against African American women. Black opposition to Hobby's appointment subsided, however, after she appointed forty African American women among the first officer trainees.[38] The WAAC followed the War

Department's policy on race: African Americans were to serve in segregated units, and Japanese Americans were barred from service from January 1942 until February 1943.[39]

Hundreds of American women applied for service in the U. S. military. The successful candidates, including African American women, began training for the WAAC at Fort Des Moines, Iowa on July 2, 1942. Again, Nisei women were not part of this group; they were categorically disqualified until the following year.

Although Waacs received military pay, food, housing, and medical care, they did not have military status. As mentioned above, Waacs were paid less than male soldiers in equivalent grades until November 1942. The fact that women were not part of the army created logistical difficulties. These problems had been anticipated by Congresswoman Rogers, who, after a strenuous battle with Congress, settled for an auxiliary status for the Corps. She made the following remarks in the *Congressional Record*: "In the beginning, I wanted very much to have these women taken in as a part of the Army. . . . I wanted them to have the same rate of pension and disability allowance. I . . . realized that I could not secure that. The War Department was very unwilling to have these women as a part of the Army."[40]

Consequently Waacs did not fall under the army's jurisdiction for promotions or punishment. Instead the WAAC director was forced to devise separate regulations for women. Most rules governing Waacs were similar to those imposed on men in the army, but differences existed, particularly in regard to overseas duty. As Morden stated, "Unlike servicemen, the auxiliaries could not receive overseas pay or government life insurance. If they became sick or were wounded, they would not receive veterans' hospitalization. If they were killed, their parents would receive no death gratuity. And, if they were captured, they would have no protection under existing international agreements covering prisoners of war."[41] Similarly, female nurses were not accorded military benefits, and female physicians were barred from entering the Army Medical Corps.

This auxiliary status of women was later challenged and changed, as was the War Department's policy of excluding women physicians from the Medical Corps. Toward the end of 1942, WAAC Director Hobby and Congresswoman Rogers drafted a bill to integrate women into the army. The bill was approved by Chief of Staff Marshall and was introduced to Congress in January 1943. In March the Seventy-eighth Congress also began hearing testimonies on appointing female physicians to the Medical Corps. Following a long debate, the WAC bill was approved by the House of Representatives and the Senate, and was signed by President Roosevelt on July 1, 1943. Public Law

78–110 established the Women's Army Corps (WAC), thereby integrating women into the army. By the time the first Nisei woman was inducted into the military, members of the WAC held the same military rank as servicemen, received the same pay, allowances, benefits, and privileges, and were subject to the same disciplinary code. A year later, on June 22, 1944, Congress granted army nurses temporary commissions and the full pay and privileges of the grades second lieutenant through colonel. Female physicians were admitted to the Army Medical Corps during the spring of 1943.

Dismantling Racial Barriers, Inducting Japanese Americans

In the same year that the WAC was established, the War Relocation Authority (WRA) began permitting larger numbers of Japanese Americans to leave internment camps and return to the larger society. Evacuees were eligible for leave permits if they fulfilled three prerequisites: they must have found employment in either the midwestern or the eastern region of the United States; they must have indicated on a loyalty questionnaire (discussed in chapter 3) that they were loyal to the United States and supported its war effort; and they were required to agree not to "affiliate" with fellow Japanese Americans.[42]

Irene Nishikaichi was at Poston for a year and a half before she left for New York City. In an effort to regain control of her life, she obtained a train ticket and fifty dollars from the War Relocation Authority, and set out to work in the home of a Columbia University professor "who wanted someone to look after a child."

> I thought I could go to night school and continue my legal secretarial
> course. I learned, after I arrived, that there were three children and I
> was supposed to share a bedroom room with them. One of the
> children had encephalitis; I guess that was the reason they wanted
> someone in the home. When I found out there were a couple of other
> kids, and I had to share the room with the kids, I said, "No way." I
> didn't know how I was going to study. I walked in and I walked out;
> no place to stay, no job, no nothing.

The War Relocation Authority had offices throughout the nation; Nishikaichi was able to find employment at one such office in New York City:

> I went to a WRA office which had already been established in New
> York City, and they needed a secretary. They referred me to an
> apartment that was willing to take Japanese Americans. I had to take
> a civil service exam. I was there in September and didn't get the civil
> service job until around November or December. In the meantime,

my mother, Nina, a midwife in the prenatal and postnatal clinics, visited mothers after their births. And one of the families . . . that had just had a child was a Baptist minister and his wife. And my mother, although she opposed my going to New York, got a [point of contact] for me at the American Baptist Society in New York. I had been going to a Christian church, but I was not a regular churchgoer. So in the meantime, while I was waiting for this civil service job, I went to the Baptist headquarters and was offered a temporary job with their foreign missionary society, paying fifty cents an hour. Some weeks I only made sixteen dollars.

When the WRA began accelerating the process of releasing evacuees, the U.S. War Department was experiencing a severe manpower shortage. In the spring of 1942, the army suffered one of the biggest defeats in U.S. military history: approximately seventy-six thousand American men surrendered to Japan in Bataan on April 9. That summer, Japan invaded the Aleutian Islands. In November 1942, the Japanese American Citizenship League (JACL) petitioned the president of the United States to reinstate the draft for Nisei men.[43]

In addition, some private citizens complained to the War Department that Japanese Americans should fulfill their obligation as citizens and should participate in the war effort. One Lilliebell Falck urged the War Department to enlist Japanese Americans, because she felt that they too had a duty to defend the nation. Falck's letter was written on the letterhead of the Daughters of the American Revolution (DAR), Golden Spike Chapter, Ogden, Utah. All DAR members are descendants of persons who helped to win American independence; Falck's grandparents had served in the Revolutionary War.[44]

In her letter to Secretary of War Stimson, dated January 29, 1943, Falck stated:

Our American children of 18 . . . and 19 years are taken out of school, and put into the service of our country. Morale is considered an essential to boys and parents. Beside our American boys, in college and universities, are Japanese boys. Our boys are taken into the military, while the Japanese students are permitted to continue their studies and professions. . . . Wherein is justice . . . ? In the demand for production, why this sort of action?[45]

More important, it was also becoming evident to the War Department that the services of all eligible persons, including Japanese Americans, were vital to the war effort, given that so many active-duty men were losing their lives in both the European and the Pacific. Thus on January 28, 1943, Secretary of War Stimson announced, "It is the inherent right of every faithful citizen, regardless of ancestry, to bear arms in the nation's battle." Still, concern

remained about the loyalty of Americans of Japanese descent. In an attempt
to determine which Japanese Americans were loyal to the United States, the
War Department in collaboration with the WRA conducted a program of registering all Japanese Americans age seventeen and older. The program was to
fulfill the dual purpose of recruiting Nisei men and women for military service and clearing loyal Issei and Nisei for resettlement in civilian communities.

For these reasons, a controversial loyalty questionnaire was administered
in January 1943.[46] Item 27 asked about the respondent's willingness to serve
in the military. Item 28 asked: "Will you swear unqualified allegiance to the
United States of America and faithfully defend the United States from any
or all attack by foreign or domestic forces, and forswear any form of allegiance
or obedience to the Japanese Emperor, or any other foreign government, power,
or organization?" It is beyond the scope of this study to detail all nuances associated with the loyalty questionnaire. Essentially, if a person answered "yes"
to both questions, he or she was assumed loyal to the United States. Con-
versely, if a respondent answered "no" to one or both questions, he or she was
considered disloyal.

The questionnaire created political controversy and confusion among
many Japanese Americans, especially the Issei, in part because the same questionnaire that the War Department used for recruiting was used by the War
Relocation Authority to resettle evacuees in the broader society. Nonetheless, the War Department allowed Japanese American men to volunteer for
military service and began to make plans for inducting Nisei in accord with
the questionnaire results. The Nisei men and women who volunteered to serve
in the armed services swore unqualified allegiance to the United States.

The opening of military doors to Nisei men was a precursor to the admittance of Nisei women, and subsequently to the induction of Issei men. In
January 1944, the War Department's policy was modified further: the Selective Service was authorized to draft all Japanese American men on the con-
dition that they were cleared individually for service. In September, Japanese
"aliens" (Issei) were allowed to volunteer for military service on the condi-
tion that they filed Selective Service forms DSS 219 and 165 with their local
board and all were cleared for service by the Provost Marshal.[47]

A Need for Nisei Servicewomen

As the loyalty questionnaire was being administered, memos were circulated
within the War Department requesting the recruitment of women linguists.
Specifically, the Chief Recruiting Branch, Personnel Division, requested that
some method be devised to recruit linguists for the WAAC to work in cryp-

tography and communications, and as interpreters. Japanese was one of the languages sought.[48] During the same period, War Relocation Authority Director Dillon S. Myer met with Assistant Secretary of War John J. McCloy to discuss the induction of Nisei women into the WAAC.[49]

During the last week of January 1943, the War Department held a series of conferences investigating the possibility of procuring Nisei men and women for voluntary induction into the army. In February the policy of excluding Japanese Americans from the army changed: Nisei men could volunteer to serve in segregated combat units if cleared by the assistant chief of staff.[50] In April, Nisei women were approved for service by the Military Intelligence Division.

Toward the end of 1943, a new image of Japanese Americans was being constructed in the media. Newspaper articles began to portray them as posing little or no threat to national security. As stated in the November 3 issue of the *New York Times,* "Fewer than half of a per cent of the 938 persons classed as enemy aliens in this country have been interned as potentially dangerous."[51] Hence the message to the American public was that the overwhelming majority of ethnic Japanese were harmless and therefore should be reintegrated into the larger society. This theme was strengthened by the induction of Nisei men into the military, although they served in a segregated unit, and later by the induction of Nisei women, who served in racially integrated units with Caucasian Wacs.

As early as January 1943, Director Hobby began collecting information on Japanese American women living in War Relocation Centers. According to a letter she received from the War Relocation Authority, 11,040 of these women between ages 18 and 45 were married, and 10,374 were single. The report also listed the occupations held by some; the majority were clerical workers (see Table 1).

Although the War Department had already begun a paper trail on the issue of enlisting Nisei women into the WAAC, officers were not sent out into the field to conduct interviews until spring 1943. In March 1943, WAAC officers began visiting the relocation camps to talk with Nisei women; during these meetings, the women expressed curiosity about the WAAC. Second Officer Manice M. Hill, for example, spoke with Nisei women at the Rohwer Relocation Center. She reported that although these women expressed an interest in joining the WAAC, they indicated that their families would have to approve such enlistment. Hill added that the Nisei women opposed any plan of segregation and felt that the segregated combat units, the 100th and 442nd, resulted from acts of racial discrimination.[52] (Additional reports that resulted from this recruitment effort are discussed in chapter 4.)

On February 21, 1943, the Office of the Surgeon General received

Table 1
Occupations of Nisei Women, 1943

Occupation	Number Reported
Editors and reporters	13
Pharmacists	12
Physicians and surgeons	6
Teachers	228
Trained nurses and students	124
Managers	129
Clerical workers	2,541
Stenographers and typists	254
Chemist	1
College teacher	4
Dentist	1
Lawyer	1
Social workers	13
Librarians	4
Draftsperson	1
Optometrists	3
Laboratory technicians	8
Religious workers	30

Source: Letter from War Relocation Authority to Colonel Oveta Hobby, January 26, 1943, RG, SPWA 291.2, National Archives, College Park, Md.

authorization to assign qualified Japanese Americans to the Army Nurse Corps. Approximately two months later, the Military Intelligence Division approved Nisei women for military service in the WAC (which had succeeded the WAAC). In June, the Military Personnel Division announced that Nisei women would be accorded the same treatment and assignment as other women and would not be racially segregated. It was further announced that all investigations of Nisei women, before and after induction, would be conducted by the Provost Marshal General's Office.[53] Finally, on July 23, Director Hobby circulated a letter to each service command announcing that women of Japanese ancestry would be accepted into the WAC. The letter stated that physical standards would be the same as for other applicants except that the minimum height would be fifty-seven inches and the minimum weight ninety-five pounds. Applicants were to be proficient in both written and spoken English.[54] Hobby also announced that the quota for Nisei Wacs was set at five hundred, and specified how this quota was to be distributed throughout the commands (see Table 2). No quota was set for Nisei nurses; also, unlike the WAAC, the Army Nurse Corps did not make any special effort to recruit from the Japanese American community.

Several structural factors help to explain why Nisei women were permit-

Table 2
Specified Quotas for the Enrollment of Nisei Women into the WAC by
Service Command

Quota	Service Command	States
10	First	Connecticut, Maine, Massachusetts, New Hampshire, Rhode Island, and Vermont
30	Second	Delaware, New York, and New Jersey
10	Third	Maryland, Pennsylvania, and Virginia (except Alexandria and Arlington, Va.)
10	Fourth	Alabama, Georgia, Mississippi, North Carolina, South Carolina, and Tennessee
20	Fifth	Indiana, Kentucky, Ohio, and West Virginia
30	Sixth	Illinois, Michigan, and Wisconsin
65	Seventh	Colorado, Iowa, Kansas, Minnesota, Missouri, Nebraska, North Dakota, South Dakota, and Wyoming
60	Eighth	Arkansas, Louisiana, New Mexico, Oklahoma, and Texas
250	Ninth	Arizona, California, Nevada, Oregon, Utah, and Washington
15	Tenth	Alexandria, Virginia; Arlington, Virginia; and Washington, D.C.

Sources: AR 170–10, August 1942, *Service Commands and Departments*, U.S. Army Center of Military History, Washington, D.C.; "Enlistment in WAC of Women Citizens of U.S. of Japanese Ancestry," 23 July 1943, RG 407, Decimal File 1940–1945, Box 4300, Folder 341.1, 342.05 WAC, National Archives, Washington, D.C.

ted to enroll in the Army Nurse Corps and finally were recruited into the WAC. The same factors help to clarify why Nisei servicewomen served in racially integrated units.

The primary catalyst for the induction of Nisei women into the ANC and the WAC was the difficulty that these organizations were experiencing in recruiting. This problem was exacerbated for the WAAC/WAC by a slander campaign against servicewomen that began during the spring of 1943: rumors that women in the military were of low moral character spread throughout the nation; and the news media depicted Waacs as sexually promiscuous.[55] Mattie Treadwell reported that an FBI investigation revealed these allegations were false. FBI agents also found that these slanders originated with army servicemen who had negative attitudes toward the WAAC.[56] Although WAAC Director Hobby worked hard to counter the slander campaign, it created a tremendous barrier to recruitment.

The Women's Army Corps needed all the qualified women willing to enroll, and Nisei women were among the most highly educated in the United States. Segregating Nisei women in the WAC was less of an issue at this time than convincing them to enlist. Of the two million military job openings in the army, the War Department estimated that six hundred thousand could "more efficiently be done by Waacs."[57] From the perspective of the War Department, women were needed to fill jobs in the rear, thereby enabling more men to be assigned to the battlefields, and many Nisei women were qualified to fill these skilled occupational positions.

Initially, serious consideration was given to recruiting Nisei women to serve in racially segregated WAAC companies, and it was further recommended that they be recruited and trained in time to replace members of the 442nd as these men deployed overseas;[58] this plan never materialized, however, as much controversy surrounded the question of segregating Nisei women. Indeed, for Nisei women interested in joining the armed services, racial integration was a serious issue. In an effort to acquire citizenship rights, these women positioned themselves as "honorary whites" rather than "constructive blacks."[59] On their loyalty questionnaire, several indicated that they would be willing to serve in the WAAC if given the opportunity, but would not serve in segregated companies. In addition, Secretary of War Stimson received letters from private citizens urging that Nisei women be able to serve in racially integrated units. One such letter was written by Allen C. Blaisdell, director of International House at the University of California at Berkeley. After expressing appreciation for the opening of military doors to Japanese American men, Blaisdell wrote:

> May I make two suggestions which are, no doubt, also in your mind: (1) That the young [Japanese American] women be accorded opportunities for enlistment in the women's branches of the armed forces. There are many of them well-trained in office skills and medical and technical professions who could be of great service in this way and should be granted opportunities for enlistment on a basis of equality with young men of their race. (2) I hope as wisdom and experience dictate that the policy of segregation can give way to the integration of these young men and women into the regularly established branches of the armed forces. They need to learn the techniques of integration and all Americans need the broadening and socially constructive experience of interrelationship. Our armed forces can thus become the training ground for the sincere democracy of the future.[60]

While the War Department had already begun conducting a study on enlisting Nisei women in the WAAC, letters received from private citizens such as Professor Blaisdell facilitated the process.

WAAC Director Hobby and other War Department officials agreed that there was no need to segregate Nisei Waacs. One reason was that the number of Nisei women enlisting into the military would be small and therefore "easily integrated" with white WAACS.[61] Another part of the rationale was that segregation "would increase racial friction and complicate administration."[62] Moreover, by the time Nisei women were being considered for induction, the War Department's policy of racial segregation had been criticized severely by the African American community. Colonel Don Faith, the commandant of the WAAC Training Center, received much correspondence from black organizations and the black press, protesting segregation in the WAAC.[63] Segregation had been a long-standing cause of dispute between the War Department and the African American community. The segregation of Nisei men was also a controversial issue for the War Department; now Nisei women were challenging the idea, too, as were some white citizens, such as Blaisdell, on behalf of the Nisei.

Officially, military doors opened to Nisei women in April 1943. The first Nisei woman was not inducted until November, however. As mentioned above, the Women's Army Auxiliary Corps had, by that time, become the Women's Army Corps, and its members had army status. Wacs, now part of the army rather than mere auxiliaries, received the same pay, medical benefits, and other allowances as men.[64] Hence, Nisei women entered the military just when women were accorded the same military benefits as men; they were dispersed throughout the integrated WAC and served mostly in the contiguous United States.

Some of the Nisei Wacs were trained as linguists at the Military Intelligence Service Language School at Fort Snelling, Minnesota. Most, however, received training in clerical, medical, supply, and other military support positions. Ruth Fujii, a Hawaiian Nisei, had the distinction of being the only woman of Japanese ancestry to serve in the Pacific Theater of Operations (Philippines and China) during the war.

Some Nisei women, such as Iris Watanabe, entered the military directly from internment camps. Stories about their induction ceremonies were featured in Japanese newspaper articles like this:

> A twenty-year-old California girl of Japanese ancestry on December
> 13 became the first evacuee to take the oath of service in the
> Women's Army Corps in the office of Colorado's Governor Vivian.
> Miss Iris Watanabe of Santa Cruz, California was one of 17 young
> women sworn in at the ceremony. Two of the others are also of
> Japanese ancestry but are not evacuees.[65]

Watanabe's induction drew considerable attention, for she was the first woman evacuee to enroll in the WAC. Reporter Harry Tarvin attempted, though without success, to interview her for an article in a mainstream newspaper. A Lieutenant S.O. Reed, commanding officer of the WAC recruiting office in Denver, forbade the interview, stating that Watanabe's induction might have a negative effect on the recruitment of white women.[66] Tarvin then went to Governor John Vivian's office, where the induction was taking place; he was accompanied by Tom Parker, then head of the WRA photographic section, and Pat Coffey, then a photographer for *Life* magazine. They were met by a Lieutenant Stanley, in charge of inductees, who advised them not to take any pictures of Watanabe on the grounds that such a picture would jeopardize recruitment of white women. Nonetheless, Tarvin asked Governor Vivian for permission to take photographs of him, first with Watanabe and then with two other Nisei women, who were attending the ceremony but not being inducted. (See illustrations 1 and 2.)

The Japanese American press applauded the War Department's decision to open its doors to Nisei women. An editorial published in the *Pacific Citizen* stated that opening the Women's Army Corps to Japanese American women was "a signal example of democracy, for it showed once again that the army of our country must and will include persons of all races, even those of enemy extraction."[67] The article listed the advantages of joining the WAC. First there were the training and work experience, which would be useful after military service. In addition, military veterans would receive preference for employment after the war, in the form of civil service points. Of particular interest to Japanese Americans was the fact that members of the WAC were free to move about anywhere in the United States: Wacs were assigned to duty in all regions of the country, and there was no policy of segregating Nisei women. (See chapter 4.)

Upon joining the WAC, the Nisei women received varying responses from significant others. Many met strong opposition from family and friends, not only because the military was a male-dominated organization, but also because the Japanese American community was divided over the issue of loyalty to the United States. On March 7, 1943, for example, Headquarters Ninth Command, WAAC Branch, in Washington, D.C., received a letter from Second Officer Henrietta Horak of the WAAC Recruiting Office in Los Angeles, regarding the survey she had administered at Tule Lake Relocation Center. Horak reported that the fifteen, thousand Japanese Americans at the location center were being registered, and she described the camp's atmosphere as one of "hate, fear, suspicion, and violence." She stated that, "74 Kebeis [have] just been jailed. [There have been] numerous beatings among the three Japanese factions (Issei, Nisei, and Kebei). One Nisei woman was beaten, allegedly because she had expressed a desire to be a WAAC."[68]

There was a great deal of dissent in the Japanese American community over the issue of military service; Nisei servicewomen often found themselves at the crossroad of this controversy. Issei parents, particularly those who were interned, often objected to their children's volunteering for service. In the words of Thomas and Nishimoto, "Those who had decided that there was no longer a place for them in America were determined that this country would not rob them of their children as it had taken their possessions. There began a campaign to prevail upon the children 17 years of age and over to say no to their loyalty question."[69] Certainly, some Nisei were embittered and disillusioned with the United States for abrogating their rights as citizens. Many young Japanese Americans who had advocated cultural assimilation before the war, had now become racialized; many of these men and women identified strongly with their parents' losses and suffering, and honored their wishes not to serve in the military.

On the other hand, a great many Nisei felt allegiance to their country of birth. Leaders of the Japanese American Citizenship League (JACL) encouraged Nisei men and women to volunteer for the armed services. Some family members of Nisei Wacs supported the women's decision to join the military; others had mixed feelings. Irene Nishikaichi recalled her parents' ambivalence:

> I knew that I would have trouble [getting parental consent] so I didn't sign up or volunteer until I was twenty-one. I . . . chuckled because my parents were kind of opposed to my going into the military. . . . I was talking about going into the service and my mother said that between the two [choices] she would rather have me leave camp [and go into service]. Other [Issei] parents were opposed to her thinking because they thought their daughters might want to follow my example. My mother wasn't exactly happy about my going into service, but later she sen[t] to me two brand new dictionaries, Japanese-English, [and] English-Japanese [which demonstrated her support].

Grace Harada also stated that her parents objected to her decision to enter the WAC. For Harada's parents and most of their Issei friends, military service was inappropriate for Nisei women:

> They just felt that I shouldn't be doing something like that, and going so far away from home. But I told them that I just couldn't stay home and do housework. I wasn't accomplishing anything I said. [Harada's brother had already joined the 442nd Regimental Combat Team.] I said [to my parents] "There is a war going on and he can't do it

alone." . . . I said what I would be doing is replacing all these men to help end the war. I tried to talk my parents into letting me go, and finally they released me and signed the consent for me to go in.

Miwako Rosenthal was finishing her sophomore year in college when she learned that she had been accepted into the WAC. She had filed the form necessary for all U.S. citizens of Japanese ancestry who were volunteering for military service (DSS Form 304A) before she began her studies. Like so many other parents, Rosenthal's mother and father objected to her entering the military.

Rosenthal had applied for entry into the WAAC in 1942; it was two years later when she finally received word that her application was approved. In her words, "I was surprised because I had been waiting for a couple of years, since I volunteered, and nothing was said so I figured they didn't want me or that I didn't pass or something. Now all of a sudden they said they can induct me. I was inducted at Fort Bliss." To avoid controversy with her parents about her induction, Rosenthal resorted to subterfuge:

> The War Department called me up at Fort Bliss and said, "You're registered, you can be inducted now." I didn't tell my parents or anything. I said I was going to go visit one of my student friends, but I went to Fort Bliss. It was at Christmastime, and they called me while I was on semester break. I went in January of 1945.

In contrast, Ellen Fuchida's family was very supportive when she decided to join the military. Her father had died, leaving her mother a widow with four children. She recalled,

> I was twenty-four when I entered service at Fort Douglas, Utah. Most of my family was behind me [but] my brother, who was overseas [with the 442nd], was ready to shoot me. He didn't count because he was overseas. . . . My friends were shocked, but they were supportive. . . . My mother said, "Okay, if that's what you want to do, go do it and do the best you can." . . . But she sure had a hard time explaining [Fuchida's going into the military] to the Issei community of Salt Lake.

Fuchida added that other Issei parents feared that her personal decision to join the military might influence other Nisei.

It is important to note that not all Nisei were willing to serve. Initially military service was voluntary for both Nisei men and women; eventually, however, Nisei men were required to register for the draft. Suffice it to mention that a few Nisei men who were inducted into the military displayed serious disciplinary problems and engaged in several acts of disruption. Such was the case with the demoralized unit that Tomotsu Shibutani discusses in *The Derelicts of Company K.*[70] The War Department faced a major challenge in attempting to enforce the policy of obligatory military service, with some Nisei men, who had no desire to enter the armed services, or, as law professor Eric Muller discovered, resisted the draft as a form of protest against mass evacuation.[71] In February 1944, the *Denson Tribune*, an internment camp paper, published the following alert:

> All Nisei men of military age who are not certain that they listed
> complete information concerning local Selective Service Boards at
> the time of registration early in 1943 are required to send name, number
> and address of their boards to the Relocation Planning Division,
> Washington, D.C. . . . A man who cannot be located and notified to
> appear for pre-induction physical examination when his order number
> appears will be reported as delinquent and is liable to severe penalties
> provided under the Selective Training and Service Act.[72]

For the next few months, Japanese American newspapers published notices of the arrest of Nisei men who refused to take their pre-induction physicals. (Examples of such articles appear in chapter 3.) Many of these men were so embittered by the unconstitutional act of mass evacuation that they renounced their American citizenship. Some internees felt that "their present situation represented a denial of their rights, and that enlistment in the Army, under these conditions, was not a privilege but an unbearable sacrifice."[73] In an attempt to avoid military service, some of the men applied for expatriation with the WRA Internal Security Division;[74] they were the exception, however.

In contrast, at the same time, Japanese American newspapers were filled with stories of Nisei women being inducted into the WAC, as in this example from the *Pacific Citizen*:

> Three women of Japanese ancestry were among a large group of
> newly-enlisted Women's Army Corps members to leave Salt Lake
> City last week for training in the WAC at Fort Des Moines, Iowa. . . .
> At Des Moines, the women will receive five weeks of basic training,
> they may be sent to one of the WAC specialist schools or to direct
> assignment to a non-combat job at an Army post. The three women
> were given an enthusiastic send-off by their families and friends who
> showered the new Wacs with many gifts. Speaking for the Japanese-
> American Wacs, Private Mukai declared, "We are thrilled to be able
> to serve in the Women's Army Corps."[75]

In another article published in the *Pacific Citizen*, Iris Watanabe, scheduled to be inducted into the WACs on December 7, 1943, was quoted, "I hope to make the land of my ancestors pay for its unwarranted attack on my country."[76] Three weeks later, the *Denson Tribune* cited Watanabe, "I am delighted to be in the WACS. It is an honor not only to me but to other Japanese Americans, and I shall be conscious of that all the time. I have always hated the militaristic clique in Japan and I resolved that I would do everything in my power to fight it, not only for myself but for my native land."[77]

Juxtaposing newspaper articles about Nisei male draft dodgers with those about Nisei female enlistees may give the false impression that Nisei women were more patriotic toward the United States than were Nisei men. In fact, however, Nisei women were no more highly motivated than their male counterparts to enter the military—in fact, probably less so, given the social stigma placed on women who went into the military. Just as some Nisei men refused to support the U.S. war effort, some Nisei women objected as well. Yet because service was not obligatory for women, the press reported only positive stories of Nisei women's induction; those who were not interested in joining the WAC did not make headline news. And the Nisei Wacs interviewed for newspaper articles were enthusiastic about joining, and it is worth noting that the women interviewed for this study expressed excitement about entering the military.

Nisei women of Hawaii, not subjected to the direct effects of mass evacuation, may have felt less ambivalence than many in the contiguous states about joining the WAC. Alice Kono of Molokai recalled that her parents were not upset when she announced that she wanted to join: "I think my dad didn't think they would take me because I was so short; so he said, 'Oh go ahead.' . . . My mother wasn't sure." Hisako Yamashita of Kauai felt independent, since her mother was deceased, and she did not ask her father's permission to join: "It was really my own decision. . . . I was very independent and I didn't even ask. I just joined. Later I heard family members say, 'Oh dear, look what she did,' but they never came out in front of me and asked why I did it."

Similarly, Ruth Fujii's father was deceased and her oldest brother was the decision maker for her family in Kauai. She had been emancipated from her home for several years and was working as a high school secretary in Honolulu when she decided to go into the military:

> Sunday morning the paper was delivered and in it said that they were recruiting girls and they were giving silk stockings away. . . . So Monday we [Fujii and a friend] went down and registered. I didn't tell anybody, not even my boss or my family. . . . And then when [the] paperwork was done I told my boss, and he said that was okay; that

they were proud that I'd made up my mind. I didn't tell my brother until I passed the physical. I guess [my family] was shocked, but they accepted it. . . . They couldn't do anything because they knew that it was my own life.

Often these women either were the target of blatant racial discrimination, in the continental United States, or were relegated to a lower social status, in the Territory of Hawaii. Thus it seems almost counterintuitive that they should want to join the American armed services. What motivated them? Each of my informants indicated that she felt a great need to show loyalty to the United States—a desire reflected in the following statement by a Nisei woman (interviewed for an earlier study):

> I was getting sick and tired of doing domestic work all the time and wanted a change. I wanted to do something more directly related with the war effort. I felt that I would not feel so restless if I got into the WACs. . . . I thought that if I joined the WACs, I would be better fitted to get a job afterward. . . . I felt that the Nisei had to do more than give lip service to the United States, and by joining the WACs I could prove my sincerity. . . . Now I can go into the WACs and be on an equal footing with everybody else, and this has given me quite a mental lift. I also feel that I am contributing something toward the real achievement of democracy.[78]

Irene Nishikaichi had read an article about the WAC, and felt that she had a special skill to share. She said:

> I saw this article in the *Pacific Citizen* [announcing that the War Department] was seeking Japanese, Nisei women for the language school. And since I had graduated the 12th grade level of Japanese school in Los Angeles, and had considered volunteering [for the military] before, I thought it was almost fate that this information should come out the month that I was turning twenty-one. I thought translating Japanese was something specific that I could do that very few women could do. If I volunteer for secretarial work, lots of others could do that. But as far as language, I thought there would be very few people to qualify. So, since I had a very specialized service that I could give my country, I felt that I should volunteer and really go through with it. I went to basic [training at Fort Des Moines], and then I went to the Military Intelligence Service Language School.

Similar reasons for joining were given by Fujiko Kutaka, Hisako Yamashita, Alice Kono, and Ruth Fujii. All were inducted in Hawaii, and all stated that they joined for patriotic reasons. As Yamashita noted, "We joined the

WAC to show that we [were] patriotic. . . . And once [the United States] won, at least we could say we didn't shy away from fighting Japan." She explained further that she became interested in the WAC during a conversation with her women friends about proving that they were Americans:

> That was the first time [the War Department] was forming a women's unit from Hawaii. I was at the University of Hawaii, and some [Nisei women] friends were talking. We said, "You know, the war started, the men . . . volunteered, . . . and why don't Japanese women join in because that would be something we'd be doing for the country. And although the enemy was Japanese and we're Japanese, . . . we're not the same people . . . we're Americans and they're from Japan, and there was a difference. . . . [We agreed] to prove that we [were] American, and to prove it we would join the army like a man. That's how it started. I said, "I'm gonna join," and I did. . . . I was the only one [from that group] who did.

Mary Yamada, the only nurse interviewed for this study, stated that she felt it her responsibility as a nurse to serve in the military and to help administer treatment to the wounded. She stated, "I just expected that if there ever was a war, that as part of my nursing career I would report for military duty. I expected to go to England with the Bellevue unit because that's where they were stationed during World War II." The same professional, moral, and ethical sentiment was echoed in the testimony of the physician Yoshiye Togasaki, who stated that her experiences in practicing medicine (outside as well as inside the internment camps) made her better equipped to treat casualties of war than doctors just completing formal training.[79]

Surely, many other reasons influenced these women's decision. Some women I interviewed were drawn by the excitement associated with travel; others were attracted by educational benefits associated with the GI Bill. Ellen Fuchida, for example, entered the military from Utah in 1944, where her family owned a grocery store. She had completed high school before studying to be a beautician, and had opened a beauty shop the day after Pearl Harbor. As stated above, her father was deceased, and her oldest brother had volunteered for the 442nd. Fuchida was searching for change:

> I joined the military mostly because I had never been out of Utah, and to do beauty work at a time like that [during the war] was useless. Most of the beauticians were going into defense force work. So I talked to my mother; I knew she was alone with four children left, but . . . we were doing all right. I was doing my beauty work in this small town, and my twenty-one-year-old sister was co-owner of a restaurant, and then my mother had the grocery business. We were so

busy and working so hard that I'd put my customer under a dryer and then run up to the grocery store [and] put up some groceries. And then at night, when everything was finished, we'd clean the restaurant. I thought I was going to drop dead. So finally I said, "I'm going off."

And Grace Harada recalled:

I had just graduated high school and I wanted to become a nurse [when] the war broke out. . . . At that time. . . . we couldn't even get a decent job. . . . I had some clerical work in high school and was trying to get some kind of office work, but because of [my] Japanese ancestry, there was nothing [available]. I was employed as a maid, doing housework. That was all we could do because there was so much [racial] discrimination. So both my sister and I worked in homes for five dollars a week, room and board.

Finally, Harada decided to go into the military because:

I was so frustrated; I wasn't happy doing housework, . . . and I couldn't go to school. I wasn't making enough, so I couldn't go on to college, and there wasn't much I could do staying there [in Pocatello]. So I decided to join the military. At the time they wouldn't accept Nisei in any of the other [military] organizations except the WAC. I tried the Marines, the Air Force, the Navy, but none of them would take the Japanese. So I finally went into the Army.

Rosenthal welcomed the opportunity to serve in the military, largely because of the educational benefits:

I went to the College of Mines and Metallurgy in El Paso. . . . Since I was in college, I thought . . . if I could get into service, that would be great because then I could get an education without worrying [how I was going to pay for it]. It wasn't easy to go to college [during the war]. Japanese couldn't get jobs or anything. [Japanese Americans] couldn't even work on the farm for ten cents an hour.

The exact number of Japanese American women who served in the WAC is unknown, although evidence (discussed in chapters 4 and 5) suggests that they never reached their quota of five hundred. Twenty-five Nisei women entered in a contingent of sixty-two Wacs from the Hawaiian Islands (see appendix). They were assigned as clerks, interpreters, and other roles.

The need for nurses during World War II was also great—so great that the ANC had to engage in a massive buildup. According to registered nurse and retired U.S. Army Colonel Mary Sarnecky:

By the end of calendar year 1941, just after the bombing of Pearl
Harbor, the authorized strength of the Army Nurse Corps was 8,237,
while the actual strength was 7,043. At the same time in 1942, the
authorized strength was 25,005, while actual strength was 19,194. In
December 1944, authorized and actual strength figures were 50,000
and 42,248 respectively. In June 1945 after V-E day, the balance
finally shifted. At that time, the authorized strength of the Army
Nurse Corps was 53,000 and actual strength was more, 54,291.[80]

By the end of the war, some fifty-seven thousand nurses would have served in
the ANC; the number of Nisei nurses in this group is unknown. Unlike the
WAC, the ANC did not recruit Nisei nurses separately. Additionally, the number of Nisei nurses was so small that segregation never emerged as a real issue.

The Nisei women documented in this book broke with subcultural norms
as well as traditional gender norms of the broader society. The testimonies
related above illustrate that many were motivated by a desire to demonstrate
loyalty to the United States and to prove their worthiness of first-class citizenship for themselves and their families. Others indicated that they volunteered because they possessed skills much needed in time of war; they believed
volunteering was the responsible thing for them, as members of society, to do.
Still others wanted an opportunity to travel and see the world.

Like other women of their cohort who entered the armed services, Nisei
servicewomen chose to enter a male domain, and, as discussed above, because
of traditional gender norms, women in the military were often a target of slander. Unlike other women, however, the Nisei servicewoman had to complete
a loyalty questionnaire. Moreover, at times, she was admonished for choosing
to serve in the U.S. military and accused of betraying her race. This was especially true of Nisei servicewomen who were living in internment camps,
where bitter riots broke out over the issue of serving in the military. As mentioned above, Second Officer Horak reported that a Nisei woman was beaten
at Tule Lake for merely expressing a desire to join the WAAC. (The intra-
racial conflict among Japanese Americans over the issue of military service is
further discussed in chapter 3.)

In the following chapters, Nisei servicewomen talk about their lives before, during, and after World War II.

Chapter 2   Before the War

When you're in your teens, you're not interested in
history. You're not interested in what your parents did or
what they thought. It's only when you get into your
fifties or possibly into your sixties [that your curiosity is
aroused]. And by then, because my parents were older
than most when they married and had children, they
were gone.

—Irene Nishikaichi

THROUGHOUT THE HISTORY of the United States, women of color have shared not only the experiences of gender inequality but also discrimination based on race and ethnicity. At the most basic level, these experiences appear to have been the same: all women of color have suffered some degree of gender and racial/ethnic oppression. On close inspection, however, their social, economic, and political realities have varied with regard to race/ethnicity and class; it is too imprecise to lump all women of color into one category and label it "minority."

An examination of Japanese American women's historical roots, family and community roles, and educational and occupational access over the last century helps to locate them in American society. Nisei servicewomen were not a monolithic group. They were from families of differing socioeconomic statuses, and had differing educational backgrounds and work experiences. In this chapter, I explore this context in an effort to understand more fully the realities of Nisei women who served in the American armed services during World War II. Who were their parents, and why did these parents immigrate to the United States? What type of households did these women grow up in?

What were their educational achievements? What were their occupational as-
pirations? How did they resolve the conflict of dual citizenship, Japanese and
American?

Parents: The Issei

The immigration pattern of Issei women to the United States differed from
that of other women of color, such as Chinese, African, and Mexican Americans. Chinese women began immigrating in the 1850s; Issei women did not
enter the United States until after the Civil War. African women immigrated
to North America involuntarily as slaves; Issei women came voluntarily in
the hopes of finding greater economic opportunities for themselves and their
families. Mexican women entered American society through the direct conquest of their homeland, which bordered on the United States; Japanese
women traveled thousands of miles from their country of origin to settle in a
country completely foreign to them.

Japanese immigration to the United States dates back to1868, during the
reign of Japan's Emperor Meiji (1868–1912). This period marked the beginning of the modern era in Japan, the start of Japan's industrial and military
development.[1] American capitalists began traveling to Japan in search of an
outlet for surplus goods, and apparently they were successful: sociologist Ronald
Takaki reported that American exports to Japan increased from $3.9 million
in 1894 to $13 million in 1897.[2] The Japanese government invited foreign
technicians to assist in efforts to modernize the country. Much of the revenue
for modernizing was obtained through a heavy tax placed on Japanese farmers, causing 367 thousand of them to lose their land for failure to pay taxes.
In 1884, the Japanese government permitted thousands of these farmers to
emigrate to Hawaii to work on sugar plantations.[3]

The new imperial regime sent Japanese students abroad to study in prepa-
ration for newly developed government positions. Virtually all students sent
to the United States under Japanese government sponsorship were chosen from
the elite class, and emigrated before 1891.[4] Many studied at eastern universities such as Harvard, Yale, and Rutgers. Other student immigrants financed
their education by working as laborers after arriving in the United States.[5]
Some Japanese students emigrated from their country to avoid mandatory military service.[6] A few student laborers left Japan as political exiles, fleeing the
restrictions the Meiji government placed on individual rights.[7] In all, the number of student laborers was small; they settled mostly in San Francisco, where
the majority of Japanese in the U.S. mainland lived until the late 1890s.[8]

Former U.S. Army doctor Yoshiye Togasaki revealed that her father was among the government-sponsored student immigrants. Both her parents immigrated to the United States in the 1880s: "My father came here as a student who had . . . graduated law school at the Imperial University."[9] Togasaki's father was en route to Europe as a government-sponsored student but traveled to the United States instead: "He was on his way to England and France for further training in French and English law, particularly in French, because his professor was interested in that. Apparently the government wanted him for future use in their structure."[10] Rather than returning to Japan, however, Togasaki's father remained in the United States.

Many push and pull factors help to explain, as they do for other groups that came to America, why Japanese men and women immigrated. Although economic hardship played a major role, it was not the only reason. Former Nisei Wac Miwako Rosenthal stated that her father emigrated from Japan to escape a Buddhist temple. As a second son, he was not eligible to inherit his family's property: it was customary for the oldest son to inherit the family's wealth. To his chagrin, he was sent to a Buddhist temple to prepare for priesthood. When he was sixteen, he rebelled and asked his uncle to give him money to study in the United States. In Rosenthal's words:

> In the late nineteenth century a lot of [Japanese] men came over as laborers, . . . much like immigrants from Mexico today. . . . They didn't have wives and they just settled in the community and worked where there were a lot of sugar beets, and lima beans, and big farming. My father escaped from the temple with his uncle's help and came to the United States and settled in Ventura County. And since he was a learned man, could read and write Japanese, he became the foreman, overseeing guys that lived in the boarding houses. And then he got elected to City Hall as a representative of the Japanese community in California, where we have our holdings; in Oxnard, Ventura County. It's a small community and they had a big sugar beet factory there. To get to Los Angeles from Santa Barbara County you have to go through Ventura County. And Oxnard is right there where the secret POE, Port of Embarkation, called Wynamie, was located during World War II. There are a lot of old Indian reservations there.

These early Japanese immigrants to the United States were a diverse group. Among them were members of the elite, skilled crafts workers, and menial servants; some of the latter were hired by Westerners visiting Japan, and later were brought to the United States.[11] Most early Japanese immigrants, however, were men, unskilled sojourners who intended to labor for money in the United States and eventually return to Japan. As expressed by the Issei women of Oregon interviewed by Linda Tamura, many Japanese viewed the United States as a place where they could travel and "get rich quick."[12]

Few women were among these pioneers. As with the first wave of Chinese immigrants, many Japanese women who immigrated during the nineteenth century were prostitutes who settled on the West Coast. The demand for Asian prostitutes was great, given the restrictions placed on immigration to the United States from Asia and the anti-miscegenation laws forbidding interracial marriage. In *The Issei*, Yuji Ichioka reported that most of these prostitutes were brought to the United States by Japanese men who transported them across the Pacific under false pretenses. Ichioka cites the stories of several Japanese women who were lured into prostitution in the 1890s. These women were often lied to and abducted from their homes, and found themselves in the United States working in brothels owned by Japanese men.[13] A similar tale of the involuntary prostitution of Chinese women is told in Arthur Golden's recent novel, *Memoirs of a Geisha*.[14]

During the late nineteenth century, several Christian institutions were established in the Japanese American community. The Japanese American Gospel Society was founded on October 6, 1877, and the First Japanese Presbyterian Church of San Francisco was inaugurated in May 1885. In 1886 the Japanese Young Men's Christian Association (YMCA) was organized. Yoshiye Togasaki's mother was part of a Christian initiative to provide a support network in the United States for single Japanese women. Togasaki's mother, the daughter of a merchant in Tokyo, and another Japanese woman, Kaji Yajiima, "were the co-founders of [a Christian organization known as] the WCTU in Japan. . . . The Christian missionary revival hit Japan just about that time."[15] Togasaki recalled, "My mother also used to preach on the street corners . . . here in San Francisco."[16] She explained:

> My mother's name was Shige Kushida. Her mother was already a widow at that time, and I would say quite progressive in the sense that my mother had been educated, but not given any degree, at the university there in Tokyo because no woman could ever be given a degree in those days, but my mother completed the classical education there. Then she came over. . . . [My mother and others] were concerned because there were so many single women here who had been persuaded to come under various pretexts or inducements and were having problems taking care of themselves.[17]

Togasaki's mother was sent to the United States by the WCTU specifically to serve as a missionary for single Japanese women who had immigrated to America "and to help protect them from moral corruption."[18]

The early phase of Japanese immigration to North America, from 1868 to 1900, was concentrated in Hawaii, where these immigrants worked as low-wage agricultural laborers.[19] Contract laborers, known as *gannen mono*, arrived in Hawaii from Japan in 1868 to work on the sugar cane plantations. Their numbers were few, and the demand for field laborers was great. Hawaii, then still an independent kingdom, entered into a treaty with Japan in 1871 allowing unrestricted immigration of laborers from Japan. Japanese immigration to Hawaii did not increase, however, until 1885, when Japan faced political turmoil and economic instability. Between 1885 and 1894, twenty-eight thousand Japanese immigrants arrived in Hawaii to work as plantation laborers; most remained after their contracts expired.[20]

Concomitant with the Organic Act, which established the Territory of Hawaii, was the outlawing of labor contracts. Japanese laborers were thus freed to travel. Some returned to Japan, while others went to the U.S. mainland. By 1900, when Hawaii became a United States territory, sixty-one thousand persons of Japanese heritage were living there.[21] Indeed, the Japanese presence in Hawaii was prominent; a Japanese community emerged, with a Buddhist temple that had been established in Honolulu in 1898. Japanese-language schools for the six-thousand-plus Nisei children in Hawaii were operated by Christian churches. Japanese-language newspapers also developed.[22]

Japanese immigration to California increased sharply in 1900, when the bubonic plague in Hawaii caused ships bound for Honolulu to detour to San Francisco. Over the next few years, Japanese immigration increased on the West Coast in response to a labor shortage; approximately 150,000 Japanese immigrants (Issei) entered the United States before 1908.[23] The number of Japanese immigrants was curtailed in 1908, following the enactment of the "Gentlemen's Agreement"; Japanese immigration declined from 10,000 in 1907–1908 to 2,500 in 1908–1909.[24] One provision of the Gentlemen's Agreement was that Japanese immigrants could bring their families to the United States; thus by 1910 Japanese immigration to the United States began to increase again, reflecting a large proportion of women and children. Thousands of Japanese women immigrated to the United States as "picture brides," women married in Japan by proxy to Japanese men already living in the United States.

Miwako Rosenthal's father was one of the Japanese immigrants who married a picture bride. He traveled to the United States at age sixteen on a visa, and established himself in a small business before writing home for a wife. According to Rosenthal:

> His uncle happened to be the husband of one of my mother's sisters.
> And so they told my mother that they had a nephew living in the
> United States and that it would be good for them to get married. My
> mother was excellent; she was good, very smart, intelligent, and very

talented. . . . My mother was a maverick for her generation. She went to college in Japan and studied how to be a good housewife. That's the way the education system was for women in those days. They just learned the art of being a good housewife. They had to be socially acceptable in all forms of the cultural arts like tea ceremony, and playing . . . Japanese instruments, and knowing how to do calligraphy, and all those things. My mother was cultured. She was much more cultured than the average first-generation women that came over as picture brides.

Rosenthal's description of education for women in Japan is consistent with other accounts in the social science literature. For example, anthropologist Ruth Benedict reported that the prescribed courses for women in Japan were "heavily loaded with instruction in etiquette and bodily movement."[25] Serious intellectual pursuits were reserved for the men. This gender stratification in education was, as is well known, common throughout the world in the nineteenth century.

Although picture brides were of varied social standings in Japan, they shared the experience of traveling to a foreign country to meet bridegrooms they had never seen. Harry Kitano described the "imported Japanese bride" as either "extraordinarily adaptable or extraordinarily dutiful."[26] By American standards, it must have been very stressful for the Issei picture bride to leave the security of her family and travel thousands of miles to be the wife of a man she had never met. Yet this may not have been so difficult for Issei women used to Japanese standards; these women were accustomed to arranged marriages.

Kitano argued that Japanese picture brides looked forward to the change that this trip would offer: "they felt liberated from former family ties." Still, like other nineteenth-century immigrants, they faced a less romantic aspect of travel to the United States: upon arrival, they were disrobed, bathed, fumigated, and given complete physical examinations. Their "bridegrooms were waiting for them on the docks, pictures in hand."[27] In her study of the Issei living in Hood Valley, Oregon, Linda Tamura learned that picture brides were often surprised to find husbands looked nothing like their photographs; middle-aged men often sent more youthful pictures of themselves.[28] Historian Eileen Tamura states that some picture brides were so disappointed they ran away from their new husbands; the Susannah Wesley Home in Honolulu provided shelter for some of these women.[29] For the most part, however, picture brides adjusted to their new home in America.

Rather than arranging for a picture bride to meet them in the United States, some Japanese male immigrants went back to Japan to be married. Ellen

Fuchida's father, for example, returned from the United States to find a wife. Fuchida stated that her parents' marriage was arranged after her father returned to Japan. Like many male immigrants to the United States, Fuchida's father promised her mother "streets of gold and brought her to mud." Recounting her mother's experience as a new bride in the United States, Fuchida stated:

> She cried for six months, but she was a very strong woman. She decided to make the best of it after she found out she was pregnant. She worked hard all of her life. . . . There were six of us: I was the oldest girl, then I had three sisters and two brothers. . . . We had a little corner grocery store. . . . My father borrowed money to start this business. . . . My mother ran the store. . . . My mother was the backbone of the family, and my father tended to be drinking most of the time. . . . She'd open the store about seven in the morning and we'd finish about seven at night. And then she would go home and sew for the family. . . . Everything we wore up until the time we left home, she made for us.

Both of Yoshiye Togasaki's parents were already living in the United States. Togasaki said they met each other in San Francisco "and decided to go back to Japan to get family approval [for marriage]." However, both her father's and her mother's family refused to grant permission for the marriage:

> Both sides completely refused. [My parents] had to be adopted, as the custom was in those days, in order to have their marriage on record. . . . So the Asada family of Tokyo, who were also Christians, adopted both my mother and [my] father . . . they then had a legal record and were properly married, and quickly came back to the United States.[30]

Japanese immigrants to the continental United States settled mostly in California. The proportion of alien Japanese living in the state rose from 42 percent of all Japanese immigrants in the continental United States, in 1900, to 63 percent in 1920, and to almost 75 percent in 1940.[31] Although very few Japanese immigrated to the United States after World War I, the crude birth rate (the number of live births per thousand persons in the total population) of Japanese Americans rose sharply. Sociologist Dorothy Swaine Thomas asserted that the fertility of Japanese Americans in the early 1920s was extraordinarily high when compared with that of women in Japan as well as with that of white women on the West Coast.[32] It was widely feared that American-born Japanese in California eventually would outnumber white people.[33] However, in the final analysis, the long-range birthrate of Japanese immigrants was only slightly higher than that of white citizens living in California, and lower than that of European immigrants. By 1940 the birthrate of Japanese immigrants living on the West Coast was discovered to be lower than the birthrate of the general population.[34]

Still, the perception of a dramatic increase in the number of children born in the United States to these immigrants, helped to fuel existing anti-Asian sentiments in California, leading to a series of exclusionary laws. In 1922 the Supreme Court decided in *Ozawa v. United States* that only immigrants of white or African origin could become U.S. citizens. The 1922 Cable Act stipulated that any woman citizen of the United States who married an Asian ineligible for citizenship would lose her own citizenship. The 1924 Immigration Act prohibited all Japanese immigration to the United States. Not until 1952, with passage of the McCarran-Walter Act, could Japanese immigrants become naturalized U.S. citizens. Some would argue that this cessation of Japanese immigration to the United States had the long-term advantage of facilitating the group's economic development.[35]

Although Asian immigrants could not become naturalized citizens, the Fourteenth Amendment to the United States Constitution provided that their children born in the United States or Hawaii were citizens. Before 1924, many Nisei children held dual citizenship; they were automatically citizens of Japan unless their parents completed documents with the Japanese consulate, rejecting Japanese citizenship on the child's behalf. After 1924, Japanese citizenship was granted to Nisei children only if the parents registered the child's birth with the Japanese consulate.[36]

Matters often were complicated for Nisei who had dual citizenship, especially after World War II broke out. Ruth Fujii learned about her dual citizenship from her uncle who lived in Japan:

> My uncle is the one who told me we had dual citizenship: Japanese
> registered in Japan and here [in Hawaii]. That was in the thirties: I'm
> a 1933 high school graduate. My uncle wrote and said that if we [Fujii
> and her siblings] wanted to come to Japan, we were welcomed. But he
> also said, "If you are not coming to Japan and you're going to stay in
> America, that is your country; you cut off your dual citizenship.". . .
> Before I graduated from high school I had cut my dual citizenship. . . .
> When I graduated . . . I had a chance to take the civil service test, and
> I couldn't take it if I had dual citizenship.

Most Nisei changed their dual citizenship to American citizenship. Those Nisei women who entered the armed services changed their dual citizenship status before induction.

Family and Community

Upon arrival in the United States, Japanese immigrants retained many values and norms of their homeland; these values were based on Confucianism and Buddhism.[37] The hierarchical structure of the traditional Japanese family was based on generation, and on age within generation, as well as on gender. Everyone played a vital role in the family's functioning. Grandparents taught young children the rituals of Japanese life. The Japanese wife controlled household affairs such as shopping and overseeing servants, and had much to say in her children's marriages (which were arranged by the families). Also prevalent were the concepts of *on* (deep obligation to superiors) and filial piety, best described, in the words of Kitano, as "a reciprocal obligation from parent to child and child to parent."[38]

In addition, family cohesion and harmony were valued over individual achievement. Interaction among family members was relatively impersonal, with an emphasis on duty and obligation over affection. Kitano asserted that there was "seldom any demonstration of affection between husband and wife or to their children. But they provided the functions of a solid family—family meals, family outings, get-togethers with other Japanese families, and an emphasis on the importance of the family name."[39]

The ideal-typical family household in Japan was both extended and patriarchal, consisting of a male head, his wife and unmarried children, his married sons, and their wives and children.[40] Wives deferred to husbands, children deferred to fathers, younger brothers deferred to older brothers, and sisters deferred to all brothers regardless of age.[41] According to sociologist Minako Maykovich, "as a rehearsal of the establishment of the patriarch's power, the male child was permitted to vent his hostilities upon the female members of his family."[42] The father was served first at meals, was given the choicest food, went first to the family bath, and received deep bows from the other family members to show respect. The eldest son was heir to the family's wealth, and shared in the father's prerogatives.[43] In return, it was the heir's responsibility to provide for his parents when they retired.[44] Non-heirs were socialized differently from heirs and often developed an entrepreneurial attitude.[45]

The Issei women interviewed by Linda Tamura spoke about the cultural norm of deferring to husbands. With reference to the "three obediences" specified in the Confucian-based treatise *Onna Daigaku*, Tamura explained that Japanese women were instructed to "obey their fathers when unmarried; their husbands when married; and their sons when widowed."[46] Tamura's Issei informants also said that they walked behind their husbands when they arrived in the United States, because that was the custom in Japan. These women were surprised at what seemed to be the elevated status of white women in their new country. Somewhat in awe, they observed white men opening doors for their wives and catering in other ways to the wants, needs, and desires of white women. To the Issei women, white women in the United States were appreciated, and appeared to be in a much more privileged position than themselves. They did not recognize the dehumanizing effects that often accompanied the pedestal on which middle-class white women were placed.

These Issei women were observing the new middle-class Victorian role for women in the United States, a role that prevailed during the nineteenth century. Marriage was defined as an alternative to work, and husbands used their wives to show off economic success. The Issei women quoted in Tamura's book did not observe the dissatisfaction of many middle-class white women with their position in society. The middle-class Victorian woman was expected to be uninterested in sex except as a marital duty. According to popular myth, she was delicate, but powerful through her virtue and righteousness. As wives, Victorian women were financially dependent on their husbands; as mothers, their primary role was to perpetuate human life. Many disgruntled white middle-class American women compared their situation with that of slaves, and felt an affinity with black men and women.[47]

The Victorian role imposed on middle-class white women in the United States was somewhat similar to that of the wealthy Chinese immigrant wives discussed by Louise Littleton, in an article originally published in the *San Francisco Chronicle* in 1893. Littleton described these wives as confined to the house and bored. It was the Chinese custom to restrict the natural growth of girls' feet by binding them, to make the girls more attractive, when they reached marriageable age, to wealthy men. According to Littleton, a small-footed Chinese woman was not expected to do anything but look stunning. Littleton wrote, about the Chinese women who immigrated to California in the late nineteenth century to join their wealthy husbands, "A wealthy man buys a small-foot wife; she comes over the seas to California as a first-class cabin passenger; when she leaves the vessel she is carried in a closely-curtained carriage to her new home, and from the day she enters it [she] is practically entombed alive."[48]

By contrast, most Japanese women immigrants to the United States were expected to work. Many found employment as domestic workers, a subject discussed at length in Evelyn Nakano Glenn's book, *Issei, Nisei, War Bride*.[49] Some worked in family-owned businesses where their labor was unpaid, but critical to the formation of a successful economic enclave that later would develop on the United States mainland, especially in California. One aspect of traditional Japanese culture that almost invariably was observed by Japanese American families was the emphasis on laboring collectively for the family unit, and Issei women often labored with their husbands in the fields during the day and cooked, cleaned, and kept house at night. This pattern held in Hawaii as well as in the continental United States. Children also were employed as unpaid laborers in family businesses, on family farms, on the mainland, and on the plantations of Hawaii.

Hisako Yamashita recalled that while she was growing up on the island of Kauai, her entire family worked:

> Actually, I was born in a pseudo-plantation town called Cape Kakaha. I grew up and went to grammar school and high school in Kauai. [Kauai] was agricultural, [producing] sugar cane and pineapple. . . . My father worked in the plantation, making only forty dollars a month. He couldn't support the family on just forty dollars . . . so he started a poultry farm. My mother took care of the . . . farm, and we all pitched in and helped. When I was a little kid I had to change the water; my sister had to feed the chickens. That's how we were brought up.

Similarly, Grace Kutaka, a former corporal in the WAC, had been reared in Kapohi, Kauai; there she lived on a plantation with her parents, who were laborers, and seven brothers and sisters. Kutaka and her siblings worked on the plantation without pay. Both Yamshita and Kutaka stated that they labored not for themselves as individuals, but for their family units.

According to Eileen Tamura, Japanese laborers were the fifth major ethnic group immigrating to Hawaii, preceded by the Chinese, Portuguese, Norwegians, and Germans.[50] Most Japanese immigrants were initially poor, starting at the bottom of the economic pyramid. At the top of the Hawaiian class structure was a small white elite, and underneath them was a middle class composed of mostly Caucasian artisans and small-business people. The lowest economic stratum was composed mainly of Asians who worked in unskilled and semiskilled jobs.[51] Andrew Lind's study of Hawaiian Japanese reveals that the majority of the Japanese immigrants spent their first few years in Hawaii on a sugar plantation; he asserted that "most of their Island-born children have lived for some years in the plantation environment."[52]

Hisako Yamashita, born in 1923, was always aware of the hierarchical structure of Hawaii's plantation economy:

> In our area, which was a dry area, there was sugar cane. . . . Asians worked in the fields. And, of course, the people who ran the plantations were all white— Norwegians mostly. The Spanish and Portuguese worked in the fields as overseers. They felt that they were above us, but not quite elite. . . . There was a definite cleavage between the

ruling class and the workers. . . . The top people who ruled the roost and ran the plantations were all white. We were always aware of that. The only way our parents said we could get out of this kind of thing was to get educated. . . . Japanese stress education a great deal, and so we were determined to go to high school and college, and become professionals.

Even so, Hawaii's Japanese had opportunities to advance economically. According to Lind, shopkeeping provided the Issei with "the most accessible stepping stones to economic security. By 1930 the Japanese were operating 49 percent of the retail stores."[53] As early as 1905, they also had "secured a strong foothold in such fields as carpentry, plumbing, tailoring, barbering, fishing, and independent farming."[54]

Alice Kono grew up on the island of Molokai, where her father worked as a carpenter: "My mom was a housewife and my dad was a carpenter. . . I had a sister and two brothers. We were all working, some of us in the office and others in the field; I worked in the office." Like the other women in this study, Kono described her family as close. As in other Japanese American families, each member worked cooperatively for the good of the whole family: "We knew what we had to do and we all did things together. There were no squabbles."

Because so many of the Japanese families in Hawaii were large and poor, children sometimes were taken into white professionals' households to live, with white professionals assuming custody of the child. Such was the case for Ruth Fujii, who would later become a Wac; she grew up in Kauai, where her mother was a widow with six children:

> Mother became a widow when my oldest brother was only twelve, and a baby came after my dad died. And so we had to be on our own. . . .
> We all worked together; we lived at home but we did our jobs. [In] those days we didn't have social security or anything like that. We lived on a sugar plantation on Kauai, . . . we all went to school, . . . we all had part-time jobs. . . . When I was in elementary school I started babysitting from when I was about eight. The doctor's wife had a little girl, and whenever she had to go anyplace she took me. I got twenty-five cents for that afternoon. . . . Whatever we earned, we took home and gave it to my mother. We were fortunate—we had our own garden, and we had our own chickens. . . . So [with] the chicken and the eggs, and all the vegetables you could think of, we never starved.

Fujii's mother was a housewife until her husband's death. "After he died," Fujii explained, "My mother did laundry, ironing, and stuff like that for the men in the plantation." In an effort to support the family, Fujii's brother left school in the eighth grade and started working on the plantation "with the grown-ups."

Not long after Fujii's father's death, her elementary school principal (a Caucasian woman named Mrs. Coby) was transferred from a school in Kauai to one in Honolulu. Fujii explained, "[Mrs. Coby] didn't want me to stay on Kauai and just be like the other girls, just graduate and get married. . . . She wanted me to go to school. So she offered to take me to live with her. She was a widow and she had a little girl." Thus Fujii left home when she was still in elementary school to live with her principal in Honolulu:

> We had only one high school on Kauai, and we lived on the west side, a ways from where the high school was. And you had to pay three dollars a month for transportation. We didn't have that kind of money. So [my mother and brother] weren't going to send me to school. . . . Mrs. Coby said, "I'm taking her home to Honolulu." My brother said "all right" because [previously], when a doctor's mother-in-law visited his family in Kauai, she wanted to take me back to live with her in Seattle. My brother said, "No, that's too far away." But when the second opportunity came, he said I could go. . . . Mrs. Coby had a two-bedroom cottage. She had a cleaning lady come once a week, but then I kept everything up. The laundry was sent out, but I washed and ironed our clothes. . . . I mowed the lawn and kept the hedge trimmed. And there were pods on the trees. I would cut them off. . . . She sent me to school, and after I graduated [from] McKinley High School, I took the civil service test and I got to be the first secretary at McKinley.

Therefore, part of Fujii's childhood was spent living in a household headed by a Caucasian woman. At the very least, this event helped to shape her outlook on life, and it may even account for the independence she displayed in stating that her family could not do anything about her decision to join the military "because they knew that it was my own life."

Family life in the continental United States differed somewhat from that on Hawaii; the degree to which the women in this study were exposed to traditional family norms varyied. Some Nisei servicewomen grew up in predominantly Japanese neighborhoods; Sue Kato, for example, was born in a Japanese farming area of North Platte, Nebraska.[55] Similarly, Irene Nishikaichi, who grew up in Los Angeles, lived in a racially segregated community:

> Until the war broke out, I wasn't really conscious of being Japanese and being American, . . . I was just myself. It wasn't until the war broke out that I would get on the bus and people would look at me, and I finally became aware that I looked different to other people. . . .

While I was in Los Angeles, except for that period after the war, I never realized [racial] differences, because for a couple of years I lived in Little Tokyo. And in a public school, 99.9 percent of the student body was Japanese American. There might have been one or two Mexicans, maybe one or two Chinese. The rest were all Japanese American. We lived in ghettos, just like the blacks; very few Japanese Americans were even allowed to buy homes. And even if you could afford to, you could only live or buy in certain areas. So we had Japanese churches, Japanese schools, and we associated only with other Japanese Americans or Japanese like our parents and their friends.

Nishikaichi's account of the Japanese American ghetto where she grew up is similar to that of Noel Campbell Mitchell, an African American woman who served in the WAC during the same period. In a published interview, Mitchell said that, before entering the military, "I had never been around white people. . . . I didn't know too much about segregation because I'd only been around blacks all of my life." As in Mitchell's case, the ghetto community in which Nishikaichi was reared insulated her from the dehumanizing influences of racism.[56]

Yoshiye Togasaki had exposure to the Japanese American as well as the white community. She recalled that both her parents were very active in community affairs: her mother helped to care for community women during childbearing and illness, and her parents cared for people in her neighborhood during an influenza epidemic. At other times, as well, her family donated their services to the community.

One of Togasaki's contributions was interpreting for community members. She recalled that women in San Francisco were highly organized and provided strong role models. Describing how she became interested in practicing medicine, Togasaki stated:

We were sent after school hours to interpret for women as they visited doctors' offices. I was sent to hospitals where women had had their surgery . . . so they would have someone who understood their language. I would get the nurse for them, ask for them the things they needed, then come on home. With this much exposure, you automatically go into medicine because you are aware of needs, you are aware of what the potential is. In addition . . . , we had in San Francisco a group of women who were well organized and who were very good role models for other women. . . . Children's Hospital for women and children was established by women, for women, so there would be a place for internship and residency. . . . This is how I happened to go into medicine.[57]

Some Nisei servicewomen grew up in predominantly white neighborhoods but were encouraged by their parents to maintain Japanese culture. Miwako Rosenthal remained in the United States with her parents and received all of her childhood education in California, but her parents wanted her to retain her Japanese cultural roots:

> My parents didn't like me associating with Caucasians. . . . I had no qualms about prejudice or anything because most of my life was spent with Caucasians in spite of the fact that there were other Japanese children around. I don't know why, but [Nisei children] never [accepted] me among them. I was usually the only Japanese in the class, so I had no qualms about being . . . different, and I was always [accepted]. The only time that I was discriminated against was when I was number one in the spelling bee in the eighth grade. And at that time they didn't let me become the representative in the spelling bee. They let [a Caucasian] girl do it. Everybody said that I should have gotten it.

Rosenthal was not discouraged by this blatant act of inequality. Discrimination began to lessen when she went to high school:

> My brother was valedictorian, and everybody said "They'll never give it to a Jap." But he got it, and the teacher that gave it to him was a civics teacher. She was so good to me, too, when I went to high school. Then, when I became valedictorian, they gave it to me. And then my sister followed and she got it too. So the three of us got it from the same high school. The teachers . . . were all good to us. I never felt any discrimination or feeling that I was any different.

Mary Yamada was born in Los Angeles. She lived in a racially mixed neighborhood, growing up with children of Mexican and Jewish descent. Yamada, whose biological father had died when she was just two years old, reflected on her family:

> My stepfather died when I was fourteen. . . . He really wanted us to go to college; he was interested in our getting education. He didn't encourage us to speak Japanese and I didn't live among the Japanese. I lived more among the Mexicans and the Jews; they were my friends. . . . I would say we were always poor as far as I can remember . . . We were in a little township, I guess you would call it, 'cause I remember we had a constable who had his office across from where we lived. . . . We had a grocery store. My mother was a midwife, and my father wasn't home much. . . . I still have letters he wrote me to take care of mama, to pay the telephone bill, to pay this and do that, you

know. And my sister was older but she was more of a social butterfly, I
would say. She was very good in athletics too.

The Yamadas' Los Angeles home was very modest, with just two rooms. They
lived in back of the family's grocery store:

> There was a screen door separating the store from our living quarters,
> if you could call it that, and the living quarters was the kitchen. The
> kitchen was our living room. That's where I took my bath, and I had
> to throw the water out in the back yard. I did my washing using that
> galvanized tub, and that washing I did outside. . . . And I remember,
> we had one bedroom for the five of us, with no wallpaper or anything,
> just rough wood. And then we had an outhouse.

Yamada grew up with responsibilities. She and her sister opened the family's
grocery store when her mother was out making house calls as a midwife:

> Whenever we came home and our store was closed, we knew that
> Mama had gone out on a call . . . as a midwife. And we never knew
> when she was going to come back. Sometimes she wouldn't come
> back 'til the following day. But we opened the store—that is—my
> sister and I. My brother was about two years younger, so he didn't do
> anything with us, really. . . . I remember opening the store in the
> morning and moving those heavy wooden crates of milk that [was] in
> glass bottles, pints and quarts. . . . I had to lift that up from the ground
> level up to the top of the box to take [them] inside the store to put in
> our refrigerator. Now we did that about seven in the morning, and
> then we would go to school.

Most of the women in this study grew up in less traditional households;
some observed their mothers serving as providers for the family and struggling
for a more egalitarian status with their husbands. Hisako Yamashita's mother,
for example, although not the primary breadwinner, was in partnership with
her husband:

> It always seems like the men are running the family but I remember
> my mother being very strong. . . . She was running the poultry farm
> and she handled all of the business with the stores. They'd order eggs
> from her and she'd have all the dozens ready for them. She handled
> that part, and she'd get money for our family. And so she would tell
> my father, "You can't tell me what to do," because she felt she was
> doing her part. And so the women became very strong too, and the
> kids [saw] all of this. . . . So now women are just as strong . . . . We
> didn't grow up meek.

Nishikaichi revealed that her father had worked in various jobs: "He had a laundry, he had a restaurant, and so forth. . . . My mother was a midwife and for most of my life she was the principal breadwinner." And, indeed, some Japanese American families depended solely on the leadership of the Issei wife and mother. In some cases, the husbands were deceased; in other cases, they were physically or mentally disabled. Ellen Fuchida's mother was the "backbone of the family" because the father was an alcoholic.

Fuchida's mother bought a house for her family:

> She was one of the first Isseis to ever own a house in Utah. It was a
> medium house with two baths, two bedrooms, . . . a full porch that
> was enclosed, where extra beds were. . . . Later on, as we grew up, that
> house became like a meeting place for all after I joined the JACL
> [Japanese American Citizenship League]. [S]he was a terrible house-
> keeper, so the girls all learned how. I was the cook. I had a sister that
> washed and ironed like a professional. I had another sister that
> cleaned house like a professional. And the other sister was a babysitter
> for my brother. We all had our jobs.

Nisei children's exposure to the Japanese culture varied. Some attended Japanese language school and were exposed to the Japanese culture by their parents; others had only limited knowledge of the Japanese culture and identified more fully with the American way of life. For example, Fuchida said that she had difficulties in relating to more traditional Nisei: "They all thought I was weird and I thought they were weird. They just seemed to be apologetic for even living at times. . . ." As indicated above, many Nisei children were sent to Christian churches for Sunday school; others were active in organizations such as the Girl Scouts or Boy Scouts. Although many Issei parents had little contact with Caucasians, they encouraged their children to acculturate to American society and to be "good Americans."

Grace Harada was born on a farm in Ucon, Idaho, on December 27, 1921. Her father died when she was only nine months old:

> My mother married my dad's cousin because that's what [my dad]
> asked her to do, so that my sister and I wouldn't have to go to
> Japan. . . . [We] could stay in the United States. . . . There was me and
> my older sister. After my mother remarried, I had three brothers and
> then a younger sister. We moved to Pocatello, Idaho. There weren't
> very many Japanese within the Pocatello area.

Fuchida also grew up in a predominantly white area. She described her mother as an atypical Issei, modern and with no desire to return to Japan. When her father died, her mother's oldest brother asked her to return to Japan with her six children, and he offered to take care of them. Her mother refused the offer saying, "No, my children would never fit into the Japanese way of life. And I can raise them myself."

Remembering how her mother was different from most other Issei, Fuchida noted, "She didn't really run around very much with the Issei in Salt Lake because we were too far out at the time. And I remember watching her putting on her hat and gloves and getting all dressed up on a Friday to go to Salt Lake with her three Caucasian friends for lunch and shopping . . . and she spoke all English."

Fuchida and her five siblings grew up acculturated to the Euro-American lifestyle:

> We all graduated from the same high school. And then, when I was about sixteen, . . . I met some of the Nisei from Salt Lake and . . . finally learned that I was a Nisei. It was kind of strange because I really didn't know any Japanese at all. [My siblings and I] went to Japanese-language school over by the Great Salt Lake, but we would cut classes and play around because it really didn't mean that much to us. I'm sorry now. . . . One time, when we were growing up, . . . when I was about a junior in high school, . . . I wondered why we were so different, because until then I had never known I was different. And [my mother] said, "Don't say anything." Just consider yourself very fortunate." And I asked: "Why?" She said, "Because you have two cultures to choose from. You have two different kinds of food you can eat." And after that I was perfectly satisfied being what I was.

Former Wac Cherry Shiozawa was a twin and one of nine children born and reared in Oakland, California. She lived in an integrated, low-income neighborhood, in which her father was very active. Looking back on her childhood, Shiozawa stated that she was "very Americanized; . . . captain of a basketball championship team in high school, and a member of the crew team."[58] Shiozawa's father worked as a tailor while her mother stayed at home caring for the children.

Almost all of the women interviewed grew up in households that practiced the traditional values of collective effort. To a lesser degree, some informants spoke of growing up in a traditional patriarchal household, with male dominance and privilege.[59] Ruth Fujii, for example, in describing her family's household in Hawaii, said that her eldest brother was twelve years old when their father died, and became head of the household. He inherited the family's house and was responsible for their mother's well-being:

> My brother's wife-to-be was told that my mother was going to live with my brother forever because he's the oldest. So he kept her [Fujii's

mother] and she kept the house, and then, when the kids came along, she dressed them, and put them on the school bus . . . [and] when they came home, she had goodies ready for them. My brother's wife was able to work [outside the home].

Research also reveals that Japanese families were able to retain some aspects of a patriarchal structure even while adapting to American life. According to a previous study, the Japanese American family was more patriarchal than the white Anglo-Saxon Protestants (WASP) family in the years preceding World War II.[60] In the Japanese American families, young Nisei women were reared to be caretakers of the home. They learned *majime* (to be serious and honest), and *sunao* (to be gentle, and obedient), and to observe *oyakookoo* (filial piety).[61]

This vertical family structure, however, was modified in response to the conditions in the United States. The Issei father's authority was undermined because he knew less about the American culture than his Nisei son. Further, the Nisei son was a citizen with rights denied to his father. In addition, the grandparents, who taught the young about the rituals of Japanese life, were not available to many young Nisei; most had remained in Japan. To fill this void, community groups sponsored Japanese schools to teach Nisei children the Japanese language and traditional, ethnic values. Not all Nisei children attended these schools, however; and among those who did, many left unable to speak Japanese, and forgot the moral lessons.[62] Hence, traditional Japanese family structure began to decline even before the United States entered the war, and was almost obliterated as a result of the mass evacuation and internment. For the most part, Nisei servicewomen growing up in the U.S. mainland were absorbing more mainstream American than Japanese culture, and identified themselves as American.

Conflicting identity was more of an issue for the *Kibei*, American-born children of Japanese descent who lived and received part or all of their education in Japan; they were often ridiculed by their peers for not understanding the American ways. Many Issei parents sent their children to Japan; given their sojourner status, the Issei generally did not sever ties with their households of origin. Evelyn Nakano Glenn has shown that immigration often was a family strategy allowing the Issei to work, make money, and contribute to the financial support of the kin in Japan:

Even those who formed conjugal families abroad still retained obligations to kin in Japan and were expected to provide for parents and other relatives there. . . In return, the relatives at home could be called upon to perform services for the immigrants. . . . [C]hildren were sometimes left behind or sent back by parents who were working in America. An Issei's parents, brothers, sisters, aunts, and uncles might be called upon to take them in and raise them for years at a time. Immigrants who became too old to work or who needed medical attention also returned and were cared for by relatives.[63]

Togasaki and one of her sisters were sent to Tokyo to live with her grandmother:

> This was partly to help my mother so she would not have her hands full with so many children, and also to provide company for my grandmother, who was getting more and more lonely because her daughter and then her only son had . . . come over by then to the United States. . . . When my grandmother died . . . we were sent to my paternal grandmother's for six months, then came back to the United States in April of 1910. At that time I entered school, not knowing a word of English, of course, but quickly picked it up because the teachers were patient. . . . and they would concentrate and drill you for pronunciation and diction.[64]

However, Togasaki probably would not be considered a Kibei, since she only lived in Japan for a few years and received all of her formal education in the United States.

In contrast, Kibei spent many years living in Japan and received at least a good portion of their formal education there. The Kibei was deeply immersed in the Japanese culture. In 1934 an estimated 13 percent of the Nisei children lived and attended school in Japan.[65] Rosenthal had two brothers, both Kibei:

> My mother took them back to Japan when they were small because she didn't want to raise her sons in the United States. And she was thinking that eventually [she and my father] would make a fortune, go back to Japan, and live very affluently. Like all the Japanese immigrants, they came here to build a fortune and then go back. My mother didn't want to stay here, so she talked my father into letting her go back for a visit, but her real intention was to return to Japan.

A study published by the War Relocation Authority in 1944 cited several reasons why Issei parents sent their children to Japan. Some parents simply felt that their children should know the customs of Japan; others wanted their relatives to know their children. Nisei girls sometimes were sent to Japan because there was a wider pool of eligible bachelors. For some parents, economics was the primary motive. American money had a high exchange value in Japan; parents worked and sent money back to Japan while relatives cared for their children. Other parents, however, believed that economic opportunities were scarce in the United States; they felt that exposure to both Japanese and American education would afford their sons an opportunity to work in Japan.

The Kibei faced the challenge of fitting into neither Japanese nor American society. Those sent to Japan during their adolescent years spoke Japanese with an American accent, and their American upbringing made them noticeably different from Japanese youths. Similarly, when the Kibei returned to the United States, they were often viewed as strange by Nisei who had not traveled to Japan. In the 1944 study, the War Relocation Authority referred to the Kibei as "a new immigrant group . . . a minority group within a minority."[66] Theirs was a conflict of identity, especially after Japan bombed Pearl Harbor. Yet, many were recruited by the War Department and served in the MISLS.

In sum, the breakdown of the traditional Japanese family structure made it easier for Nisei servicewomen to break with subcultural norms. For the most part, they had been reared in the Western culture and identified strongly with being American. For many of them, having to choose between Japan and the United States was not a great source of anxiety. The Nisei woman who identified strongly with the Japanese culture during World War II—and there were some—did not don the uniform. The decision to join the military would have caused more mental anguish for the Kibei; still, some were inducted into the American armed services and served with distinction.

Education

Historical studies have shown that, on the U.S. mainland, Issei parents sent their children to school more often than any other ethnic group. In addition, Nisei children stayed in school longer, and were more likely to graduate and attend college than other immigrants' children.[67] The Nisei child was encouraged to do well in school by parents, teachers, and other community members. Formal education reinforced social conformity; as Harry Kitano observed, every element of the Nisei child's environment "sanctioned conforming behavior and school success."[68] Consequently Nisei children often were high academic achievers. According to Richard Bell's study, published in 1935, Nisei students' academic achievement and intelligence level were equal to those of Caucasian students in 1930.[69] Citing studies conducted at Stanford University in the 1920s and 1930s, Roger Daniels claims that "in both attitude and achievement, Nisei pupils were well above the norm."[70]

This is true of the women in this study. Yoshiye Togasaki, who graduated from the University of California at Berkeley in 1929, spoke of her father's commitment to educating all of his children well:

> My father's principle was "I will not leave you any money, I will not leave you any wealth, but I will give you any education you wish to aspire to, and no questions asked." I originally entered as pre-med, but shifted over into the so-called Bachelor of Public Health. . . . There were about eleven or twelve Nisei women graduating [from] Berkeley that year and about twice as many Nisei men. . . . By the time I was going to medical school, in 1931, things were pretty tight. . . . I went to my father and said I wanted to go to medical school. He said, "Well, how do you think you are going to do it?" I said, "I have some money saved." . . . He said, "If you give me what you have, I will help you and I'll take care of it for you."[71]

Togasaki attended and graduated from the Johns Hopkins University School of Medicine and started a private practice in Los Angeles in 1941. In regard to her sisters, who had also become physicians, Togasaki stated: "My older sister Kazue finished [medical school] in 1934, and after her internship, she opened her office in San Francisco in 1935. My other sister finished [medical school] also . . . she practiced in Sacramento. She was younger than I."[72]

Miwako Rosenthal's parents consistently emphasized high educational attainment. Her brother studied medicine and became a pediatrician; as she stated, "My sisters were also professionals. They went to nursing school and so forth. One of them went to the University of Chicago; another one went to St. Mary's College to study nursing, and then . . . to the University of Minnesota. When we moved to Texas, I went to the College of Mines and Metallurgy. It's one of the branches of the University of Texas; it was an engineering school."

Mary Yamada attended elementary, junior high, and high school in Los Angeles. After graduating from high school, she attended the University of Southern California until the cost became prohibitive. She attempted to find employment as a domestic worker to finance her college education:

> I was at the University of Southern California through half of my junior year, and not having a father, . . . we didn't have much money, and I tried to work my way through college. . . . It was quite an adventure; at that time I was seventeen years old, . . . a sophomore trying to work my way through college. . . . I walked from Los Angeles to Hanford, from Hanford to Fresno and Sacramento and all these other places up to Oakland, and up as far as San Francisco. . . .
> Anyway, I covered about thirteen cities and towns during the summer when I was trying to earn money.

Yamada found it difficult to get work, even as a domestic: "I thought anybody could be hired as a domestic but even then you needed references. . . . I was sixteen when I entered the university as a freshman and I had no references."

Unable to find a job in California, Yamada moved to New York City and enrolled in a nursing program at Bellevue Hospital: "I was taking a pre-med course at Southern Cal and . . . I couldn't afford to study medicine at Berkeley. . . . So I thought [that] by becoming a nurse, I could earn money to continue my education. At Bellevue, after eight months they gave us a stipend, twenty dollars or something like that." Yamada remained at Bellevue Hospital and worked her way into advanced positions:

> I stayed at Bellevue for three years and then became a ward instructor, and then after ward instructor I was an assistant supervisor in surgery, and then after that I became chief, supervising pediatrics. At that time I happened to be going to Columbia University to finish my education. I had over fifty credits, so I got my bachelor's degree. . . at Teacher's College of Columbia . . . in 1939, and then I got my master's in [1942].

Irene Nishikaichi had aspired to become an attorney, but her family's economic position forced her to enroll in secretarial school instead. Nishikaichi altered her educational plans out of concern for her parent's welfare:

> I decided my parents were so much older [than I] that [I'd] better start earning a living. And so I went into legal stenography. When I got into City College, the person who was teaching shorthand said that she was planning to become a secretary before she got talked into becoming a teacher. I learned that at L.A. City College I could take what was called a semiprofessional course and an academic course. So I combined typing and shorthand with a regular academic course.

The emphasis on educational attainment also prevailed among the Nisei living in Hawaii. Hisako Yamashita explained that her parents, and other Issei parents she knew, stressed education:

> In grammar school [we] worked hard and studied hard, and then [we] were supposed to go to college to be a teacher. That's what [our parents] always said to us. . . . I was second to the last in a family of nine. [Education] was put in my mind so much that I said, "I'm going to college and I'm going to be a teacher." . . . And a lot of [us] became teachers. Three-fourths of the teachers for Hawaii were of Japanese [descent]. . . . and then they became doctors, dentists, and social workers before the war. . . . and the family stressed all these things . . . all of the time.

However, in Hawaii educational opportunities for the Nisei children were sometimes limited, because they lived in rural areas far from schools. In addition, the burden of such family responsibilities as caring for siblings or working to contribute to the family's income often stood between the Nisei and formal education. In the words of Eileen Tamura: "Despite the Japanese interest in education, continuing in school (in Hawaii) during the first three decades of the twentieth century was difficult because most Nisei youths had to help their families make ends meet."[73] Tamura further asserted that the loss of potential earnings was but one issue facing Issei parents; the extra expenses incurred by parents to pay for school fees, books, and sometimes boarding was yet another burden.[74]

On the other hand, Nisei men and women living in Hawaii had greater opportunities for occupational mobility in the years preceding World War II than those living on the U. S. mainland. Although mainland Nisei students excelled in college before and after the United States declared war on Japan, they were seldom able to find employment commensurate with their education. This was due in part to the relatively small population of Japanese Americans in the continental United States, and in part to the virulent racism practiced on the mainland. Despite their educational achievement, Nisei men and women often fell prey to racial discrimination excluding them from occupations for which they were trained. Togasaki recalled her difficulty in finding employment after she completed medical school:

> While I was in Los Angeles in my residency I was taking all kinds of examinations for the State of California, or cities, or counties. I was interested in public health work. . . . I was informed, "Sorry, we would like to employ you, but other members of the staff and the community will not accept you." . . . And then, finally, to cap it, the chairman of Maternal and Child Health, State of California, came down to Los Angeles while I was working there at the county hospital to interview me. He said, "Miss Togasaki, would you please take your name off the Civil Service list because we are in the position where we cannot employ another person with your name there." I said, "That's too bad."[75]

Anthropologist Lane Ryo Hirabayashi wrote a similar account of Richard Nishimoto, who graduated from Stanford University with an engineering degree:

> In 1929, when Nishimoto graduated in engineering, it was already the custom for businesses and corporations to come to Stanford to interview members of the senior class. One associate of Nishimoto's

recalled that all of the class members received job offers after interviews except for Nishimoto. When he asked the reason, he was reportedly told: "Look at your face. It's Oriental. No one will hire you."[76]

These acts of discrimination, however demoralizing they may have been, did not appear to alter the Issei parent's position on education. Nisei children still were expected to attain and maintain high levels of academic achievement. The educational achievement on the part of Nisei women helps to account for their recruitment by the War Department and assignment to military intelligence and to administrative positions in other units. Being encouraged to excel in school, and having access to quality education, provided Nisei women the educational aptitude and achievement to qualify for military service.

Occupational Niche

Like the Hawaiian Japanese, most Issei immigrating to the continental United States during the nineteenth century entered the rural labor force, in this case in the Pacific Coast and the intermountain states. In some cases they replaced Chinese laborers on the railroads, in the mines, and in the lumber industry. Immigrants to urban areas worked mostly as domestic servants. According to historian Sucheng Chan, there were three types of Japanese domestics, "school boys," "day workers," and those who found long-term domestic work.[77] Chan describes "school boy domestics" as young men from poor families who worked as live-in servants while attending school. "Day workers," according to Chan, performed domestic tasks for a daily wage while living in Japanese-operated boarding houses.[78] Long-term domestic workers usually filled permanent positions in restaurants or in Japanese-owned companies.

By 1908 the Issei had established themselves in all areas of California's agriculture, had secured tenancy and sharecropping arrangements, and were supplying most of the state's seasonal labor. Roger Daniels estimates that Japanese Americans controlled about 1 percent of California's agricultural land, but controlled, through their intensive labor, about 10 percent of California's crops, valuing approximately 67 million.

One way Japanese American landowners profited was by leasing land to tenant farmers. As described by demographer Dorothy Swaine Thomas:

> Japanese tenants . . . cleared, drained, and leveled waste land and
> reduced it to cultivation. They installed pumping plants and introduced irrigation systems. They transformed land from extensive
> farming to more profitable intensive cultivation of vegetables, berries

and fruits, and they pioneered in developing new crops. They
accepted inferior housing, . . . Above all, they paid high rents.[79]

Japanese landowners found it more profitable, Thomas argues, to lease
the land to tenant farmers than to farm it themselves. To increase their profits, the Issei usually conducted specialized types of farming that required little
capital investment.[80] Tenancy continued to increase profitability until the 1913
passage of the California Alien Land Law, prohibiting Issei from owning agricultural land. (The Issei could own urban real estate, however; that right was
protected by a Japanese-American commercial treaty.) Yet the Alien Land Law
was often ineffective; Japanese immigrants could work around it by purchasing land in the name of their American-born children and retaining control
as legal guardians. This law also permitted leasing and sharecropping contracts,
a loophole designed to protect the interests of white landowners who leased
land to Issei.

The 1920 amendment to the 1913 Alien Land Law was far more devastating to Japanese farmers. It prohibited Japanese immigrants from purchasing or leasing agricultural land, holding stock in agricultural landholder
companies, transferring or selling agricultural land to one another, or being
appointed guardians of minors who had title to such land.[81] Nonetheless, as
Daniels indicates in one of his many studies on the subject, Issei farmers could
evade this law through legal methods such as forming corporations, which
could hold land while the Issei farmers held the stock. Therefore it is not surprising that, just before the United States entered World War II, Japanese
Americans retained a strong hold on West Coast agriculture.

Japanese immigrants also owned and operated highly competitive businesses in the continental United States. Among the more common Japanese-
owned enterprises in the early 1900s were hotels, restaurants, barbershops, shoe
shops, supply stores, and laundries. By 1929, Los Angeles had the largest Japanese population on the West Coast, 30 percent of whom were engaged in urban trade.[82] Bloom and Riemer found that in 1941 approximately 36 percent
of all employed Japanese in Los Angeles were self-employed.[83] The older and
more established a Japanese American man was, the more likely he was to be
self-employed.

Much of the Japanese Americans' success with their small businesses is
attributable to some continuity in the traditional Japanese household structure. This was evident in Hawaii as well as the continental United States.
Japanese Americans did not separate work from family life: wives and children worked for no additional income. The traditional Japanese cultural values of diligence, frugality, and commitment to long-term goals also facilitated

the Issei efforts to attain economic success in the U.S. In addition, Japanese Americans' exclusion, regardless of qualifications, from mainstream occupations helps to explain why they devoted so much energy to their small businesses; many such businesses were established by well-educated Issei unable to find employment in their professions. Yoshiye Togasaki's father, for example, had graduated from the law school at the Imperial University before he immigrated to the United States. He went into the import business, dealing in "retail foods . . . canned and dried foods, Japanese foods, Oriental foods, . . . soy sauce, . . . tea, et cetera" to support his family. Similarly, engineering graduate Richard Nishimoto owned and operated a fruit-and-vegetable market in Gardena, California.

Further, the rise in self-employment among Japanese Americans on the West Coast is explicable in part by the cooperation among community members. Bonacich and Modell have identified several elements of Japanese-style cooperation that help to explain how the Issei were able to advance from laborers to farm owners and entrepreneurs. First, Japanese immigrants developed capital through partnerships; with this capital they formed *tanomoshi*, or rotating credit associations. Second, they could make use of cheap labor from within their ethnic group by recruiting through communal channels. In addition, they exercised a labor paternalism that allowed workers to accept low wages and long hours, knowing that the employers would provide for their basic needs. Finally, Japanese entrepreneurs trained workers through an apprenticeship program.[84]

This Japanese system of employment allowed Issei business owners to compete with rivals by charging lower prices in the open market and offering higher bids on purchases and rentals. Japanese underbid white barbers, restaurant operators, and laundromat owners. Issei businesses were able to expand rapidly, and in some economic spheres these businesses could monopolize the market. The highly educated Nisei living on the mainland were, like well-educated Issei, excluded from occupations for which they were trained; often they worked in family businesses or on family farms. By 1942, many Nisei had developed small businesses on the West Coast, primarily in produce retailing, as successful as those of their parents.

Ellen Fuchida worked in her parents' grocery store along with her siblings when they were growing up:

> This was a family business, and everyone was expected to do their
> part. From the time we were ten we were expected to put in hours at
> the store, either putting things on the shelf, or wiping the shelf off.
> And after we got out of school we had to give at least two years [of
> service] before we went off onto a life of our own. . . . We were paid,

but not regular wages. We just got paid whatever we needed, a pair of shoes or whatever, and whatever spending money we wanted. We [didn't get] . . . a regular salary; it was family work.

When they were older, Fuchida and her sister opened successful businesses of their own. As mentioned earlier, when Japan bombed Pearl Harbor, Fuchida owned and was operating a beauty salon in her family's house. Her mother still ran the family's grocery store, and one of her sisters owned a restaurant. Before she joined the WAC, Fuchida worked in all three family entreprises: "We were going night and day. . . . We were making money hand over fist."

Indeed, Japanese Americans made economic gains early in their years in the United States. Euro-American small farmers, large corporate farmers, and small businesses felt the pinch of Japanese American competition. Consequently, Japanese American restaurants were picketed in San Francisco in 1906, and anti–Japanese-laundry leagues were formed in several cities by employees of white-owned laundries.[85] Bonacich and Modell argue that business and labor united temporarily in a movement to destroy the ethnic-Japanese economy,[86] and that the evacuation of Japanese Americans was a result of the threat of successful small Issei businesses felt by business and labor. According to Bonacich and Modell, the Japanese Americans' peculiar position in American society as a "middleman minority" caused them to be economically concentrated and socially isolated, and thereby vulnerable to racist attack during World War II.[87]

Historian Roger Daniels published statistics showing that Japanese American employment in 1940 was concentrated mostly in agriculture (51%), followed by wholesale and retail trade (24%) and service (17%). Although most of the businesses were small fruit and vegetable stands, Daniels asserted that a few of the larger businesses grossed $1 million or more annually. Also according to Daniels, first-generation families owned farms and businesses to a greater degree than did the general population.[88] Bonocich and Modell, as well as Daniels, argue that the success enjoyed by Japanese American businesses intensified negative sentiments toward them during World War II. Trade unions and professional organizations refused membership to Japanese Americans, forcing them to form their own. Consequently, Japanese Americans developed ethnic solidarity in racially isolated communities.[89]

As illustrated in these studies, the Japanese American community had advanced to the stratum of lower middle class within one generation. Economic competition, combined with ethnocentrism and political dominance on the part of the white power structure, thus certainly helps to explain why Japanese Americans were evacuated from their homes and incarcerated.

In contrast to those who settled on the mainland, Japanese immigrants to Hawaii were able to protect their economic interests through political involvement. Japanese laborers who remained in Hawaii after 1900 were able to strike for better working conditions and higher wages, because the National Labor Relations Board services in Hawaii were free of racial bias. Labor organizers recruited Hawaiian Japanese workers to demonstrate for labor rights, and the Hawaiian Japanese responded enthusiastically. This was clearly the case in 1943, when a unionized transportation slowdown took place, involving five hundred bus drivers, 65 percent of whom were of Japanese descent.[90]

Several white Hawaiians expressed concern about the potential political and economic power of the Hawaiian Japanese, who held jobs important to the city's day-to-day activities. This scenario was much different from that of the Japanese immigrants living on the mainland, forced to work in an ethnic enclave and excluded from mainstream occupations. Largely through their strong representation, Nisei men and women living in Hawaii had begun the process of occupational assimilation before World War II.

Still, whether in an ethnic enclave or an occupation in the mainstream labor force, Nisei men and women were gainfully employed before the war, and they were well educated. They were the sons and daughters of parents who had immigrated to the United States freely and opted to stay. African Americans by contrast had very little access to economic institutions, were forced to attend racially segregated schools that were below the national standards, and were excluded from the political process. They were descendants of black slaves who had been victims of internal colonialism, forcibly severed from their countries of origin.[91] Unlike the economic frailty suffered by most African American communities, Japanese American communities were economically sound. In the aggregate, Japanese Americans controlled 10 percent of California's agriculture, held stocks in corporations they themselves formed, and owned competitive businesses. It is not unreasonable to speculate that, had Japan not bombed Pearl Harbor and had the United States not declared war on Japan, the Nisei might not have struggled so hard to be a part of the U.S. war effort. However, Japan did bomb Pearl Harbor, and the United States did declare war on Japan. These events, as well as Executive Order 9066, created an environment of urgency, forcing the Nisei to choose unequivocally between their citizenships—Japanese and American—and between the culture of their parents and that of America.

Chapter 3

Contradictions and Paradoxes

It is our duty to obey the laws and regulations of this country and to cooperate in all war tasks, especially in respect to food production with all our might. We are with our younger generation who are American by birth here and we have an obligation to bring them up. Many of them are serving in the United States Army and performing other services wherever they may be fitted. We are here with you, ready to do our part and we hereby pledge ourselves to do whatever we are permitted to do.

—Japanese American residents, Brawley-
Westmorland District, Imperial Valley[1]

WHY WERE JAPANESE AMERICANS treated so inhumanely during World War II, and what effect did this treatment have on the political attitude of the Nisei? In this chapter, I discuss events that led to the United States involvement in World War II, and the reactions of the Nisei to the United States declaration of war on Japan. In addition, I examine racial antagonism in the United States, and discuss how Japanese Americans were treated by the U.S. government, as compared with other racial/ethnic groups. Last, I explore the consequences of the internment camps on the political attitudes of Japanese Americans, and how these attitudes influenced some Nisei women to join the military.

The events that led to the United States' involvement in World War II stemmed from a long history of tense relations with Japan. Political friction between these two nations dated back to the late nineteenth century, when the United States acquired territory in the Central Pacific and East Asia as a result of the Spanish-American War. The acquisition of the Philippines gave the United States access to Chinese markets, protected by the U.S.'s newly formed Open Door policy.[2]

Part of the growing fear of Japanese Americans in the United States before and during World War II was that Japan had a strong military. Japan was not viewed as a threat to U.S. commercial and political interests until it defeated Russia in the Russo-Japanese War of 1904–1905. This event was followed by a series of other Japanese military victories: the acquisition of the Caroline, Mariana, and Marshall Islands from Germany in World War I; the conquest of Manchuria in 1931; and the invasion of mainland China in 1937. The United States was concerned that Japanese control of the East would impede American trade in the region and would deny Americans access to natural resources such as oil, tin, rubber, and bauxite, which were abundant in southeast Asia.

The United States became even more alarmed when Japan entered an agreement with Germany and Italy to provide mutual political, economic, and military assistance if one of these nations was attacked by a power not involved in the European war or the Chinese-Japanese conflict; this agreement was known as the Tripartite Pact.[3] Historians agree that diplomatic relations between Japan and America worsened when Japan signed the Tripartite Pact, on September 27, 1940.[4] In retaliation, President Franklin D. Roosevelt imposed economic restrictions on Japan, freezing all Japanese assets in America on July 23, 1941, and placing an embargo on the export of oil and gasoline to Japan the following month. American citizens then living in Japan were urged to return to the United States, because of strained relations between the two countries and the threat of war.[5]

In October 1941, Japan sought diplomatic talks with the United States, proposing that Premier Fumimaro Konoye meet with President Roosevelt immediately to discuss the U.S. relaxation of the trade embargo.[6] In return, Japan was willing to withdraw its troops from Indochina at the close of the war with China. The United States stipulated that it was interested in negotiations only after Japan had clarified its obligations under the Tripartite Pact and indicated that Japanese troops would be withdrawn from China as well as from Indochina.[7] The two countries did not reach a resolution in October, or in November. By 7 December 1941, the United States and Japan were at war.

In the years preceding the Japanese attack on Pearl Harbor, the political mood of the United States was isolationist. In a somewhat pacifistic climate, American foreign policy in 1938 tended to support the status quo. Historian Stephen Ambrose remarks that the United States, anxious as it was to put an end to Japanese aggression in China, "did not have the military muscle to fight even a one-front war."[8] After December 7, 1941, however, the country's political attitude changed dramatically.

A Blatant Violation of Civil Rights

According to Roger Daniels, the anti-Japanese movement in the United States actually began in 1892 with labor leaders and was expanded by middle-class politicians: "the three major California political parties—Republican, Democrat, and Populist—took a stand against all Asiatic immigration in 1900, as did the National American Federation of Labor."[9] Daniels argues that this anti-Japanese movement did not exert much influence beyond the Far West until 1905: at that time the national media characterized Japanese immigration to the United States as an invasion.

In the previous chapter, I discussed the laws enacted to prohibit Japanese immigrants from owning agricultural land. These acts of racial antagonism were rooted in efforts to exclude Japanese immigrants from receiving the economic rewards associated with hard work in America. Sociologist Edna Bonacich has appropriately explained this racial antagonism in terms of split labor markets, which were and still are characteristic of the United States.[10] Whereas African immigrants had already been relegated to a socially inferior position through chattel slavery, followed by the implementation of a caste-like system known as Jim Crow, efforts were made to fully exclude the Japanese immigrants from the American economic and political process.

Several accounts describe racial discrimination against Japanese Americans before the 1940s. The occupational discrimination faced by Yoshiye Togasaki and Richard Nishimoto was discussed in chapter 2. Similarly, former Wac Haruko Sugi Hurt expressed the frustration associated with trying to find adequate employment even before Japan bombed Pearl Harbor. In a *Rafu Shimpo* newspaper article, Hurt was quoted that her life before the war "was very bad, depressing, with one menial job after another."[11] In the same article, former Wac Miwako Yanamoto revealed that Americans of Japanese heritage were treated like "second-class citizens, even before the war. . . . Japanese [Americans] couldn't go to a lot of places then. There was the Alien Land Law which kept Issei from buying land—my parents couldn't buy a house."[12]

The stereotypical images of Japanese Americans were only worsened by the war. Almost immediately after the attack, Japanese Americans were demonized. White Americans stopped doing business with the Japanese-owned stores they had patronized previously. Except for Japanese farmers, who helped supply food to the War Department, Japanese businesses such as nurseries, florists, and stores dependent on patronage from outside the Japanese community suffered great losses. Because of the social stigma associated with being of the same ethnicity as the enemy, Japanese Americans became outcasts not only to Euro-Americans but to other minority groups as well. This was particularly noticeable in the fear of mistaken identity exhibited by other Asian Americans. To avoid being taken as persons of Japanese heritage, Americans of Chinese, Korean, and Filipino descent began wearing identification badges.

These acts of discrimination against Japanese Americans cannot be explained solely in terms of enemy alien status. The United States was at war with Germany and Italy also: four days after Japan bombed Pearl Harbor, Germany declared war on the United States. Yet Italian and German Americans were not subjected to the same degree of ethnic antagonism as the Issei and the Nisei during World War II. Furthermore, although the so-called "alien" segment of the Italian and German American population was targeted for scrutiny and for possible evacuation, American citizens of Italian and German descent were not.

Anti-German sentiment did exist. The growth of pro-Nazi German organizations in the United States, which began as early as 1923, fueled American resentment toward the German American community during both world wars. Kurt Georg Wilhelm Ludecke visited the United States in the early 1920s to recruit German nationals for a proposed Nazi party in Germany.[13] Pro-Nazi organizations such as the Friends of New Germany and the German-American Bund sprang up in the 1930s. Whether or not these organizations were engaged in illegal activities, they helped to stigmatize the German American community as a whole. In the words of Timothy Holian, a scholar in German American studies, the existence of these organizations "helped to create an hysterical fear of Nazis in the United States, which in turn placed other uninvolved German-Americans in the position of also being cast into suspicion."[14]

Anti-German sentiment also was attributable to the destruction of American ships by German U-boats in the first six months of the war. In 1992 the Commission on Wartime Relocation and Internment of Civilians reported that, from January through June 1942, German submarines destroyed thousands of tons of American ships along the eastern coast of the United States. As reported by the commission, "This devastating warfare often came alarmingly close to shore. Sinkings could be watched from Florida resorts and, on June 15, two American ships were torpedoed in full view of bathers and picnickers at Virginia Beach."[15] According to Samuel Morison, the destruction caused by German U-boats on the Atlantic Ocean was far more devastating than the bombing of Pearl Harbor.

Yet Japanese Americans were treated far more severely by the American government and the American people, during this historical era, than any other ethnic group.[16] The treatment of Japanese Americans during World War II is more analogous to that of German Americans during World War I. Though the treatment of the two groups differed markedly, some parallels can be drawn. During World War I, the U.S. government imposed an array of restrictive measures on German "aliens" that resembled those placed on Issei and Nisei during World War II. These restrictions included exclusion from sensitive military areas, the need for government permission to change residence, and internment for minor violations of these regulations.[17] Historian Frederick Luebke wrote:

> At the beginning of the war, the President had acted under the ancient Alien and Sedition Act of 1798 to restrict their activities. Later, as spy hysteria intensified in the fall of 1917, Wilson issued new orders requiring all German aliens fourteen years and older to register with the government. On the assumption that all were potential enemy agents, they were barred from the vicinity of places deemed to have military importance, such as wharves, canals, and railroad depots. Moreover, they were expelled from the District of Columbia, required to get permission to travel within the country or to change their place of residence, and forbidden access to all ships and boats except public ferries.[18]

In some states, German nationals were disenfranchised and lost their voting privileges, privileges that the Issei did not have.[19] These restrictions were imposed on German nationals and usually did not apply to their American-born children. During World War II, by contrast, restrictions were placed on Japanese immigrants as well as on their children born in the United States.

This is not to understate the severity of discrimination against German Americans during World War I. Anti-German sentiments permeated American cultural institutions, affecting the lives not only of German nationals but of all Americans. The United States engaged in a form of ethnic cleansing. For example, in an effort to rid the United States of German cultural influences, the playing of music by Bach and Beethoven was banned, and German books were burned.[20] Several states outlawed instruction in the German language and prohibited citizens from speaking German in public.[21] German Americans became pariahs in the United States during World War I, just as Japanese Americans would, two decades later.

Although the U.S. government and private citizens sometimes infringed on the civil liberties of German and Italian Americans during World War II, these infractions did not approach the magnitude of the mass evacuation suffered by Issei and Nisei during the same period. The Alien Registration Act of 1940 required European nationals and other noncitizens to register at their local post office, where they completed a questionnaire and were finger-printed. However, as Timothy Holian observed in his study of German Americans, "registration of German legal resident aliens took a low profile as focus shifted to the increasingly hostile positions of the U.S. and Japanese governments. Issues concerning Japanese Americans and Japanese aliens replaced a preoccupation with German and other European aliens during mid- to late 1941."[22] Even after Hitler declared war on the United States, German Americans were not subjected to the same injustices as were Japanese Americans. In regard to Italian Americans, historian George Pozzetta has pointed out that only in very rare cases did government regulations force unnaturalized Italian residents to move out of family homes and evacuate restricted zones.[23]

Some scholars argue that the evacuation of some 120,000 Japanese Americans during World War II was racially motivated.[24] Surely, at some level this mass evacuation can be connected to such racist acts as the dispossession of Native Americans, the enslavement of African Americans, and the mistreatment of Mexican Americans. Racism, however is an incomplete explanation for this event. Overt acts of anti-Asian discrimination during World War II were directed specifically toward Japanese Americans. Because China and Korea were allies of the United States, and the Philippines was a U.S. territory, the status of Americans of Chinese, Korean, and Filipino descent actually improved during the war. The U.S. government viewed other Asian groups as victims of Japan, similar to the United States.

Approximately seven hours after the bombing of Pearl Harbor, Japan bombed the Philippines. This act strengthened political ties between the United States and the Philippines, and in turn improved the sociopolitical image of Filipino Americans. Forty percent of the male Filipinos living in California registered for the draft in 1942. As reported in a recent U.S. Department of Defense document:

> In 1942, the First Filipino Infantry Regiment and the Second Filipino
> Infantry Regiment were formed. As members of the Armed Forces,
> Filipinos were allowed to become citizens, and on February 20, 1943,
> 1,200 Filipino soldiers stood proudly in "V" formation at the parade
> ground of Camp Beale as citizenship was conferred on them.[25]

Similarly, Chinese Americans were accepted into the armed services and served in racially integrated units. Chinese Americans' loyalty was unquestionable, as the Republic of China also declared war on Japan the day after the attack on Pearl Harbor.

The U.S. military welcomed the service of Korean Americans. Korea had become a Japanese protectorate in 1905, and Korean Americans hoped that the destruction of Japan would lead to the restoration of Korean independence. Thus Korean Americans strongly supported the U.S. war effort against Japan. Some Korean Americans knew the Japanese language and were enlisted by the War Department to work in intelligence. Korean American women served predominantly in the American Red Cross, while the men were concentrated heavily in the National Guard. As reported by the U.S. Department of Defense, 109 Americans of Korean descent formed the Tiger Brigade of the California National Guard. "On August 29, 1943, Korean National Flag Day, the Los Angeles mayor raised the Korean flag to honor the men of the Tiger Brigade as they marched past City Hall."[26]

The racial climate was quite different for Japanese Americans, who not only were excluded from military service during the first year of the war, but also were ostracized in their civilian communities. Former Wac Grace Harada recounts the hardships that she and her family endured as they were forced out of their community. She had just graduated from high school in Pocatello when the war broke out, and aspired to attend nursing school. Harada discovered that she would not be able to attend nursing school because her father had lost his job, and she was unable to find gainful employment:

> My father worked for the railroad. And when the war broke out, he
> had worked [there] for almost thirty years. . . . Oriental [Japanese
> American] workers were all forced to quit their jobs and were more or
> less left on their own. . . . We went to Pocatello because my sister and
> some of my parents' friends were there. We had no place else to go; we
> weren't going to camp and we weren't accepted anywhere else.

Surely racism partly explains the severe treatment suffered by Japanese Americans in the United States before and during World War II, but it does not explain why the sociopolitical status of other Asian American groups improved as their countries of origin allied themselves with the United States. The ill treatment Japanese Americans were subjected to during World War II was not comparable to that accorded other racial/ethnic groups in the United States; rather, members of other Asian American groups were treated favorably, as were German and Italian Americans.

The extreme form of racial antagonism faced by Japanese Americans during World War II was multifactored. Indeed, race was one factor. Economic achievements that Japanese Americans had made before the war was another factor. These achievements, as noted in the previous chapter, were made in spite of legislation imposed by the U.S. government to impede Japanese Americans' efforts, and reflect the enormous capacity of the Japanese immigrant to adapt to the American economic system. Adaptive capacities, in the words of Charles Wagley and Marvin Harris:

> are those elements of a minority's cultural heritage which provide it with a basis for competing more or less effectively with the dominant group, which afford protection against exploitation, which stimulate or retard its adaptation to the total social environment, and which facilitate or hinder its upward advance through the socioeconomic hierarchy.[27]

In theory, an ethnic group with the greater adaptive capacity is likely to emerge as the dominant group in society.[28] It follows that, due to their economic achievements, Japanese Americans were viewed as a threat to the Anglo-dominated power structure. The military strength of the Japanese government was another factor, with fears in the dominant society exacerbated by Japan's military victories.

The oppression experienced by Japanese Americans in the continental United States was less widespread in Hawaii. Although the bombing of Pearl Harbor brought their lives to a temporary standstill, the Nisei in Hawaii were not ostracized. The women interviewed for this study indicated that they remained part of their Hawaiian communities even after the bombing. Former Wac Hisako Yamashita, for example, was in her last year of high school in Kauai when Japan bombed Pearl Harbor. She recalled, "school stopped completely. We didn't go back to school but they said we all graduated. So we all graduated the following year." Yamashita and other Japanese Americans did not experience the same racial intimidation as those living on the mainland. Yamashita stated just the opposite: "We felt very secure, to tell you the truth. . . . We were known as the dominant group. . . . We didn't have this feeling of minority [suffered by] the Japanese in California."

A similar account was given by former Wac Ruth Fujii, who was living in a racially integrated dwelling in Honolulu during the Japanese attack. On the day of the bombing, she reported,

> I was living in a cottage with a bunch of girls. . . . We already had first aid training, and I had a first aid certificate. . . . I was going out to a drug store around the corner to buy some Christmas paper when the girls next door said, "Where are you going, Ruth?" And I said, "I'm running to the drug store." They said, "No, don't." So I went back in, and that's when I found out about the bombing. The first thing we did was get our first [aid kits. We] ran to the school, and we volunteered.

In contrast to the immediate isolation of Nisei living on the mainland, the

Nisei of Hawaii were only one of many ethnic groups working side by side in the rescue and recovery efforts after the bombing of Pearl Harbor. Therefore it was not surprising that Fujii's first response to the attack was to aid in the rescue efforts along with her Caucasian housemates. Unlike those on the mainland, citizens in Hawaii were initially unified by this catastrophic act rather than separating along ethnic lines.

Certainly, there were some private expressions of hostility against Japanese Americans in Hawaii after the bombing. Lieutenant Commander Cecil Coggins, stationed there before and during World War II, observed that, after Pearl Harbor, negative attitudes toward Hawaiian Japanese began to develop: "Plantation overseers who for years had called their workmen friends suddenly recalled that they never 'trusted those damned Japs.'"[29]

Similarly, newspaper articles reported an upsurge of anti-Japanese feeling in Hawaii. Much of the hostility stemmed from the fact that Japanese Americans in Hawaii were exercising their citizenship rights. One newspaper article in particular summarized the concerns:

> Anti-Japanese feeling in Hawaii had been noted by military and civilian agencies. Among the most important charges are that Japanese in Hawaii [were] becoming "too important," "too complacent," and "too independent." Racial harmony in Hawaii was dependent on maintenance of economic and social balance which has been upset by the war. The acute manpower shortage, emphasis on the American principles of equality, gradual elimination of old country attitudes of humility and obedience, and unionization of labor in Hawaii were major influences leading Japanese to a new appreciation of their rights and privileges under the U.S. flag, and a new willingness to demand those rights. As a consequence, many Japanese Americans were no longer willing to accept a dual standard in wages or the traditional principle of benevolent paternalism.[30]

Still, these expressions of individual racism were never institutionalized in Hawaii as they were in the continental United States.

Nisei Demonstration of Allegiance to Their Homeland

Nisei living on the mainland responded to the Japanese attack and the ostracism that followed by emphasizing their American citizenship. Frustrated by stereotypes and prejudices, some Nisei became enraged when their national identity was questioned. Ellen Fuchida stated that her brother was extremely offended when Caucasian customers visiting the family's grocery store challenged his loyalty to the United States. The store was located near their home in a predominantly white neighborhood. Before the war, said Fuchida, white customers were "friendly." During the war, some customers picked fights. Fuchida said, "When [Caucasian] males called [my brother] a 'Jap,' he would say, 'Step outside,' . . . And then he would hit them . . . , call up the sheriff, and ask them to come and pick up the body."

In an editorial published in the *Rafu Shimpo* on December 22, 1941, American Japanese were encouraged to forget their racial identity and identify with being American: "It behooves us to reason that the idea of stressing racial identity in this country does not conform to the democratic principles. People from all parts of the world came to this country to lose their racial identity, to become Americans. . . . We want everyone to forget his racial identity in order to fight enemies of America."[31]

This reaction by Nisei was like that of German Americans, particularly during World War I, when many of their ethnic organizations either disappeared or were Americanized.[32] Unlike Japanese Americans, however, many German Americans anglicized their surnames to assimilate into the mainstream of American society. U.S. Army General John J. Pershing, for example, changed his name from Pfoerschin.[33] Japanese Americans, by contrast, remained an identifiable minority.

Another dissimilarity between European and Japanese immigrants during World War II is that the former had the privilege of becoming naturalized citizens. Italian Americans are a case in point. At the beginning of World War II, the United States government declared that all unnaturalized Italians were "alien enemies." This designation called for registration, and imposed limitations on travel and property ownership. Consequently, Italian aliens became naturalized citizens at an accelerated rate. As revealed in George Pozzetta's study on Italian Americans, "during the period 1940–1945, some 281,354 Italian aliens became naturalized. . . . In 1944 alone, 106,626 became citizens, the largest single-year figure in American history."[34]

Issei had no opportunity to become naturalized citizens until 1952. Yet, although they were denied U.S. citizenship, they encouraged their children to take pride in their American heritage. Before the mass evacuation, Issei parents helped to instill nationalism in their children by enrolling them in civic organizations such as the Girl Scouts and the Boy Scouts. Some of these organizations gave moral support to their Nisei members when the question of Nisei loyalty surfaced. Boy Scout Troop 379, for example, was composed of Nisei boys of the Daishi Mission in California. In December 1941, just days before the United States declared war on Japan, these boys were selected as Troop of the Month. In recognition of the patriotic deeds performed by these Nisei boys, and in support of the boys and their communities, Scout Executive

Ernest E. Voss of the Los Angeles Metropolitan Area Council publicly com-
mended them in a statement published in *Rafu Shimpo*:

> Those of us who know the Japanese for what they are know that they
> are not in sympathy with the military and naval clique which has
> brought about the present state of affairs. All of our Scouts and
> Scouters join with me in expressing to you and your boys our appre-
> ciation of your true worth as patriotic fellow Americans. None of us
> condemn you or your ancestors. We want you to wear your uniform
> with pleasure and honor to yourselves and to the Scout Movement.
> We want you to participate in our common understanding which will
> help contribute to victory.[35]

In spite of the racial discrimination confronting Japanese Americans, the
Nisei made an organized effort to acculturate to white America. This movement is discussed in the following editorial by Warren Tsuneishi, published
in a Japanese newspaper in 1941:

> The greatest single failure of Americans of Japanese ancestry is that
> they don't participate enough in the affairs of their own community.
> They stick too closely among others of the Japanese race. . . . We have
> arrived at this conclusion also and have acted accordingly, refusing to
> join the Japanese Student Club on the [University of California at
> Berkeley] campus (a small gesture on our part, to be sure), in the
> belief that this group, among others, offers too good an "excuse" for
> NOT JOINING the activities in the wider campus community. . . . Very
> undiplomatically, we have voiced our opinion, attacking the J.S.C.
> [Japanese Student Club], and other groups as well; the Berkeley
> Fellowship (the "largest Nisei group on the Pacific Coast which meets
> regularly"), exclusive Nisei churches, Nisei clubs, and the Nisei
> Citizens League. And finally, we have begun to question the Nisei
> press which we feel "exclusivizes" the Nisei and cuts down his social
> horizon.[36]

Many Nisei viewed the United States' declaration of war against Japan
as a crucial test for demonstrating their patriotism.[37] Shortly after a state of
war was formally declared, representatives from the Southern District Council of the Japanese American Citizenship League (JACL) met to repudiate Japan and to offer services to the United States. Leaders of this civic organization,
all Nisei, formed an "Anti-Axis Committee" to affirm their citizenship and
express loyalty to the United States. Their stated objectives were to cooperate with all national, state, and local government agencies; to coordinate activities of all Americans of Japanese descent as well as of Japanese "aliens"

(immigrants); and to secure national unity by fair treatment of "loyal Americans."[38]

The committee went on to take charge of all press releases, and instructed Japanese Americans in appropriate individual and group conduct. Members of the Japanese community were urged, through newspapers, to condemn their ancestral country; they were told that "blood ties mean nothing now."[39] The following passage from a Japanese American newspaper summarizes this sentiment:

> We have lived long enough in America to appreciate liberty and justice. We cannot tolerate the attempt of a few to dominate the world. We have faith in free institutions, in individual freedom, and we have the courage of our convictions to back up our words with deeds of loyalty to the United States government! . . . Fellow Americans, give us a chance to do our share to make this world a better place to live in![40]

Similar positions were taken by Japanese Americans in other parts of the country. In New York City, for example, the 150 Nisei members of the Japanese American Committee for Democracy condemned the history of Japanese aggression and pledged their efforts and strength to the successful defense of America.[41]

Individuals of Japanese heritage expressed loyalty to the United States in many ways. In Santa Barbara, a Japanese mother was applauded for showing patriotism to the United States when she wrote a letter to her daughter's school asking for the exclusion of a Japanese dance routine that her daughter was to perform in a school program. The letter stated, "At this unhappy time, I'd like to keep all things Japanese as foreign to my children as is humanly possible so that in spite of their physical make-up, I can instill in them the fact that they are truly American."[42]

Several Euro-Americans rushed to the aid of Japanese Americans. One such individual, writer and philosopher Donald Culcross Peattie, spoke at a Santa Barbara JACL meeting, broadcast live on December 7, 1941, by radio station KTMS. He urged the white citizens of Santa Barbara not to penalize loyal American citizens of Japanese descent. Addressing the Japanese-American community in the same talk, however, he stated that (white) Americans had a right to ask that Americans of Japanese descent "prove their loyalty to the hilt. They more than any others . . . must show unfailing support to the United States government in its fight against Japanese military aggression."[43] Japanese Americans indeed showed that they were loyal citizens of the United States; however, the government began to isolate them.

On December 11, 1941, the *Rafu Shimpo* informed the Japanese community that property owned by Issei would not be transferable, according to a ruling by the Federal Reserve Branch. In addition, small Japanese foodstuff-handling businesses with no more than ten workers would be allowed to operate only on a cash basis. Four days later, the *Rafu Shimpo* published Attorney General Francis Biddle's announcement: "[The] presidential proclamation issued under Section 21, Title 50, United States Code, provides that in the event of a declaration of war, or when an invasion or predatory incursion is perpetuated, attempted, or threatened against the territory of the United States by any foreign nation or government . . . nationals of the hostile nation shall be liable to apprehension as alien enemies." It was reported that the expected proclamation would contain regulations for the conduct of all such aliens. Among the restrictions, those called enemy aliens would be forbidden to use or possess firearms, to travel by airplane unless authorized by the attorney general or the secretary of war, and to enter military areas such as power plants, vessels, piers, factories, and foundries.

It was also reported that enemy aliens deemed dangerous by the attorney general or the secretary of state would be held in the custody of the Immigration and Naturalization Service, pending review of their cases by review boards. Permanent detention would follow the review when detainees posed a strong threat to the country's internal security. Enemy aliens could not leave or enter the United States unless authorized by the president, and could not change their workplace unless granted permission by the attorney general.

The United States Evacuation of Japanese Americans

On February 20, 1942, the Secretary of War authorized Lieutenant General John L. DeWitt, Commanding General, Western Defense Command, to establish military areas within his command "as the situation required." General DeWitt established his first two military areas in the following month: Military Area No. 1 consisted of the western halves of Washington, Oregon, and California, and the southern half of Arizona; Military Area No. 2 included the remaining territory of those states. This action imposed travel restrictions on all enemy aliens and all persons of Japanese ancestry in these areas; any change of residence had to be reported in advance.

Later the War Department decided that all persons of Japanese ancestry were to be evacuated from critical areas on the West Coast. Among the stated reasons was that the country's most important shipbuilding and aircraft plants were located in these areas, as were the vital port installations of San Francisco and the air fuel resources of the California oilfields. Although War

Table 3
War Relocation Authority Internment Camps

Name of Camp	Location
Central Utah (also known as Topaz)	West central Utah
Colorado River (also known as Poston)	West central Arizona
Gila River (also known as Rivers)	East central Arizona
Granada (Amache)	Southeastern Colorado
Heart Mountain	Northwestern Wyoming
Jerome (also known as Denson)	Southeastern Arkansas
Manzanar	East central California
Minidoka (also known as Hunt)	Southeastern Idaho
Rohwer (also known as McGee)	Southeastern Arkansas
Tule Lake (also known as Newell)	Northern California

Department officials realized that the majority of the evacuees were U.S. citizens, they claimed that, if Japan dropped parachutists in civilian clothing among the Japanese civilian population, the result would be mass hysteria and violent acts against innocent people. Consequently persons of Japanese ancestry were evacuated from the western half of Washington, the western half of Oregon, the southern half of Arizona, and the entire state of California, allegedly for their own protection.

As stated above, mass evacuation was first conducted on a voluntary basis. This was followed by a mandate that all people of Japanese ancestry living in restricted areas must evacuate to army-operated assembly centers, which would provide temporary shelter for evacuees until they were transferred to internment camps (see Table 3). On March 18, 1942, the War Relocation Authority (WRA) was established by Executive Order 9102 to assist in the supervision and maintenance of evacuees, and to manage the ten relocation centers where the evacuees were to be settled.

By November 1942, all of the Japanese evacuees had been transferred from assembly centers to relocation camps. In general, the relocation centers were communities with many of the same institutions as in the larger society: schools, libraries, hospitals, newspapers, churches, a governing body, and the like. Living facilities were poor; family quarters had no running water and few items of furniture beyond the army cots provided by the WRA. Everyone ate in the mess hall; children tended to eat with their friends rather than with their families.

Cherry Shiozawa recalled that, when the evacuation orders came, she and her family stored their personal items in the basement of their house. "At one point we thought of selling our home and moving east, but Father and I were against that idea. A black painter checked on our house periodically. While

we were in camp, people tried to break in to get [our] washer." Shiozawa and
her family were evacuated to Topaz relocation center, where she worked as a
recreation leader. She said, "The worst thing about camp life was the lack of
privacy."[44]

When Mary Yamada's family was evacuated from Los Angeles, she was
already living in New York. She visited her family at the internment camp
on two occasions:

> I was in New York and my family went to Heart Mountain, Wyo-
> ming. . . . I went to visit them twice. . . . I went when my sister was
> being married, and at that time they were beginning to give them
> three-day passes from the camp. . . . We were able to go to Billings,
> Montana, and she was married in a Methodist church in Billings. . . .
> The other time I went was after I was accepted by the Army. I then
> went to Heart Mountain to get my mother out, to bring her to New
> York. . . . And by then my sister and brother-in-law were here so she
> stayed with them. . . . They moved into the apartment where I used to
> live.

Irene Nishikaichi was living in Los Angeles with her parents at the time
of evacuation. She was still enrolled at Los Angeles City College when Japan
bombed Pearl Harbor. Nishikaichi described how she and her family felt when
they were evacuated to Poston, the WRA camp in west central Arizona; she
was nineteen years old at the time.

> We went on the bus to Poston, Arizona. It was stressful when we first
> went into camp. We were wondering how long the war was going to
> last. [We would ask ourselves,] "Are we going to be here for five years,
> ten years, the rest of our lives?" and "You know, they're talking about
> sending us back to Japan." "What's going to happen to us?" I went to
> work within the first weeks.

Poston, also known as the Colorado River War Relocation Center, was
the second largest of the ten WRA camps. It was located on the Colorado
Indian Reservation, and until December 1943 was managed by the Office of
Indian Affairs (OIA) under contract with the WRA. According to anthropologist Lane Ryo Hirabayashi, the camp housed almost eighteen thousand
residents at its peak, and existed from May 1942 through November 1945.[45]
Most of the water in the camp came from the Colorado River. The land was
desert, and the temperatures ranged from 20 degrees in the winter to125 degrees in the summer.[46]

Hirabayashi characterized Poston as unparalleled among internment
camps, in that its key administrator emphasized limited self-governance among

residents. In compliance with the WRA policy banning Issei from holding elective office (because of their status as Japanese nationals), only Nisei men could serve as community leaders. This practice created dissension between the first and the second generations, as it stripped the Issei of the leadership role they had enjoyed in the prewar Japanese American community. The issue was resolved when the WRA gave the Issei residents power to hire and fire community leaders through advisory boards.[47]

The WRA provided work for willing adults. As Japanese Americans entered Poston, they were required to sign an oath that they would be productive members of the community.[48] The occupational opportunities provided were open to women as well as men. Harry Kitano observed that, among the negative consequences of mass evacuation, there was one positive aspect: for the first time, Nisei could fill a variety of social roles. The best jobs often were assigned to Nisei who had arrived early at the camp.[49] Nishikaichi remembered her work assignment at Poston:

> Since I was the first [employee] in the office, I was [made] the office manager over six secretaries. I enjoyed the work; we had wonderful attorneys to work with. One of them became a California appellate judge later. I was doing the kind of work that I was trained for, and enjoying it. The other secretaries and I are still in touch with each other, especially the ones who are in this area. And, as I say, the attorneys were wonderful people.

One consequence of the internment camps was that Japanese American men lost their position as primary providers for their families. This role was taken over by the federal government, since it provided for the residents' basic needs. Salaries for internees were relatively low; sometimes WRA officials refused to pay them at all. Japanese Americans felt resentment when Euro-American staff members earned much higher salaries for the same work; this friction sometimes resulted in protest by internees in the form of work slowdowns.

Another major consequence of the internment was that it *racialized* Japanese Americans.[50] Prior to the mass evacuation, Japanese Americans did not identify themselves as a racial group. The event of mass evacuation forced them all into one category regardless of social, economic, or political background. In the words of Lane Ryo Hirabayashi:

> All pre–World War II distinctions—whether of region, occupation, class, religion, or creed—were essentially erased because all persons of Japanese descent, whether or not they were U.S. citizens, were subject to basically the same regulations that characterized their

institutionalization in a racially segregated setting operated by
agencies of the federal government.[51]

The process of becoming racially distinct resulted in a bifurcation in the Japanese American community, a bifurcation that erupted when the loyalty questionnaire was administered. (See below.)

It is important, at this point, to reiterate that the treatment of Japanese Americans on the U.S. mainland differed from that of Japanese Americans in Hawaii. The Hawaiian Japanese were not subject to mass evacuation. This is not to say that Japanese Americans were not interned in Hawaii; rather, the internment of Hawaiian Japanese was limited to known enemy agents and others considered potentially dangerous to U.S. military interests. Ruth Fujii recalled that the FBI searched the homes of some Japanese Americans living in Hawaii at the time of the bombing: "I knew that they [the FBI] were going around to the Japanese homes . . . so people burned a lot of precious things. . . . My brother hid my father's picture because he was on a horse [in a] military outfit." Similarly, Hisako Yamashita reported that Japanese schoolteachers and principals were taken into custody: "I know Mr. Kaluta, the principal of the Japanese school I was going to was taken right away. And the . . . Buddhist ministers, and the leaders of the community, they all disappeared."

Among the Hawaiian Japanese targeted for detention were representatives of the Japanese government, the consular agents, Shinto priests, Buddhist priests and priestesses, Issei language school teachers and principals, organizational leaders, and fishermen.[52] Andrew Lind has explained that Shinto priests were suspect because "they were active exponents of the divinity of the Japanese emperor and of Japanese nationalism."[53] Buddhist priests and priestesses, as well as Issei language school teachers, were recent products of the educational system and were viewed as "sympathetic to the ideals of the military regime in Japan."[54] Fishermen were considered a threat to American security because they were knowledgeable about the ocean and could aid the enemy in the event of an actual invasion. In all, fewer than 1,500 Japanese Americans were detained by the FBI in Hawaii during the entire war period; 879 of these were Issei and 534 were American citizens.[55]

Unlike the mainland, however, Hawaii was placed under martial law after the Japanese air strikes. Among other inconveniences, a curfew was imposed on all residents, public establishments were closed, and mail was censored. Secretary of the Navy Frank Knox made more than one request to remove Japanese Americans from Oahu. The Commanding General of Hawaii, Delos Emmons, replied that such an evacuation would be dangerous and impracticable. Emmons asserted that "large quantities of building materials would be needed at a time when construction and shipping were already taxed to the limit." Further, additional troops would be necessary to guard the evacuees.

Another major factor why Japanese Americans in Hawaii were not evacuated en masse is that they made up a large proportion of the Hawaiian population and were indispensable to the economy. Japanese Americans living on the mainland accounted for approximately 3 percent of the population; those living in Hawaii made up 35 percent. The Commission on Wartime Relocation and Internment of Civilians reported in 1992 that of the 158,000 ethnic Japanese living in Hawaii when Japan attacked Pearl Harbor, fewer than 2,000 were taken into custody. By the end of the war, 1,875 Hawaiian residents of Japanese descent had been evacuated to the mainland, "1,118 to WRA camps and the remainder to Justice Department camps." These numbers are extremely low in proportion to the relatively large population of Japanese Americans in Hawaii, and when we consider that some 120,000 Japanese Americans were interned on the mainland.

The Commission reported that part of the reason for the difference in treatment of ethnic Japanese in Hawaii was the approach taken by General Emmons in diffusing political pressure:

> The commanding general in Hawaii, Delos Emmons, restrained plans
> to take radical measures, raising practical problems of labor shortages
> and transportation until pressure to evacuate the Hawaiian Islands
> subsided. . . . [H]e appeared to have argued quietly but consistently for
> treating the ethnic Japanese as loyal to the United States, absent
> evidence to the contrary.[56]

Hawaii also was more ethnically diverse than the mainland. Ethnic differences were tolerated more, because Hawaii had not been "infected with the same virulent antagonism" found on the West Coast.[57] For example, Ruth Fujii's friends were of many ethnic backgrounds: "I had friends of Japanese descent, but there were other friends of mine of other nationalities except colored [African Americans], because we didn't have any colored people here then."

Registration or Renunciation?

In February and March 1943, the War Relocation Authority administered a controversial questionnaire to all Issei and Nisei age seventeen and older living in the relocation camps. The purpose was to register all evacuees of Japanese descent and to determine who was loyal and who was disloyal to the United States war effort. The WRA used questionnaire results to facilitate the release of loyal evacuees from the internment camps. Although the questionnaire was titled "War Relocation Authority Application for Leave Clearance," it was almost identical to an earlier form prepared by the War Department for Nisei men of military age, "Selective Service System: Statement of United States Citizens of Japanese Ancestry," used to recruit for military service.

The questions creating the controversy were worded as follows:

27. If the opportunity presents itself and you are found qualified, would you be willing to volunteer for the Army Nurse Corps or the WAAC (Women's Army Auxiliary Corp)?

28. Will you swear unqualified allegiance to the United States of America and forswear any form of allegiance or obedience to the Japanese Emperor, or any other foreign government, power or organization?

The "Application for Leave Clearance" form was administered to Nisei women living in WRA camps, and to Issei men and women. Nisei men were administered the "Selective Service System: Statement of United States Citizens of Japanese Ancestry"; the only difference in the two questionnaires is that question 27 for men read, "Are you willing to serve in the armed forces of the United States on combat duty, wherever ordered?" The awkward wording of questions 27 and 28 created a great deal of confusion for the Issei. Both questions were inappropriate for the Issei, who were denied citizenship in the United States, but at the same time were being asked to renounce their allegiance to Japan.

The Japanese American community was divided over the issue of serving in the military. The majority, however, were in favor, arguing that by sharing the burden of defense, the community was assuring that future generations of Japanese descent would have equal citizenship rights. This sentiment was similar to that expressed by African American leaders throughout American history. During World War I, for example, W.E.B. Du Bois declared, "If the black man could fight to defeat the Kaiser . . . he could later present a bill for payment due to a grateful white America."[58] Similarly, during World War II, Representative Adam Clayton Powell and educator Mary McLeod Bethune advocated that African Americans serve in the military to demonstrate patriotism and later to reap the benefits of full citizenship. Some Nisei, too, hoped to use the military as a vehicle for social change.

Still, evacuees expressed widespread resistance to registering. Nisei interned at Topaz Relocation Center in Utah sent a petition to the War Department requesting full restoration of civil rights and assurance of protection for their families as a prerequisite to proceeding with the registration.[59] They later acquiesced and issued a statement accepting the registration as an indication of the government's good faith.[60] Other Japanese Americans were relentless in their opposition to serving in the military. They felt that they, as a people, had already demonstrated their patriotism by showing no resistance to evacuation from their homes. Further, they viewed mass evacuation as a curtailment of their citizenship rights; to serve in the military under such conditions was "not a privilege but an unbearable sacrifice."[61] In an attempt to avoid the military draft, some of these Nisei men and women answered "no" to questions 27 and 28 on the questionnaire. Some applied for expatriation (a matter discussed in greater detail below).

The primary opponents of military service were the parents of the Nisei and the Kibei. Issei parents objected because they depended on their children to provide for them; many felt that their families' security would be further jeopardized if their children were to enlist in the military. They were also worried about being forced to return to a hostile civilian society after losing all of their assets; if they were categorized as "disloyal," they would not be forced to leave the WRA camps and resettle. Some Issei opted to repatriate to Japan.

Pressure was placed on the WRA by Congress, the War Department, and the press to segregate all persons of Japanese ancestry who were "disloyal" to the United States. (Later this pressure was relieved by the Senate.) On July 15, 1943, the WRA designated Tule Lake Relocation Center for "disloyals"; the "loyal" evacuees at Tule Lake were to be transferred to one of the other WRA camps before resettlement in a civilian community.

Many "loyal" evacuees, however, remained at Tule Lake after the arrival of "disloyals"; they are referred to in the social science literature as "Old Tuleans." Many had no desire to relocate; they were the most firmly established of Tule Lake evacuees, occupying the best jobs and the most desirable living quarters. Among those transferred to Tule Lake were evacuees who had requested to leave the United States and go to Japan, who had answered questions 27 and 28 in the negative or not at all, who had been denied leave clearances, or who had been recommended by the Department of Justice for detention.[62] In addition, some of the family members of these individuals were also transferred to Tule Lake. Surely not all of these transferees (known as "newcomers") were disloyal to the U.S. war effort. Some of the "newcomers" transferred to Tule Lake not for political reasons, but solely to stay with members of their immediate family. Many scholars argue that the inaccurate labeling of "loyal" Japanese Americans as "disloyal" stemmed from a poorly implemented registration program.[63] In 1946 the WRA published statistics showing that of the 18,422 persons segregated at Tule Lake, 12,489 were Nisei and 5,933 were Issei.[64]

Among these so-called "segregants" were persons who were genuinely loyal to the United States, those who were genuinely disloyal, and those who had mixed feelings about supporting the United States.

Several disloyal segregants belonged to a pro-Japanese militant group. These individuals felt that Tule Lake was exclusively for evacuees who wished to pursue the Japanese way of life. The camp administrators allowed members of this group to establish Japanese language schools and to observe some cultural customs and activities. The administrators felt that in this way the evacuees were preparing themselves for their future life in Japan.

A problem developed when the pro-Japanese forced other evacuees to support their segregation efforts. Using terrorist tactics, such as threatening lives, and beating up their opponents, the pro-Japanese internees prevented loyal evacuees from registering and forbade them to volunteer for military service. Due to the resulting turmoil, Tule Lake was placed under martial law on November 13, 1943. Members of the militant pro-Japanese group continued to apply pressure to all Nisei residents to renounce their U.S. citizenship. These efforts were facilitated by the rescinding of Executive Order 9066 on December 17, 1944, and by the announcement that all WRA camps would be closed within a year.

Anxieties about resettling in a hostile civilian society and fear of entering the military encouraged the undecided Nisei to renounce American citizenship. A few thousand Nisei reportedly did so during the war. Joseph Yoshisuke Kurihara, a Hawaiian-born Nisei, is a case in point; his life history is published in *The Spoilage*, Dorothy Swaine Thomas and Richard Nishimoto's study on the evacuation and resettlement of Japanese Americans during World War II. Kurihara had moved to California in 1915 and had worked as a fruit picker in Sacramento. He migrated to Michigan in 1917 and entered the army, eventually receiving an honorable discharge. Later he returned to Los Angeles, California, where he earned an accounting degree from Southwestern University and opened an accounting firm. Kurihara was a successful businessman when, in 1942, he was evacuated to Manzanar. He became active in anti-administration and anti-JACL movements before renouncing his American citizenship and sailing to Japan in 1946.[65]

Although none of the Nisei Wacs were among those labeled disloyal, some had "disloyal" family members. One of Hisako Yamashita's older brothers had moved from Hawaii to California while she was still a child; while growing up in Kauai she only knew of him at a distance. After the United States declared war on Japan, the brother and his family were forcefully evacuated and interned. Yamashita remembered her brother's rage: "He had five kids and he was so mad that they were interning him that he opted for Tule Lake. My family was very unhappy at that point. They wrote to him and said, 'Send your kids to Hawaii,' and they would bring them up. No, he wouldn't. . . . The first ship that went back to Japan, they were on it."

Yamashita, who served in the WAC from December 1944 to October 1946, had an opportunity to visit Japan in 1961. There she learned of her brother's difficulties in adjusting to Japanese life:

> I visited Japan because my father had gone there to retire. And when I finally saw my brother's family, and talked with the kids, one of the girls said, "When my father first stepped foot in Japan he hated it." He regretted his decision to renounce his citizenship but at that point they couldn't do anything. And his children grew up in Japan. . . . After the war the Nisei in California challenged the loss of citizenship and took it up with the Supreme Court and got the citizenship back. And so all of those kids, my nieces and nephews, got their citizenship back and they all live in California now. . . . My brother died while he was in Japan.

In some cases, Nisei men renounced their U.S. citizenship in an effort to avoid military service. For example, a Nasumi Tokeuchi wrote a letter to the president of the United States, dated August 20, 1944. She stated that her husband, Ryoichi Yamaguchi Takeuchi, had just passed the pre-induction physical and soon would be sent to the army. She claimed that he had dual citizenship and was more willing to give up American citizenship than Japanese. Mrs. Tokeuchi explained that she and her husband had been mistreated by the American public, and requested that he be discharged from the military even if it meant that he would be sent to a concentration camp. This letter and others like it were sent to the War Department and placed in a category labeled "Japanese American Enlisted Men Who Make Disloyal Statements in Order to Avoid Overseas Combat Duty." In this case, the letter was forwarded to the commanding officer of the army reception center in which Takeuchi was to be processed, for action.[66]

Historian Donald Collins estimated that eight thousand people of Japanese heritage left the United States for Japan during and immediately after the war. In his study of those who renounced U.S. citizenship and expatriated to Japan, Collins found that both the Issei and the Nisei had difficulty in adjusting to their new life:

> Japan had just lost the war. Houses, buildings, and factories had been devastated. Food had to be supplied from outside the islands. Every major city except Kyoto had been subjected to the American bombing and fire raids. Because of the severe food shortage, the Japanese

government continued wartime rationing which allowed each person one-third the calories served as a minimum to American soldiers. Unemployment was also widespread.[67]

Perhaps even more so than the Issei, who were born in Japan, and the Kibei, who had attended school there, the Nisei expatriates suffered culture shock, for they had been socialized in the American culture. As in the case of Yamashita's brother, many Nisei who left the United States for Japan wanted to return home.

Most of the renunciants still waiting to be deported to Japan when the war ended changed their minds and filed lawsuits to cancel their renunciation of citizenship. San Francisco civil liberties attorney Wayne M. Collins represented the renunciants, arguing in court that they had been victims of duress by the United States government. After years of litigation, Collins succeeded in helping most of these renunciants to restore their United States citizenship by the mid- to late 1950s.[68]

Picking Up the Pieces: Nisei Reclamation of Citizenship

Roger Daniels reported that the process of leaving the concentration camps began in the summer of 1942 and continued even as more evacuees were entering. He described four categories of inmates who were qualified for release from the camps: college students, agricultural workers, Japanese linguists, and Japanese diplomats, who were sent back to Japan in exchange for American diplomats.[69]

After spending a year and a half at Poston, Nishikaichi was released under the War Relocation Authority's indefinite leave program. As described in chapter 1, she traveled to New York City to work as a nanny for a Columbia University professor with three children, and hoped to continue her legal secretarial studies at night. Finding herself in an impossible situation, however, Nisikaichi "walked in and walked out," and subsequently interviewed for a job with the WRA in New York City:

> When I went for the interview, I met a girl that I [had known] at City College. She was a member of a Japanese American males' and females' social club. (From high school days, we [Japanese American girls] had these clubs. We would have socials and would invite the boys' clubs. Even after we left high school we would have socials.) She invited me to go home with her that night. She informed me that a friend of hers, [whom] I knew through a social club in L.A., was coming to New York and needed a roommate. So [her friend] and I

roomed together, and our rent was fifty dollars a month. The subway in New York was a nickel. At sixteen dollars a week, toward the end of the week if you [bought] a candy bar, you were not going to have the nickel to go to work to pick up your paycheck for Friday.

From New York City Nishikaichi transferred to the WRA office in Rochester, hoping that she could persuade her parents to leave the internment camp and join her: "Since my father was a cook, I thought possibly they could get a domestic job. I was in Rochester for a whole year but I couldn't persuade my parents to leave the camp."

Some evacuees, particularly the Issei, who had lost their homes and their businesses, felt secure in the internment camps. They were reluctant to leave even when the War Relocation Authority announced that the camps would be closed on or before January 2, 1946. Former internee Richard Nishimoto has written that many evacuees at Poston reacted negatively to that news, "varying from being violently vociferous to being passively defiant."[70] Of evacuees at Tule Lake, Donald Collins has written: "Faced with prospects of violence and economic impoverishment in West Coast communities, the residents of Tule Lake fought to remain within the security of their concentration home."[71] Nishimoto and Dorothy Swaine Thomas have published the words of some evacuees at Tule Lake: "We'd like to sit in Tule Lake for a while. We don't want to relocate. The discrimination is too bad. I see letters from people on the outside. There are fellows in Chicago who want to come back [to camp] but who are not allowed."[72] Japanese American Citizenship League officials opposed the closing of the internment camps because they felt that many evacuees had been so impaired by captivity and the loss of their assets that they would not be able to live on their own.[73]

Although policies excluding Japanese Americans from the armed services had been rescinded, and although the all-Japanese American 442nd Regimental Combat Team received favorable publicity in the media, prejudice against the group persisted. This was especially true in California, where many evacuees feared returning home because of reported incidents of anti-Japanese crimes. (Some of these reports appeared in the February 1945 issues of the *Los Angeles Times*.)[74] The U.S. government was faced with the task of rearticulating the image of Japanese Americans; from that of enemy alien to that of innocuous citizen.

Another major barrier to resettlement in the border states was white business owners' fear of Japanese American economic competition. This issue was described in a commentary by Larry Tajiri, published in the *Pacific Citizen*, July 22, 1944:

It appears that some of the people who have profited from the
evacuation of persons of Japanese ancestry from the west coast are
having cold chills over the prospect that evacuees may return in the
not too distant future. This may account for the frenzied attempts on
the part of California race-baiters to forestall, if not prevent permanently, the return of the evacuees to the homes, businesses and lands
they have tilled and developed for two generations.[75]

In the article, Tajiri alleged that the American League of California, an organized group of produce dealers and wholesale florists, was interested in keeping Japanese Americans from reestablishing themselves in these businesses.
Indeed the wholesale distribution of farm produce and floricultural products
had (as noted in chapter 2) been an economic mainstay of Japanese Americans in southern California before the mass evacuation. Tajiri claimed that, in
the year preceding the evacuation, "wholesale produce dealers of Japanese ancestry in Los Angeles did business in the extent of $26,000,00. And it has
been estimated in Los Angeles that in the year after the evacuation Los Angeles consumers paid $20,000,000 more for 10,000 carloads less of farm prod-
ucts."[76] This industry, Tajiri argued, was cause for the antagonistic sentiment
promoted on the West Coast against Japanese Americans: white agricultur-
ists were acting in their own economic interest.

The U.S. government banned the resettlement of Japanese Americans
in California, parts of Washington, Oregon, and Arizona until a December
1944 Supreme Court decision to lift the ban for Nisei not charged with disloyalty.[77] Several organizations worked against the resettlement of Japanese
Americans on the West Coast, such as the No Japs, Inc., the American Federation, the Japanese Exclusion Association, and the Japanese Problem League.
Aware of these organizations, the War Relocation Authority concentrated its
resettlement efforts in communities in the midwestern and eastern regions of
the country.[78] Relocation offices were established in cities such as Chicago,
New York, and Milwaukee, and collaborated with humanitarian organizations
to foster community acceptance of the resettling Japanese.

Sometimes the problem of resettlement was exacerbated by Niseis' desire
to assimilate into white America and to distance themselves from blacks. Some
refused to live in neighborhoods where African Americans resided. In her study
of the Nisei generation in Hawaii, Eileen Tamura claimed that the Japanese
ideas about skin color were formed long before they came in contact with
Westerners; "Japanese saw themselves as white-skinned, which they considered beautiful; they viewed black skin as ugly."[79] In an editorial published in
the *Pacific Citizen* in January 1944, Marie Harlow Pulley, a Chicago woman
advocating the elimination of racial segregation in the United States, warned

that the Nisei resettlement program "may be endangered by their anti-black sentiment."[80] She declared that the liberal groups working for the Nisei were the same groups that had been working on the "Negro problem" for years. Pulley offered to rent part of her home to four Nisei; her house was located in an old Chicago neighborhood that included both white and black homeowners. Pulley determined that Nisei harbored an extremely rigid, strongly developed prejudice against African Americans. She said that when they saw children of "Negro professional people playing quietly in some of the yards, the Nisei were not interested in leasing the house."

> The Nisei have been quick to pick up America's superficial qualities, and it followed that they easily accepted the undemocratic and truly un-American aspect of prejudice toward Negroes. . . . Nisei stand at the crossroads with the two counts of color and identity against them. They are alienating the energies and interests of the only really friendly group in this country.[81]

To help eliminate the problems associated with resettlement, relocation officers served as liaisons between the resettling evacuees and the communities where they settled. Jobs were offered to Japanese evacuees through the relocation offices; most numerous were war plant positions and domestic work. The United States Department of Interior reported the efforts as successful:

> As a means of affecting community attitudes, relocation officers gave talks to business, professional, social, civic, church and fraternal groups, met with employers individually and in groups, enlisted the aid of unions when possible, and spoke to employees in plants where employment of Japanese was contemplated. Newspapers were provided with information in regard to the [resettlement] program. This public relations program was sufficiently successful so that in most communities opposition did not crystalize or become organized movements.[82]

The news media wrote articles in support of the reintegration of Japanese Americans into the overall society. Referring to Asian students who attended a local college, the *Chicago Tribune* stated in May 1944, "Oriental faces are all that set those students aside from any others on the campus. They take the same courses, make good grades, and participate in campus activities."[83] Similarly, in an editorial in the *Pacific Citizen* on January 13, 1945, Larry Tajiri claimed that the evacuees returning home were well received by their Caucasian neighbors: In Fowler, California, "an ex-serviceman returned with his wife and children a day or two before Christmas and neighboring families brought gifts for the children." Similarly, a Methodist church located in southern California reportedly welcomed its Japanese American neighbors.

Many Americans were beginning to feel that, although some people voiced opposition to the resettlement of Japanese Americans on the West Coast, anti-Orientalism in California was largely a dead issue. As Tajiri stated:

> There has been a vocal opposition to the return of the evacuees, but
> daily it becomes more apparent that these oppositionists consist
> largely of the lunatic fringe of West Coast reaction, who are reminis-
> cent of the Ku Klux Klan of another day. The people who came down
> to the evacuation trains to see the evacuees off to their assembly
> centers and relocation camps, the women who wept with evacuee
> women when the trains pulled out, are welcoming their friends home
> again.[84]

Surely the evacuees mentioned by Tajiri were families who had retained their homes. The majority of the evacuees, however, had lost the homes, businesses, and employment they had possessed before evacuation. Moreover, as Tajiri observed, many of the Japanese Americans who still owned their homes found that, during the resettlement, "many of these homes were occupied by war workers, largely of minority groups, who found that the homes left vacant by the evacuees were the only ones available. In many cases commercial buildings left empty by the evacuation have been cheaply converted into dwellings where slum conditions prevail."[85] Tajiri was referring to African Americans and Mexican Americans who leased houses owned by Japanese Americans from the local government in California's urban areas. He stated, however, that the growing antagonism between Japanese Americans and other racial minorities was being ameliorated by African American leadership: "Negro leaders on the west coast already have taken the lead in recommending Federal interracial housing. The tightness of the housing situation in urban areas can be relieved through large-scale Federal programs."[86]

While the mass evacuation of Japanese Americans by the United States government was unconscionable, the internment camps were not analogous to the concentration camps in Germany where Jews were executed during the war. In the words of a former Nisei Wac:

> [Japanese Americans] talk about being incarcerated and all that, but I
> don't think one should say that, because they don't know the true
> value of that word. By saying incarcerated, [one implies that Japanese
> Americans] were treated like what you see in the movies, where the
> Jews were just killed off, exterminated. Internment camps were
> nothing like that. [Japanese Americans] had a free choice of moving
> to camps if they wanted to, or going to other places. . . . And for me [a
> Japanese American] to say that may [make me sound] like a traitor.

On the other hand, this mass evacuation, which had been commonly referred to as "internment," is perhaps more appropriately labeled "incarceration," as it often is in contemporary literature on this topic, because "internment" can legally be applied only to aliens. During World War II, the United States government confined American citizens of Japanese descent, as well as their Issei parents. Unlike German and Italian evacuees, Nisei were confined without a hearing; mass incarceration was based simply on ethnic origin and geographic location. This act of mass evacuation was later found to be unjustified, as "there were no documented acts of espionage, sabotage, or fifth column activity committed by Japanese Americans."[87]

Several scholars assert that relocation camps had a liberating effect on the lives of Japanese American women.[88] Daisuke Kitagawa characterized life in relocation camps as "really and truly a well-earned and highly deserved holiday" for Issei women.[89] Similarly, Dorothy Swaine Thomas and Richard Nishimoto observed that "Issei women found pleasure in the new leisure, freedom from the burdens of cooking and the worries of providing for a family. And they spent much time at knitting, sewing, handicraft, and English classes."[90] According to Valerie Matsumoto, living in relocation camps resulted in "more leisure for older women, equal pay with men for working women, and disintegration of traditional patterns of arranged marriages."[91]

Nisei women living in internment camps were viewed by the War Department as potential recruits, as these women were often seeking shelter and employment in an effort to resettle in the civilian community. Indeed, these events of World War II spurred feelings of what Leslie Ito has referred to as "super-patriotism" among the Nisei.[92] Not only did the bombing of Pearl Harbor, and the ensuing mass evacuation, alter the lives of those who became Nisei servicewomen, but these events served as driving forces for their enlistment.

Chapter 4

Women's Army Corps Recruitment of Nisei Women

It's a wonderful opportunity for my people to participate actively in the greatest battle for democracy the world has ever known. By serving in the WAC, I've found the true meaning of democracy—the principle of share and share alike. I'm sure that Japanese American girls who join the WAC will develop, as I have, a broader outlook and an increased pride in their native land. Before I joined up I felt useless and restless because I wanted to do something for my country. I wouldn't exchange for anything the experience I've gained in the WAC.

—Pvt. Chizuko Shinagawa[1]

ALTHOUGH THE WOMEN'S Army Auxiliary Corps had existed since July 1942, the first Nisei woman was not inducted until November 1943. By contrast, American women of German or Italian descent were eligible to join the WAAC/WAC without any restrictions. Even though the United States was at war with Germany and Italy, women whose parents were natives of these countries were not subjected to the same scrutiny as Nisei women. Euro-American women of all ethnic backgrounds blended into the socially constructed category labeled "white," and their assignments in WAAC/WAC units were based almost exclusively on level of skills.

The scenario was different for Nisei women. This chapter discusses the procedures used by the War Department to recruit and induct Nisei women into the WAC, and highlights the biographies and personal statements of several women who joined.

Determining Loyalty, Determining Interest

As mentioned in the previous chapter, Nisei women were required to demonstrate their loyalty to the United States before they could volunteer for the WAAC/WAC. Early in January 1943, the War Department announced that a special effort would be made to recruit linguists for the WAAC. Although these recruits would also perform other, related duties, their primary responsibility would be to work in cryptography and communications. Japanese was among the eight languages specified for such work in a memorandum sent from the WAAC's Chief Recruiting Branch, Personnel Division.[2]

Later that month, the War Department formed operating teams to recruit Nisei women from internment camps. Each team consisted of one member from the War Relocation Center, one military officer, two sergeants of the loyalty investigative branch of the combined service commands, and one American male soldier of Japanese ancestry. The objective of these recruiting teams was to determine if Japanese American women supported the U.S. war effort and whether they would serve in the military if given the opportunity.

Also in that month, while loyalty questionnaires were being administered at internment camps, WAC Director Hobby began examining statistics, on Nisei women, received from the War Relocation Authority. WAC headquarters had requested this information to help in deciding whether to induct Nisei women and in determining what occupations to assign them to if accepted. In compliance with Hobby's request, the WRA compiled occupational statistics from the 1940 census, revealing the occupational distribution of Nisei women as follows: 2,541 clerical workers, 254 stenographers and typists, 228 teachers, 129 managers, 124 trained nurses, 30 religious workers, 13 editors and reporters, 13 social workers, 12 pharmacists, 8 laboratory technicians, 6 physicians and surgeons, 4 librarians, 4 college teachers, 3 optometrists, 1 chemist, 1 dentist, 1 draftsperson, and 1 lawyer.[3] These statistics showed that Nisei women were well educated and skilled in the occupational fields necessary to the military.

As the Women's Army Corps was moving from a policy of excluding Nisei women to one of inclusion, the civilian population expressed support for Nisei women's service in the WAC. Several people wrote Secretary of War Stimson urging him to recruit Japanese American women. One such letter, written by DAR member Lilliebell Falck, who claimed to be a friend and advisor to Japanese Americans, stated, "while American boys are taken out of . . . universities to serve in the military, Japanese students are permitted to continue their studies and professions." Falck protested the exclusion of Nisei men and women from military service, not knowing that the process of inducting them was well under way. Shortly after her letter was received in January 1943 by the War Department, Nisei men were authorized to serve in a combat battalion.

Among the many letters sent to the War Department about the exclusion of Nisei women from military service was one by Henry C. Blaisdell in January 1943. Blaisdell was then director of the International House at the University of California at Berkeley. He expressed his "hearty and appreciative approval" of Stimson's announcement that Nisei men had been "accorded the privilege of enlistment in the American army," then requested that Nisei women be accorded the same opportunity to prove their loyalty to the country, and to do so in nonsegregated units. Secretary Stimson replied informing Blaisdell that enlistment of Nisei women in the WAC was "presently being studied."[4]

In the U.S. military, policies on the utilization of women of any ethnic group were contingent upon those governing the utilization of men of that group. Hence, before a Woman's Army Corps was formed, there were army corps consisting solely of men. Before African American women were inducted into the WAC, African American men were inducted into the army. Thus, before Nisei women were inducted into the WAC, Nisei men would be reinducted into the army. On February 1, 1943, President Roosevelt informed Secretary Stimson that he fully approved the War Department's proposal to organize a combat team consisting of loyal American citizens of Japanese descent.[5] Fifteen hundred Nisei men were taken from among Hawaiian volunteers, and several thousand were inducted from War Relocation Centers (first as volunteers and later as draftees); this Nisei combat team, later known as the 442nd Regimental Combat Team, would consist of infantry, artillery, engineers, and medical personnel.

On the day that President Roosevelt approved the formation of the Nisei combat regiment, an interoffice memorandum was sent to WAAC Director Hobby, recommending that plans be made for recruiting Nisei women. It was recommended that two to four WAAC companies be composed entirely of Japanese Americans. It was further recommended that the Nisei women be trained at Fort Des Moines, and that they be recruited and trained so as to be ready for duty soon after male Nisei units were in the field.[6] A few weeks later, a letter was sent to the War Department from Sergeant Kenneth Uni, assigned to recruitment duty at the Manzanar Relocation Center, further encouraging the induction of Nisei women; Sergeant Uni stated that Nisei men were reluctant to join the military because they felt that Nisei women also should be allowed to.

In finally sending WAAC officers to relocation centers, War Department officials accelerated the recruitment of Nisei women. These officers were charged with investigating Nisei women's attitudes toward joining the WAAC. Nisei women were told that no decision had been made by the War Department as to their possible enlistment, and that the decision depended partially on their desire to serve. Each officer subsequently submitted reports of her findings, similar to the report of Second Officer Manice M. Hill (in chapter 1). Hill reported that Nisei women at the Rohwer Relocation Center expressed a great deal of interest in serving in the WAAC but indicated that their families would have to approve; such concern about families' approval, Hill stated, was natural to Nisei under normal conditions, but was even stronger during the war years: feelings of responsibility toward parents were even more pronounced for Nisei during that time because the parents were aliens in an uncertain and insecure position. Hill noted further that, because the sons of the interned Issei were likely to be drafted, the daughters were more reluctant to join a military organization and leave their parents alone in the relocation center.

Still, Nisei women at Rohwer wished, according to the report, to learn more about the WAAC and indicated that they would possibly serve in the military; military service was of particular interest to those who had business training, had been employed outside the home, or had been in college before the evacuation. Hill emphasized that Nisei women opposed any segregation: they viewed the formation of an all-Japanese combat unit for Japanese men as an act of racial discrimination.

Similarly, on March 6, 1943, Third Officer Emily Miller surveyed Nisei women at Camp Jerome in Arkansas. Her scheduled meeting had been announced in the camp's newspaper, and women from age 21 to 45 were encouraged to attend. Miller reported that the women of Camp Jerome were intelligent, interested in the WAAC, and responsive, and that there were approximately fifteen hundred Nisei women in the camp in the 21–to–45 age bracket. Most were married and thus, according to their values, ineligible to join. Several single women expressed enthusiasm about joining, but they stated emphatically that they would not serve in an all-Japanese American unit. Some women were concerned about provisions for practicing their religion, Buddhism. Caucasian personnel at Camp Jerome expressed great admiration for the Nisei and told Miller that they would have no objections in being assigned to units with them. Finally, Miller noted that most of the Nisei women were below five feet tall, the lower limit for women recruits, with an average height of about 4'10".

On March 7, 1943, a letter to Headquarters Ninth Command, WAAC Branch, in Washington, D.C., was received from Second Officer Henrietta Horak of the WAAC Recruiting Office in Los Angeles. Horak had administered the survey at Tule Lake Relocation Center; she reported that

all information on the WAAC was administered during group interviews and
at open meetings, to which parents and Kibei were also invited. Officer Horak
stated that six "exceptionally intelligent" women, three of whom had been
trying to join the WAAC ever since it had been organized, appointed themselves as "constructive rumor spreaders."[7] In a few hours they had posted information folders about the WAAC in forty mess halls, a fact that contributed
to the large turnout.

During her two-day stay, Officer Horak spoke with 217 Nisei women; 30
indicated that they were ready to join the WAAC immediately, and claimed
that they already had obtained parental consent. Many women interviewed
by Horak mentioned that Issei sometimes obstructed what Horak termed the
practice of good American citizenship: military service, for example, would
conflict with their parents' wishes. Some of the women requested that they
be given special consideration regarding height, weight, and eyesight; Horak
observed that some of the most desirable applicants were "two inches under
five feet, as is characteristic of the race."

After administering a total of three hundred questionnaires to Nisei
women at Tule Lake, Horak summarized and tallied them. Among the women
surveyed, 218 said they would swear allegiance to the U.S., and 82 said they
would not, nor would they forswear any form of allegiance or obedience to
the Japanese emperor or other foreign government, power, or organization.
When asked whether they would serve in the WAAC, 125 said they would
do so if the opportunity presented itself; 175 said they would not.

Horak also interviewed approximately 217 Nisei women at the Manzanar
Relocation Camp in east central California. From the responses she received
at both relocation centers, she concluded that many women there were prepared to enlist immediately.[8] Horak claimed that the women interviewed at
Manzanar represented the "highest type" at any relocation center; the majority were college graduates or had college training. Several of these women had
been requested by Colonel Rasmussen, of the Military Intelligence Service
Language School, to apply for teaching positions. Others, according to Officer Horak, were well trained in office work, classifications, physical education, and other occupations.[9] Indeed, these women were strongly sought by
the WAAC.

One stated reason why some of these women would not serve was that
they were applying for repatriation to Japan. Others said they had invalid
parents to care for. Still others said they did not know English well enough.
Other reasons given included pregnancy, poor health, marriage, and parental
objection.[10]

Third Officer Margaret E. Deane of Headquarters Utah surveyed Nisei women at Topaz Relocation Center in west central Utah. In an effort to present the corps in the most favorable light, she first met with fifty Nisei women project leaders to inform them of the purpose of her visit and to solicit their cooperation. She held another meeting with all English-speaking female residents, at which she explained the WAAC program and answered questions about the possibility of Nisei women enlisting.

Deane reported that approximately two-thirds of the women eligible for the WAAC indicated willingness to join. Like other WAAC officers surveying Nisei women, she found that they were not willing to serve in segregated units. These women wanted to assimilate into the mainstream population; they stated that at home, in the San Francisco Bay area, they were dispersed throughout the white population. They feared that they would encounter racial discrimination if assigned to segregated units. Nisei women also were quick to assert that racial integration was in keeping with democracy, the very reason the war was being fought.[11]

The War Department scheduled several other visits to internment camps. Officer Deane was sent to interview women at Hunt Relocation Center in Idaho, where she found 37 Nisei women, out of 58, eligible and seriously interested in enlisting in the WAAC. Similarly, when Second Officer Joyce Burton interviewed Nisei women interned at the Heart Mountain Relocation Center in northwestern Wyoming, many stated they were interested in serving if granted the "privilege." Like other Nisei women who expressed a desire to serve, these women said they were loyal citizens of the United States. They welcomed an opportunity to serve in the WAAC to prove their loyalty.

Most of the Nisei women interviewed on these visits were more interested in joining the army than in working in civilian jobs: they perceived that the army would offer more protection and more physical security, as well as the assurance of fifty dollars per month. Most of the women prided themselves on being "modern American women who had outgrown oriental ideas."[12] Some feared that their living in internment camps placed them at risk of reverting to traditional "Oriental" ideas because they were forced to live in such close contact with the "old Japanese school."[13]

This last wave of loyalty investigations had two objectives. First, the War Department sought to determine the loyalty of Nisei women; second, it wished to ascertain whether these women would be willing to serve in the WAAC or the Army Nurse Corps if given the opportunity. Largely influenced by the sentiments expressed by Nisei women in these official reports, WAAC Director Hobby recommended that Nisei women be accepted for enrollment and service in the WAAC, subject to all rules and regulations governing the enrollment of white women.[14] She further recommended that the surgeon general issue special weight and height requirements applicable only to women of Japanese descent. Finally, Hobby recommended that Nisei women, unlike Nisei servicemen and African American servicemen and women, serve in racially integrated units.

Subsequently, Assistant Secretary of Defense Lt. Gen. Joseph D. Hughes proposed that Japanese Americans be permitted to serve in the WAAC. In a letter dated April 7, 1943, Hobby acknowledged receipt of Hughes's letter, and assured him that integrating Nisei and Caucasian women in the corps required no special planning. The Military Intelligence Division approved this action the following week. In June, the War Department Personnel Division approved acceptance of Japanese Americans into the WAAC. The War Department further decided that loyalty investigations of Japanese Americans were to be conducted at the Office of the Provost Marshal rather than that of the Military Intelligence Division.

All Nisei women inducted into the WAC during World War II had indicated on their loyalty questionnaires that they were loyal and supportive of the U.S. war effort. If they had indicated that they were not loyal to this effort, or that they were not willing to serve in the military, they would not have been inducted. This screening process was more complicated for Nisei men because they were obligated to serve in the military when the draft was reinstated for them in 1943; consequently some Nisei men who indicated on their questionnaire that they were not loyal to the U.S. war effort were drafted, anyway. But, because women were never drafted and entered the military only on a voluntary basis, they underwent a more thorough screening.

Induction into the WAC from the Continental United States

The process of joining the WAC was cumbersome: Nisei women had to fill out volumes of paperwork before they could be accepted. This could take several months. Irene Nishikaichi had left Poston and was living in New Jersey when she entered the WAC. She described the lengthiness of the process:

> I volunteered in September of '44. I didn't get inducted until April of
> '45. I would keep going to the recruiting offices and asking what
> happened. The recruiter would say, "You just have to wait." So finally
> I couldn't wait anymore and I had the WRA person look into it. In
> the meantime, the [West] Coast was opened for [Japanese Americans]
> to return [to their homes] and so all the records were sent from
> Washington, D.C., to Los Angeles and my records got lost some-
> where. It took six months to get the paperwork straightened out, and I
> had to take the army physical twice because it's only good for 90 days.

I finally got inducted in April. [President] Roosevelt had died and I was inducted under [President] Truman.

The first Nisei woman to become a member of the WAC was Frances Iritani, who was inducted on November 10, 1943, in Denver. Twenty-year-old Iris Watanabe was the first Nisei evacuee to join the WAC; she and two other Nisei women (Bette Nishimura of Rocky Ford, Colorado, and Sue Ogata of LaSalle) were inducted on December 13, 1943, in the office of Colorado Governor John F. Vivian. Watanabe had been a resident of Santa Cruz, California, until March 1942, when she was evacuated. She had been sent to the Salinas assembly center in California before being transferred to the Poston Relocation Center in Arizona. After living at Poston for nine months, Watanabe was transferred to Amache Relocation Center in Colorado. She left Amache to take a job in Chicago, where she was notified that she had been accepted into the WAC. Her mother and younger sister were still interned at Amache when Watanabe was inducted.

By December 23, the first group of Nisei Wacs began their training at Fort Des Moines. The five women, who ranged in age from twenty to twenty-four, were Iritani, Watanabe, Nishimura, Ogata, and Fukuoka. Fukuoka previously had been an evacuee at the Manzanar Relocation Camp. She stated in a newspaper interview that she joined the WAC because "I wanted to serve my country. I also thought that all Japanese Americans might find it easier to return to a normal way of life after the war if we did our share during the war."[15] Irene Tanigaki, of the Colorado River Relocation Center and subsequently Chicago, entered in January 1944. In February, Kay Keiko Nishiguchi of Garland, Michiyo Mukai, the daughter of an Ogden, Utah, restaurant owner, and Priscilla Yasuda of Provo were inducted in Salt Lake City. These three women received an enthusiastic send-off from their families and friends. Mukai is cited as saying, "We are thrilled to be able to serve in the Women's Army Corps."[16] After basic training, Mukai was stationed at Wright Field, Ohio, where she was appointed associate editor of the Wright WAC newspaper.[17]

A few weeks later, Florence Y. Kato, formerly of Los Angeles, was inducted in southeastern Colorado, where she lived with her parents at the Grenada Relocation Center. Dr. Masako Moriya, formerly a dentist at Gila Rivers Relocation Center in east central Arizona, also joined. She had received her B.S. degree from the University of California at Berkeley, and practiced dentistry in San Francisco until she was evacuated; she volunteered for the WAC on January 10, 1944. Diane Moriguchi, originally from Gardena, California, worked as a pharmacist at the Gila Rivers community hospital and hoped to be assigned to a WAC medical detachment. Toyome Murakami of Idaho was the twentieth member of the Pocatello Japanese American Citizenship League (JACL) to join the WAC. Mary Ryuko Uyesaki, a former evacuee, was working as a secretary in the Catholic Rural Life Office in Des Moines when she volunteered. When asked by a newspaper reporter what she felt about the WAC, Uyesaki said, "It's grand and in this way I feel I am doing something."[18]

Although Nisei women initially showed a great deal of enthusiasm about enlistment, they entered the WAC at a very slow rate. By February 17, 1944, only thirteen had enlisted.[19] The Japanese American press encouraged Nisei women to join the WAC, emphasizing the benefits of military service, as in the following excerpt from the *Pacific Citizen*:

> WAC requirements are not hard. . . . Age 20–49. Citizenship of course. Marriage, either married or single. Dependents, no children under 14. Character must be good. Education, two years of high school and a satisfactory aptitude rating. High school requirement waived when aptitude shows equivalent ability. Health good. . . . Because so many Nisei girls in the WAC are crack secretaries they have been given that type of work. But there are exactly 155 Army jobs that the WACs handle. They need women for jobs such as technicians, public relation experts, chemists, photographers, interpreters and translators, librarians, draftsmen, radio operators, airplane mechanics, accountants, chauffeurs, dieticians, and stock clerks. . . . The WAC has specialist schools for enlisted women. They include the administrative specialist school, the cooks and bakers school, and the motor transport school. In addition, army schools give special courses in photo lab work, coding and decoding, finance, medical and surgical, dental and X-ray technique. In other words, you can start training now for that after-the-war job. . . . There are a dozen good reasons for joining the WAC . . . there is no segregation in the WAC. You will bunk with, train and live with hundreds of girls from all over the country. It will prove an educational, inspiring and broadening experience unlike any other. It will enliven your personality and broaden your horizon. . . . This is a way to back up your brothers and husbands now overseas or at Shelby or any other Army camp. The Nisei Wac will be further testimony to the faith and loyalty of all Japanese Americans.[20]

In an effort to increase the enrollment of Nisei women, the War Department assigned Nisei Wacs to recruiting duty. Private Chizuko Shinagawa, who was inducted on August 16, 1943, was sent to Denver in May 1944 to urge Nisei women to enlist. In a press release, Shinagawa stated:

> It's a wonderful opportunity for my people to participate actively in the greatest battle for democracy the world has ever known. By

serving in the WAC, I've found the true meaning of democracy—the principle of share and share alike. I'm sure that Japanese American girls who join the WAC will develop, as I have, a broader outlook and an increased pride in their native land. Before I joined up, I felt useless and restless because I wanted to do something for my country. I wouldn't exchange for anything the experience I've gained in the WAC. All Americans, whatever their ancestry, must remember that they will be judged in the future by the part they play now. If we shirk our plain duty to our country in a time of its greatest need, we must be prepared to have our loyalty questioned. Indeed, I think it should be questioned.[21]

Other Nisei women began to register, as the WAC increased its recruitment efforts, and some of their names appeared in Japanese American newspapers in the following months. On March 17, 1944, two Nisei sisters, originally from Kent, Washington, and living in Chicago, joined the WAC. Alice Miyoko and Neba Fumi, daughters of Mr. and Mrs. Kihachi Shimoyama of Minidoka Relocation Center in southeastern Idaho, enlisted in Palatine, Illinois; they had one brother already in the army.[22] Kathleen Iseri, a former evacuee of the Gila River Relocation Center, was employed as a secretary in the local WRA office in New York. She was also enrolled in the evening division of New York University, studying English literature.

Iseri entered the WAC exactly one year after she left the internment camp. She stated in a newspaper interview that she was proud to be an American citizen:

I have volunteered for the Women's Army Corps because I am proud that I am an American citizen. I firmly believe in her institutions, ideals, and traditions. True, I had to leave my home on the West Coast at the onset of the war and live in a relocation center. But would Hitler or Tojo have given me the opportunity to leave such a camp—to help establish new homes for the other Americans of Japanese ancestry, who like myself, were evacuated from the West Coast? . . . I hardly think so. . . . There are thousands of American boys of Japanese ancestry serving in our armed forces, . . . and it is in the tradition which they have set that I, as a soldier of the United States Army, Women's Army Corps, shall proudly serve my country.[23]

Mary Arakawa of Cheyenne was the first Japanese American woman to enter from Wyoming. She had lived in Los Angeles before being moved to the Heart Mountain Relocation Center in northwestern Wyoming; she left the center to work as a nurse's aide in the home of Dr. and Mrs. H. L. Goff in Cheyenne. At the time of her enlistment, she had three brothers serving in

the United States Army.[24] Anna Takano, a dictaphone operator in Philadelphia, left her job to start basic training at Fort Oglethorpe in September 1944;
Takano, an evacuee, had been affiliated with the American Friends Service
Committee.[25] Mary Yamagiwa of Barrington, Illinois, volunteered for the WAC
in October 1944. Kathryn Tanaka, formerly of Pismo Beach, California, was
the first Nisei to enlist in Michigan; Tanaka, who came to Detroit from the
Gila River Relocation Center, was sworn in on December 7. She had worked
as a secretary in the Michigan office of the YWCA; at the time of her induction, she had a brother in the army and two sisters working in Detroit.[26]

Cherry Shiozawa, who volunteered for the WAC in 1944, married a soldier before joining the military. She explained, "Francis [my husband] was
drafted into the army, and we got married when he got leave." Shiozawa said
that she volunteered because her husband was on orders to go overseas; "We
were able to get together on furloughs." She went to Fort Oglethorpe for basic training and then to permanent duty in Ohio.[27]

Private Iritani, the first Nisei woman to join the WAC from an internment camp, appeared on a radio program, "WAC of the Week," which was
broadcast live from Tyndall Field, Florida. In a broadcast in August 1944,
Iritani, a former evacuee, stated:

> I am proud of my American citizenship. I have a brother fighting with
> the infantry somewhere in Italy. Both of us feel we are fortunate to
> have this chance to fight for our country. Being of Japanese parentage
> in this country has given us both full advantages of American youth.
> Everything I have came as a result of being an American. More than
> anything else, I want the children that I may have to enjoy the
> privilege of American rights. I want to be assured that when they read
> in their history books of the attack on Pearl Harbor, they need not be
> ashamed. They will have the right to be proud of their citizenship.[28]

Shizuo Yagi was the first Nisei women inducted in Milwaukee, where she
settled after leaving the Gila River Relocation Camp. She was sworn into the
WAC on September 30, 1944, and started her basic training at Fort Des
Moines on October 11.[29] Three months later it was reported that a second
Nisei woman from Milwaukee, Toshiko Nancy Etow, had joined the WAC;
Etow, originally from Watsonville, California, also was living at Gila River
when she was inducted. Her parents were interned at the Colorado River Center in Poston, Arizona; her brother had joined the army and was waiting to
be called. Etow, who was to be assigned as a medical technician in the WAC,
was cited in a Japanese American newspaper, "I thought I could best utilize

the nurses' aide training I had at the Colorado Project in service for my country by becoming a medical aide in the WAC."[30] On October 26, 1944, Aiko Nelly Sasuga became the sixth woman from Poston to join.[31] Takako Taxie Kusanoki joined the WAC from the Granada Relocation Center, where she had written for the camp's newspaper, *The Granada Pioneer*.[32]

Some Nisei WAC inductees were college graduates. Kumi Matsusaki entered in January 1945. She had graduated from high school in Las Cruces, New Mexico—where her parents were living at the time of her induction—and received a degree in pharmaceutical science from the University of Colorado in 1940. Matsusaki is cited, "I wanted to be a doctor, but it was too long and costly a proposition, so I settled for pharmacy and worked my way through college as a waitress and typist on the campus."[33] Upon completing her studies, Matsusaki worked at Beth-El Hospital in Colorado Springs, and then at St. Luke's Hospital in Denver. She considered joining the military, at her father's suggestion. Referring to her father, Matsusaki stated, "He's such a staunch patriot that he was actually unhappy over having no sons to lend to the war effort."[34] Tamie Tsuchiyama graduated from the University of Hawaii and studied at the University of California at Berkeley before the mass evacuation. She spoke several languages and was a reader in the anthropology department at the University of Chicago when she volunteered for the WAC. She expressed no preference regarding military assignment, declaring that she just wanted to do her "bit."[35]

In March 1945, the *Pacific Citizen* published an announcement that six Nisei women had volunteered for the WAC, with an interest in working as hospital technicians. The women, all in basic training at Fort Des Moines when the article was written, were Kisa Noguchi, Tsuruko Mizusawa, Margaret Uemura, Yaye Furutani, Amy Okada, and Haruko Sugi. All had been employed before their induction.

Twenty-five-year-old Noguchi was working with the field staff of the Carnegie Institute in Boulder, Colorado, when she decided to join. She was a graduate of the University of Colorado, and was studying for her master's degree when she joined the Carnegie staff. At the Carnegie Institute, she was responsible for making archaeological drawings for a study on Central American pottery. One of Noguchi's sisters was already in the WAC, stationed near Tampa, Florida.[36]

Mizusawa, a former evacuee at Poston Relocation Center, came originally from Garden Grove, California. Before joining the WAC, she was living in Minneapolis, where she held a job as a bindery apprentice. She had a brother who was stationed at Fort Snelling, Minnesota, when she was inducted.

Uemura, born in Spokane, Washington, had traveled to Denver for college. At the time of her induction, she was working as an assistant laboratory technician at Colorado General Hospital of the University of Colorado at Denver.

Furutani, born in Oxnard, California, studied art in Santa Barbara for three years before attending a private art school in Tokyo. Shortly after she returned to California, Furutani traveled to Hawaii and married Brownie Furutani, a newspaperman. The following year they returned to California, and were planning to go back to Hawaii when Pearl Harbor was bombed. Furutani applied for military service with her husband in El Paso. He was rejected for army service and returned to Hawaii; she joined the WAC. Furutani's parents were living in El Paso at the time of her induction. A sister, Peggy Tokuyama, a registered nurse in Rochester, Minnesota, also volunteered for military service; two brothers-in-law also were in the service.[37]

Okada studied nursing for a year in Seattle before being evacuated to Minidoka Relocation Center in southeastern Idaho. After leaving the center, she lived in Salt Lake City; she moved to Chicago and finally to Indianapolis before entering the WAC. Her fiancé, Frank Hidaka, and one of her brothers, Frank, were in France when she was inducted. Okada had another brother who already had received an honorable discharge from the army.

Sugi, a native Californian, worked as a saleswoman and dressmaker in Los Angeles before the war. She and her family were evacuated to the Jerome Relocation Center in southeastern Arkansas after the United States entered the war. Sugi's brother, Yoshitsugi, was in the army and was stationed at Fort Knox, Kentucky, with an armored replacement division. Sugi was fluent in Japanese and hoped to be assigned where she could use her linguistic ability.[38]

Two additional Nisei Wacs featured in the Japanese American newspapers were Julie Tanaka and Miwako Yanamoto. Tanaka joined the WAC after relocating to Des Moines in June 1945. Before the evacuation, she lived with her family in Los Angeles. She and her family were evacuated to the Manzanar Relocation Center, where Tanaka worked in the Caucasian mess hall. Her mother, younger sister, and a brother had resettled in Denver at the time of Tanaka's induction. Tanaka had another brother, who was in the Merchant Marines.[39]

Yanamoto, twenty-one years of age, left Rochester, New York, on April 30, 1945, for basic training at Fort Des Moines. Born in Los Angeles, she was a student at Los Angeles City College at the time of the mass evacuation. She and her parents were relocated to Poston; Yanamoto worked as a secretary in the law department while there. In September 1943 she left the internment camp and settled in New York City, where she worked in a WRA office. Later she transferred to the WRA office in Rochester. Yanamoto said, "I am very happy to be accepted into the WAC and to have the opportunity to take a more active part in the war effort."[40]

Finally, Mimi Asakura of Santa Barbara, and later of the Gila River Relocation Center, was inducted into the WAC in August 1945. Before her induction, she had been a secretary at the Indianola Methodist Church office in Columbus, Ohio.[41]

These Nisei women of the continental U.S. were from different walks of life. Some had been interned; some had not. They were all well educated. They lived in different regions of the country. Regardless of their differences, these women all had a strong desire to demonstrate their loyalty. They volunteered to play an active role in the war effort.

The Hawaiian Contingent

Women living in the U.S. territory of Hawaii were not recruited into the WAC until October 1944. On October 3, the *Honolulu Advertiser* published an article indicating that women living in Hawaii were enthusiastic about joining the WAC:

> More than 50 Island girls with ambitions to trade the hibiscus in their hair for khaki-colored Wac hats kept a staff of male recruiters busy at the Armory yesterday as the Women's Army Corps opened its first enlistment campaign in the Territory. . . . Opening day of the enlistment program saw a constant line of applicants passing shyly, resolutely or thoughtfully among the desks of the recruiting headquarters. . . . Most of them were in their early twenties, but a few were not much under the 40-year limit, and recruiting officials hope there will be more of the older ones as the campaign gets underway.[42]

One of the reasons these women gave for wanting to join the WAC was a desire to travel to the continental United States. As one enlistee said, "I've always wanted to go to the States, and this way I could do something for the war and have my expenses paid too."[43] Some of the women had husbands or other relatives in the armed services and had been waiting for the day when they too could wear the uniform. Grace Kutaka, a teletype operator at the *Honolulu Advertiser* at the time of her enlistment, stated, "I have two brothers in the army, one overseas. I want them to know that I am doing my part."[44] Michic Yagami, a cashier with a life insurance company, said, "I want to serve the country."[45] May Fukagawa, a switchboard operator at the USO (United Service Organizations) Army and Navy Club, said simply, "I want to be in the service."[46] Atsumi Miyashiro, a clerk for a manufacturers' agent, stated, "I have always wanted to be in the WACs."[47] Elaine Oda, employed at a Honolulu department store, said, "I want to do something for my country."[48]

There was a political controversy over whether WAC recruitment in Hawaii would deprive the workforce of women when there was a critical need for labor. James Blaisdell, then president of the Hawaii Employers' Council, expressed this concern: "We are opposed to taking women needed in essential employment in Hawaii for shipment to the Mainland when they will have to be replaced by other women shipped from the Mainland."[49] Newton Holcomb, territorial director of Hawaii's War Manpower Commission, proposed that only women not employed at their maximum skills in essential industries be eligible to enlist in the WAC. The War Department, however, maintained that the women of Hawaii should not be discriminated against in any way, and should have the same opportunity to serve as women in other parts of the United States.

By December 1944, sixty-two women from Hawaii had been inducted into the Corps, entering from the islands of Oahu, Kauai, Maui, and Molokai (see the appendix for the women's names and serial numbers). These women were of various ethnic backgrounds: German, Portuguese, Chinese, Korean, Filipino, Irish, English Portuguese, and German Chinese, as well as Nisei.[50] Most, however, were of Japanese descent, and their military experience did not differ from that of Japanese American women who had entered from the mainland. A newspaper article reported that all of the women were well educated, having completed at least two years of high school. Some had postgraduate college education. All spoke fluent English in addition to their parents' native tongues.

Some military officials expressed concern as to where the Hawaiian women would receive their basic training. This concern was reflected in a letter, dated December 9, 1944, from Colonel O. N. Thompson, commanding general of the headquarters of U.S. Army Forces, Pacific Ocean Areas, to the adjutant general of the War Department. Thompson requested that WAC inductees from the Hawaiian Islands be given their basic training in southern states. His rationale was that the change in climate would be less severe there than in the north. A transmittal sheet dated December 18, 1944, signed by a Major C. W. Ardery, authorized the Hawaiian Wacs to receive basic training at Fort Oglethorpe, Georgia, provided that they arrived at the training center before February 7, 1945.

Implicit in Thompson's request was the stereotypical notion that women were frail and needed protection from the cold environment. This seemingly special provision was challenged by the acting assistant chief of staff, Brigadier General W. W. Irvine, on January 2, 1945. In a letter addressed to the director of training, Irvine stated that military necessity made consideration of climatic conditions unfeasible in assigning personnel for training or permanent duty. The issue was put to rest on January 11 by Colonel Vance L. Sailor, chief of the War Department's Appointment and Induction Branch; Sailor confirmed that fifty-eight Wacs had been recruited from Hawaii and shipped to Fort Oglethorpe. He added that the recruiting program had been terminated and there would only be one shipment of Hawaiian Wacs to the training center.[51]

The newly formed Hawaiian WAC unit was led by three Caucasian Wacs, who were assigned to the Air Transport Command. These Wacs were in charge from the time the women were inducted in Honolulu until they arrived at their basic training unit at Fort Oglethorpe. Captain Margaret Steele, formerly of Albany, New York, was the company officer in charge. The noncommissioned officers were Sergeant Maxine Sharp, from Grand Junction, Colorado, and Corporal Bobbie Mahler, from Long Island, New York. Before leaving Hawaii for the mainland, Captain Steele issued a press release about the Hawaiian Wacs:

> The Wacs already have developed remarkable morale and efficiency. Their drilling after 12 days is equal to any other Wacs I have seen after five weeks. . . . They kept their barracks at Fort Ruger beautifully and we left it in completely GI condition despite this morning's excitement and rush. . . . We have two softball teams and two dodgeball teams, and the girls weren't in camp 24 hours before they were planning a company party. . . . I don't think we'll have any tears today, even when that ship finally puts out to sea. . . . I think the girls are well adjusted now to the Army and to each other.[52]

One of the Hawaiian Wacs, Lillian Mott-Smith, was a well-known educator on the island of Maui. She was born in England and had lived in Hawaii for twenty-two years when she was inducted. (Her son later graduated from the U.S. Naval Academy.) From the time the Hawaiian Wacs were inducted until the end of the war, Mott-Smith wrote articles about the women's assignments and about other events for the *Honolulu Star Bulletin.*

The Wacs sailed from Hawaii to California and stayed four days at Fort Stoneman. Much of this time they spent in washing, ironing, drilling, attending church, and writing letters. On the fourth day, the Wacs boarded a train for Fort Oglethorpe. They had two cars to themselves; many rode in "deluxe compartments used only for peacetime luxury travel." Mott-Smith described the days on the train as filled with "card games, map and route markings, group singing and hulas." She described the dining cars' large windows that revealed such beautiful scenery as "snow-capped hills covered with symmetrical pines and snow carpeted earth." The Wacs made several stopovers where they purchased souvenirs, some from Native American shops.

The women also visited the USOs in many cities en route to Georgia.[53] During a travel delay in Amarillo, Texas, they visited the local USO and were greeted by the director, E. D. Frederick. Frederick formerly had served as USO director on the island of Oahu. Three Hawaiian Wacs, Privates Johnson, Yang, and Kim, had been junior hostesses at that USO and had worked for Frederick. In the article "Hawaiian WACs Find a Friend Between Trains in Amarillo" the *Amarillo Daily News* announced that the three members of the company and Frederick spent an hour "talking over old acquaintance and renewing friendships."[54]

On the trip to Fort Oglethorpe, the women's loyalty and patriotism were not questioned by the public. The following statement, published in the *Amarillo Daily News*, seems to capture the general sentiment about the Hawaiian Wacs' war experience: "They all know what war is about. Nearly all were at Honolulu, Dec. 7, 1941, and saw the Japanese attack on Pearl Harbor. One of the girls who is a practical nurse spent three weeks at a tuna canning factory where she helped treat the wounded and injured."[55]

Wherever the Wacs stopped, they were well received. Some of the more musically talented entertained male soldiers stationed in the areas they passed, at the local USOs. On January 19 the Wacs stopped in Memphis, where they visited the USO and "entertained servicemen with Hawaii's favorite songs and dances."[56]

The travelers were met by heavy fog when they arrived in Chattanooga. There they transferred to trucks, which transported them to their final destination, Fort Oglethorpe, the Third WAAC/WAC Training Center.[57]

Nisei Air Wacs

Most WACs were assigned to either the Army Ground Forces or the Army Service Forces, but a large proportion, approximately 40 percent, were assigned to the Army Air Forces (AAF). As men were transferred from the air forces to the ground forces, particularly during 1944, Wacs were recruited to replace them. Most of the AAF Wacs were sent to air bases directly from basic training, to work in jobs for which they already possessed skills. A smaller number (approximately two thousand) were sent to AAF technical schools and assigned in military occupations such as weather observers, weather forecasters, electrical specialists, cryptographers, bombsight maintenance specialists, and other technical and mechanical jobs considered atypical for women. Army historian Mattie Treadwell has reported that opportunities for technical jobs in the AAF increased for women toward the end of the war because men less often met the aptitude requirement.[58]

Approximately 50 percent of AAF Wacs held administrative or office jobs; only a small fraction were assigned to flying duty. The first two "flying Wacs" were assigned to Mitchell Field in Montgomery, Alabama, as radio operators, participating in B–17 training flights. A few additional WAC radio operators, mechanics, and photographers were assigned to flight duty, in the United States and overseas; some received Air Medals.[59]

Nisei women were among those accepted for duty with the Army Air Force; they were assigned upon completion of basic training. Cherry Nakagawara, formerly an Oakland, California, resident, and wife of a Nisei soldier stationed at Camp Bowie, was accepted for the AAF in January 1944.[60] Air Wac Tamako Irene Izumi was inducted in Texas; her husband, Sergeant Heiharchiro Izumi, had been stationed at Forth Worth for three years.[61] Shizue Sue Shinagawa, formerly a schoolteacher, left the Poston Relocation Center, where she lived with her parents, to be inducted into the WAC and report for duty with the Air WAC upon completion of basic training at Fort Des Moines.[62] Chidori Ogawa, a clerk in a Minneapolis store, was accepted into the Air WAC in May 1944. She was born in Honolulu, graduated from the University of Hawaii, and migrated to San Francisco in 1935; later she was forced to evacuate. Forced to leave San Francisco during the mass evacuation, Ogawa moved to Minneapolis.[63]

The induction of Nisei Wacs into the AAF was particularly newsworthy because this unit was completely closed to Nisei men. In an article published on January 15, 1944, the *Pacific Citizen* applauded the Women's Army Corps for assigning Nisei women to all units, including the AAF. The article, which highlighted Cherry Nakagawara's induction, stated, "[N]isei women are eligible to serve in all units of the WAC as attested to by the acceptance of a [N]isei, Mrs. Cherry Nakagawara, for duty with the [A]ir [C]orps, a unit so far closed to men of Japanese ancestry."[64]

The recruitment process attracted many skilled, enthusiastic Nisei women to the WAC. The realities of training and duty followed enlistment. The military experiences of Nisei women had similarities as well as differences from those of other women of color.

Chapter 5

Service in the Women's Army Corps

I was on KP Duty when I received a message to report to headquarters. After I walked over to headquarters, I was told to go to the barracks and pack, "We're taking you to the train station." So I packed, not knowing where I was going. I later learned that MacArthur had requested fourteen Wacs to do secretarial work. I was sent to the Philippines.

—Ruth Fujii

Basic Training

The rigorous schedule of WAC basic training began at 5:30 A.M., when the women prepared to fall into formation for 6:00 A.M. reveille. After reveille they cleaned and tidied their personal areas, picked up cigarette butts and other trash outside their quarters, marched to breakfast, and then began classes. The women studied military first aid, personal hygiene, military customs and courtesy, map reading, defense against chemical and air attack, supply, organization of the army, and other subjects. They broke at midday for lunch and resumed classes until supper. They also drilled and participated in ceremonies and parades. After supper the Wacs were required to study and prepare their uniforms for the following day.[1]

This schedule was the same for all members of the WAC, regardless of racial or ethnic background. African American Wacs, who served in racially segregated units, described the same routine.[2]

Miwako Rosenthal recalled:

They sent me to the First WAC Training Center at Fort Des Moines. I was the only Japanese American in the company. The sergeant and high-ranking officers were very good to me. There were . . . other Japanese Americans from other states that were assigned to different WAC detachments at the time. . . . [W]hen I got to Fort Des Moines it was bitterly cold and snowy, and I got so excited with the snow that I ran outside, skidded on the ice, and broke my rib. They sent me to sick call and then they just put a bandage around it and relieved me from doing all this KP stuff because I couldn't lift those big pots. They were surprised to see an Oriental, you know? And this little tiny one at that; I wasn't big, I'm not quite five feet. They received me perfectly fine.

Although most of the interviewees stated that basic training was stressful and somewhat unpleasant, Rosenthal enjoyed it: "I had a wonderful time." She said that she would never forget one incident in particular:

I was short, and the first dress parade we had, they arranged us by size . . . I was on the tail end of this company. I was running like the dickens to keep up. My officer saw me doing that and had empathy for me. The next time we had to march in a dress parade, she had me put in charge of quarters. So I stayed in the office while the rest of the company did their marching. I didn't have to be in the parade because it would have ruined the whole parade with me running like crazy to keep up with the rest of four hundred Wacs marching in dress formation.

Rosenthal accepted charge-of-quarters duty because she did not want to disrupt the parade. She did not perceive this assignment as an act of racial discrimination, even though she was receiving differential treatment: "I understood that I wouldn't be able to march because they were really tall people."

Like Rosenthal, most women interviewed for this study were the only Nisei in their basic training companies. Ellen Fuchida recalled, "Fort Des Moines was for WACs only; there were no men there at all. I was the only Nisei in this whole group [WAC company] of mine. There was a WAC contingent from Hawaii, but I never saw them."

All of the interviewees stated that they were not treated any differently than Caucasian Wacs. They thus gave a far different account of the racial climate at Fort Des Moines than did African American Waacs/Wacs, who were assigned to racially segregated companies. In 1944, for example, African American Wacs alleged that they were forced to billet in crowded quarters, were subjected to racial slurs, and were not permitted to charge books out of Service Club "[N]umber 1."[3] No such allegations were made by Nisei Wacs.

Unlike the African Americans, the Nisei were not forced to house, socialize, and eat in facilities separate from white Wacs. Except for exclusion from the WAC officer corps, Nisei women were fully incorporated into the WAC. In contrast, African American women were trained as officers but were segregated and restricted from leading white Wacs.

Basic training lasted about six weeks. Grace Harada stated: "There were only women at Des Moines, just hundreds and hundreds of women. We trained from five in the morning until evening. We had physical exercise, marching, and all these different things that you do in the military, learning discipline. I was the only Oriental [in my basic training company]. We didn't have any problems at all."

Irene Nishikaichi was also the only Nisei woman in her company; she too speaks of being treated no differently than the other women:

> I didn't notice any difference. I didn't feel any animosity or hostility or anything. I was the only Japanese American in my company. There was one other Japanese American from Poston assigned at Fort Des Moines. Her mother and my mother were friends, and so my mother sent me her address at Fort Des Moines. But she had already gone through basic, and was actually assigned there for permanent duty. I looked her up and I saw her once during the time that I was at Fort Des Moines. She was the only other Nisei American that I saw during that period. After basic I went to the language school.

Rosenthal, too, said she did not experience racial discrimination while in basic training. She felt that she was accepted by Caucasian Wacs largely because of her personality: "I have that kind of personality. If somebody doesn't like me I make it a point to find out why . . . and make him like me." Further, Rosenthal felt that being the only Nisei in her basic training unit meant she did not suffer discrimination: "I think I was more privileged being Japanese American than being white because I was the only one. I wasn't discriminated against because I was the only one."

All members of the multiracial Hawaiian Wac contingent were assigned to the same company, which also included some Caucasians from the mainland. Unlike other Nisei Wacs, those who traveled with the Hawaiian contingent were assigned together. They were not racially segregated; as mentioned above, the group represented members of all racial and ethnic backgrounds (except African descent). They went through basic training as a unit, for convenience.

Ruth Fujii, a secretary in the WAC, recalled that the Wac officers, although they did not treat Nisei and Caucasian Wacs differently, commented on the mannerisms they observed in the Nisei women, "We're different, and so the officers were surprised that when we had inspections we never got nervous. . . . So one Caucasian girl told me that the commanding officer of the Fort wanted to know how come we were so poised."

Grace Kutaka remembered that the Japanese Americans in the Hawaiian contingent were not treated differently than Caucasians. She stated, in a letter about basic training, published in the *Honolulu Advertiser* in April 1945:

> We were like sisters, and we shared everything that we had. . . . Before
> leaving basic we had a party, with some of the Hawaii girls doing the
> hula and the Mainland girls putting on a skit. It was swell and one of
> the C.O.s said she never did see any group of girls who cooperated
> better. She was quite amazed at how we all worked together.[4]

The Hawaiians arrived at Fort Oglethorpe on the morning of January 22, 1945, in time for breakfast. Their accounts of basic training reflect good humor and jocularity. One of the women interviewed by Lillian Mott-Smith at Fort Oglethorpe described the first two days of basic training:

> Army food is good, contrary to all reports. . . . It's heavy and starchy,
> but we enjoyed it . . . many of us had gained weight, which wasn't too
> complimentary to our stock uniforms, which had been made for us in
> Hawaii. After breakfast we were taken to our barracks . . . The bunks
> were a problem. They were hard to make, and bumped heads were the
> results of absentmindedly forgetting that there was another one
> above. . . . We rose by way of flashing lights being unceremoniously
> turned on at six in the morning. (To many of us, this was the middle
> of the night.) We were given a half hour to dress, make our bunks,
> clean our areas and report for inspection. . . . Then we stood in line . . .
> for breakfast, which was served on aluminum trays, cafeteria style. . . .
> After mess we often had extra duties, such as latrine cleaning,
> classroom dusting, yard KP. Everything was rush, rush, rush.[5]

Like all Wacs during that time, these women learned military customs and courtesies, hygiene, map reading, and military drill. They also had daily physical training (PT). One of the Wacs described the exercises they were required to do as "stunning blows to flabby muscles." They were convinced that "death was sweeter than the complete dip."[6]

Three of the women I interviewed were inducted into the WAC from Hawaii. Alice Kono remembered that all of the trainees and cadre (instructors) at her basic training installation were women: "I don't remember seeing any men there." Kono recalled how demanding the drilling and the classes were, as were the additional duties required of Wacs in basic training. Through all of the stress, these women seemed to retain their good humor. It was not unusual for them to poke fun at each other. One of the Hawaiian Wacs described Kono performing additional duty during the first week of basic training: "More duties confronted us at four-thirty each day. One of the funniest sights I ever saw was small Alice Kono from Molokai carrying mop, broom, and bucket going to clean the theater. She was in a PT dress much too big for her and she looked like a miniature chimney sweep."

The Hawaiian Wacs had been at Camp Oglethorpe for a little over a month when an Earl Finch of Hattiesburg, Mississippi, arranged for ten of the women to have dinner with GI musicians of the 171st Infantry Battalion, a unit of Nisei male soldiers stationed at Camp Shelby, Mississippi. The men were on their way to Nothington General Hospital in Tuscaloosa, Alabama, to entertain wounded combat veterans of the 100th Battalion and the 442nd RCT. One of the members of the 171st, Technician Fourth Class Robert Terauchi, described the meeting:

> Although the Wacs were restricted from passes since they were new arrivals, Mr. Finch arranged to have ten of the girls have supper with us at the hotel, the choice being left to lady luck and a lottery system. The girls were already seated when we entered the dining room, as we were a little late. What a racket we made when we met for the first time!—a typical Hawaiian greeting. . . . Knowing we like sashimi (raw fish), Mr. Finch had some prepared for us, and everything was just perfect. . . . After supper we went to the Fort to meet the rest of the girls. The first word we heard as we entered the service club was "Aloha". . . All of the girls were asking which islands we were from and if we knew certain people back home. . . . A program for the evening was pre-arranged and the girls started the show with their vocal and hula numbers as we accompanied them with the musical background. It was like being home again. . . . The show being an informal one, we spoke in *Hapakanaka* (Pidgin English) all the way, and the *Haole* (white) audience had a hard time trying to understand the lingo. S./Sgt. Ken Okamoto did a hula duet with Evelina Gunderson, one of the Wacs from Hawaii. The dance was a sensation and they made a wonderful team.[7]

Immediately after the social gathering, the soldiers of the 171st left for Nothington General Hospital.

Despite their good humor and graciousness, some of the Hawaiian Wacs found basic training unfulfilling: It was not socially or culturally stimulating enough. Although they did not express regret for having served, they rarely looked back with pleasure. Consider this statement by Hisako Yamashita:

Most of the time we were in the fort training. . . . On weekends, we could go to Chattanooga for a day and come back. That was all. . . . I think it was a restricted life. Life in the barracks was dreary. It seemed secure and yet so barren to me. . . . There was nothing that would enlighten me, or make me think really hard on anything other than just living from day to day. And that, to me, made it an unpleasant experience even though I was in for patriotic . . . duty. I'm glad I did it and it's over.

Grace Kutaka, on the other hand, had nothing but praise for her experience, as in this letter to the *Honolulu Advertiser*:

I always think I'm a lucky girl to have had the opportunity to join the Wacs. You learn a lot of things, and you learn to conserve time too. I know what some people think of us, but I'm proud of myself and the uniform. I found out now that it is up to the individual to [retain the lessons learned]. . . . By the time we get back to civilian life, we will bring the GI ways with us. . . . Miss all of you at the *Advertiser*. . . . Miss also the lovely Hawaiian music. Oh—last night there was a boy with a guitar, and boy! Did I feel lonesome! Take care of Hawaii for us till we come back.[8]

Permanent Duty Assignments

Wacs were assigned to their duty stations by a process known as the bulk allotment system.[9] Under this system, tables of allotment (TA), sometimes known as manning documents or tables of distribution (TD), showed military positions by grade, title, military occupational specialty, and branch.[10] Commanders received a quota of WAC spaces by grade, and then submitted requisitions for Wacs with specific skills. Women were allowed to fill any noncombatant position they were fit to perform. The military occupations in which women were authorized to serve included (among others) clerical, administrative, mechanics, radio operators, intelligence analysts, photographers, carpenters, painters, parachute riggers, and postal workers.[11]

Nisei women filled a variety of military occupations in the WAC. Private Lillian Higashi was assigned as a chaplain's assistant at Fort Knox. She was studying to be a language teacher, specializing in French and Spanish, when she joined the service. Higashi was responsible for counseling military men who were in trouble, performing a stenographer's duties, driving the chaplain's car, and projecting motion pictures. In a newspaper article she stated, "I like my people, and I love my work."[12] Dorothy Nakasato of Honolulu was a clerical worker in the discharge section of Camp Kilmer, New Jersey.[13]

Private Kumi Matsusaki had a degree and work experience in pharmaceutical science. After basic training she was stationed at Nichols General Hospital in Louisville, Kentucky, as a technician. Comparing her military duties with those required previously in her civilian jobs, Matsusaki stated, "I was already accustomed to handling war time pharmaceuticals like penicillin and sulfa derivatives; they were in use at St. Luke's. But it's something new to be compounding and dispensing drugs in bulk, not by prescription."[14]

Mitsue Houchi of Wailuku, Maui, also entered the WAC with previous medical training. After basic training she was assigned to the Beaumont School for medical technicians in El Paso, Texas. She received an additional month of training at the Army Service Force (ASF) Regional Hospital at Camp Crowder, Missouri, before being assigned to the Army General Hospital at Camp Carson, Colorado, for permanent duty in the dermatology section. Houchi later was assigned as a medical Wac at the Separation Center at Fort Des Moines, where female military personnel received medical examinations when returning to the United States from overseas areas for discharge.[15]

Katherine Tanaka, mentioned above, also was assigned to the medical field. She had attended a dental technician course at the Fitzsimmons General Hospital in Denver, Colorado, before joining the WAC. After basic training, she was permanently assigned to Camp Polk, Pennsylvania, as a laboratory technician. Corporal Kay Keiko Ogura, formerly of the Manzanar Relocation Center, worked as a surgical technician at Camp Joseph Robinson, Arkansas. Private Miyoko Sadahiro of Layton, Utah, is of particular interest. Before the United States entered the war, Sadahiro had been a student at the Women's College in Hiroshima. She studied there for fourteen months and was a passenger on one of the last ships to leave Japan for the United States before Japan bombed Pearl Harbor. Sadahiro was assigned with the WAC medical detachment, and worked as an assistant in an army hospital laboratory.[16]

Although a variety of military occupations were open to Nisei Wacs, the War Department wished to utilize the women primarily in clerical positions. In the words of a War Department memorandum dated January 30, 1945:

> Japanese American women who apply for enlistment in the Women's Army Corps will be encouraged to enlist for general assignment in the clerical field in order that Military Intelligence may have full opportunity to utilize their services in Japanese language work, and that those not used by Military Intelligence may be assigned to the largest extent practicable to administrative and clerical duties.[17]

The memo stated further that no recruiting effort would be directed toward enlisting Japanese American women in the WAC for duty with the Medical

Department. Authorization was given for women, like Kumi Matsusaki, who already had the requisite qualifications and wished to enlist for direct assignment to an army general hospital. The number of Nisei women in the medical field, however, was not to exceed the authorized quota.

The women I interviewed served mostly in clerical positions. A few worked in intelligence, translating war documents. One of the interviewees actually taught Japanese at the Military Intelligence Service Language School (MISLS—see below). Some were sent, after basic traninng, to advanced training before reporting to their permanent duty stations. Fuchida, for example, completed basic training and stayed at Des Moines to complete clerical school; then she was assigned to Dugway Proving Ground, a military facility in Utah established to test biological warfare. According to Mattie Treadwell's official history of women in the WAC, written in 1954, Wacs were first assigned to the Chemical Warfare Service (CWS) at Dugway in April 1943. There they served as laboratory technicians and draftspersons, and were "trained to participate in field observation during the mortar and rocket shoots, noting wind direction and air temperature."[18] Fuchida was assigned clerical duties at Dugway, and worked for a doctor:

> At that time, Okinawa was the main battle front and the terrain at
> Dugway was just like Okinawa. There were caves all over, and in
> these caves they would put three goats; one with a Japanese gas mask,
> one with an American gas mask and one with no gas mask. They'd all
> three come out dead and then they would be taken to my boss's office
> to be looked at. I had to record whatever he wanted recorded—
> clerical work.

Although she met "a lot of nice people" at Dugway, Fuchida did not enjoy her assignment: "It was horrible. I didn't know there was a place like that in Utah. It was ninety miles from nowhere into the desert." What Fuchida disliked most was the location:

> It really wasn't that bad of an assignment, but I felt that there must be
> more to going into service [than] being assigned to a place worse than
> where I left. It was so isolated, you had to make your own enjoyment.
> I think I did fairly well at nearly all the assigned tasks that I had. I did
> what I was supposed to and I was promoted to PFC. I seemed to be
> accepted. There were quite a few men and women at Dugway Proving
> Ground, and a lot of them were doctors and professional people.
> Everybody seemed to be enjoying what they were doing out there.

Although there were social activities on the installation, Fuchida went home most weekends. "It would take me hours to get home. . . . I just lived for the weekends." Although Fuchida did not attend the weekend dances, she had many friends at Dugway with whom she stayed in touch for many years after service. From Dugway, Fuchida was assigned to the Military Intelligence Service Language School at Fort Snelling, Minnesota.

Some of the Wacs were assigned directly to a permanent duty station from basic training. Harada was sent to Fort Benjamin Harrison, Indiana, to work in the ordnance department:

> There were all these vehicles at Fort Benjamin Harrison, being sent
> overseas. And we were getting them ready and in good condition to
> be used. I helped with supplying parts. It was warehouse-type of work:
> if they needed certain parts for these vehicles, I would have to make
> sure that everything was accounted for as it went out. Fort Benjamin
> Harrison was a very nice place; there was only one WAC detach-
> ment. . . . I enjoyed it there; I didn't have any difficulties. We all were
> doing clerical work. I was a little unhappy because I wanted to get
> into medical work, and my heart was on becoming a nurse. I thought
> if I went into the military maybe they might train me enough so that I
> could do work in the medical field. But since I had already had some
> typing, clerical, bookkeeping, and shorthand in high school, [the War
> Department] naturally just put me into clerical work. Well, I did get
> one promotion there, so I guess I was doing all right.

Harada was at Fort Benjamin Harrison only a few months before she was re-assigned to the Military Intelligence Service Language School at Fort Snelling.

Rosenthal left basic training for Camp Polk, Louisiana, where the army had weapon carriers. There she was assigned to the dispatcher's office, and also worked as a chauffeur for one of the male officers. Rosenthal lived in the WAC detachment at Lake Pontratrain, New Orleans, while working at Camp Polk, Louisiana. Many African American civilians were working on base:

> That was a tremendous place to work. There was nothing but black
> civilians coming around for jobs every morning. . . . They would
> congregate there to see what jobs I could give them. They were
> civilians because they didn't have enough military men to do that
> kind of work on the post. Blacks were hired as wage board [workers].
> Wage board was their Government Service rating; they were like the
> janitors and the custodial help, those jobs that you don't have to have
> a degree for. Wage board workers have even numbers: . . . two and
> four and six and eight, like that. And Government Service profes-
> sional ratings go from odd numbers: [they] start from five and go up to
> GS 15, which is high-ranking, equivalent to a general, I guess.

Figure 1. Iris Watanabe being inducted into the WAC in the office of Colorado's governor, John Vivian. Watanabe is shown with Governor Vivian. December 1943. *RG 165, Box 49, National Archives.*

Figure 2. Iris Watanabe (left) being inducted into the WAC in the office of Colorado's governor, John Vivian. Watanabe is shown with two other Nisei women, who are attending the ceremony but not being inducted, and Governor Vivian. December 1943. *RG 165, Box 49, National Archives.*

Figure 3. Two Japanese American sisters, Emiki (left), 24, and Rose Tanada, 21, viewing a poster of the Women's Army Corps in which they enlisted. They were residents of Chicago. Photo taken 23 January 1945. *RG 208, Box 106, National Archives.*

Figure 4. Anna Takano (left), being sworn into the Women's Army Corps by Lieutenant Jane Gillespie in front of the Liberty Bell, during a ceremony in Philadelphia, 12 May 1944. *RG 208, Box 106, National Archives.*

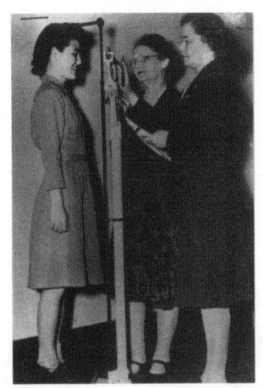

Figure 5. Mrs. Tamako Irene Izumi, being weighed for induction into the Air-Wacs (Army Air Force). Her husband, Sergeant Heihachiro Izumi, had been serving in the Army Air Force for nearly three years. *RG 208, Box 106, National Archives.*

Figure 6. Florence Kanashiro Kahapea (right) in front of the Treasury Department, Bureau of Engraving and Printing, Washington, D.C., 1946. *Courtesy of Kahapea's daughter, Coralynn Jackson.*

Figure 7. Florence Kanashiro Kahapea (left), 1946. *Courtesy of Kahapea's daughter, Coralynn Jackson.*

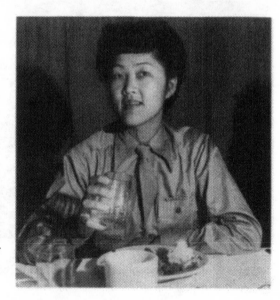

Figure 8. Tosuko Alice Kono of Molokai, Hawaii, in the mess hall, Fort Oglethorpe, 28 March 1945. *Courtesy of the U.S. Army Women's Museum, Fort Lee, Virginia.*

Figure 9. Eleven Nisei Wacs, one Caucasian Wac, and one Chinese American Wac are ready to board a Tran-Pacific plane to Japan. All were graduates of the Military Intelligence Service Language School at Fort Snelling, Minnesota. January 1946. *Courtesy of the Defense Language Institute Foreign Language Center, Monterey, California.*

Figure 10. Second Lieutenant Mary Yamada (right), Army Nurse Corps, Princeton, New Jersey, 24 September 1946. *Courtesy of Mary Yamada.*

Figure 11. Second Lieutenant Mary Yamada, Army Nurse Corps, Fort Hamilton, New York, 12 May 1947. *Courtesy of Mary Yamada.*

Figure 12. Second Lieutenant Mary Yamada, Fort Dix, New Jersey, during basic training for the Army Nurse Corps. May 1945. *Courtesy of Mary Yamada.*

Figure 13. Nisei Wac graduates of the Military Intelligence Service Language School at Fort Snelling, Minnesota. They are leaving for Camp Ritchie, Maryland. To the right is their commanding officer, Captain Nestor. 1945. *Courtesy of the Defense Language Institute Foreign Language Center, Monterey, California.*

Figure 14. Nisei Wac section of the soprano and alto departments of the choir, shown singing at Fort Snelling, Minnesota. 1945. *Courtesy of the Defense Language Institute Foreign Language Center, Monterey, California.*

Figure 15. Florence Kanashiro Kahapea at Camp
Ritchie, Maryland, 20 February 1946. *Courtesy of Kahapea's daughter, Coralynn
Jackson.*

Figure 16. Florence Kanashiro Kahapea (right). *Courtesy of Kahapea's daughter, Coralynn
Jackson.*

Rosenthal noted that she had no difficulties in doing her job. She felt that she was able to communicate well with the African American workers "because I am Japanese, and they didn't treat me like a white." According to Rosenthal, African American civilian workers had a difficult time working with white soldiers because the latter were condescending:

> If you've had any experience with blacks or any nationality like
> Hispanics or anything, they've got a chip on their shoulder if you treat
> them like they're lower than yourself. They get defensive. They
> weren't defensive with me because I was a minority. I didn't order
> them; I asked them. And they were all willing to do what I asked
> because they wanted to get paid. They wanted to get a job. There
> were more guys there than there were jobs. And every morning they
> would try to get there first so that they'd be first in line to get the job.
> I was a PFC when I went there, but then I got promoted to a corporal.
> And then . . . I left for the Military Intelligence Service Language
> School.

Like other Nisei Wacs, those from Hawaii filled a variety of military occupations after completing basic training. Some of the Hawaiian Nisei were the only women of Asian descent in their assignments. Grace Kutaka served at Mason General Hospital in Brentwood, on Long Island, before being transferred to duty at Hickam Field as a teletype operator: "When I saw the skyscrapers my mouth flew open! New York was exciting and the girls there were friendly. Spring in New York was lovely, with the green grass and pretty flowers."

From basic training, Ruth Fujii went to advanced training in clerical work at Fort Des Moines. Later she was assigned as a secretary to an executive officer at Camp Hood, Texas. Fujii did not like her assignment:

> It was miserable at Camp Hood. . . . no ocean, no mountains. I was so
> uncomfortable and it wasn't pleasant in the office. . . . That's the only
> time I faced some racial discrimination. I don't know [if it was
> because] I was a Wac or because I was Japanese. . . . But the colonel I
> was assigned to had just come back from Europe and then I replaced
> this man's secretary. And so he made it rough for me, but I didn't say
> anything. He called me in for dictation so I went in with my pad. . . .
> He used all the big words that others [other secretaries] wouldn't
> understand, but I took it all. . . . And then I sat down and ran it off.
> And then I gave it to the office manager . . . and covered my type-
> writer. I walked out, back to my barracks. I didn't say goodbye or
> anything. . . . Later the office manager called me and said the colonel

wanted to see me. So I said "Okay, I'll come over after I take a
shower. . . ." So I took a shower and I went in and you know what he
asked me? "Where did you learn English?"

Fujii did not bother to explain to the colonel that English was the primary
language in Hawaiian schools. She resented his ignorance.

In March 1945, the first Wacs arrived in Manila. After serving only a
few months at Camp Hood, Fujii applied for overseas duty and was stationed
there, in the Southwest Pacific Area (SWPA):

> I got assigned to General Marshall's group. . . . There were about nine
> of us girls. It was a small outfit they used to call MAGIC—Military
> Advisory Group In China. . . . I was a secretary to four colonels . . .
> [and] each had locked files. I had four files: personnel, intelligence,
> training and plants with pits, and supply . . . and had to memorize all
> four.

Fujii explained that the office in which she worked was under heavy security:
"Nobody was supposed to go behind the railing in our office. . . . They could
sit outside but could not cross the bar."

During our interview, Fujii recalled that an officer from Japan with the
same last name as hers was on trial while she was stationed in the Philippines:

> Being of Japanese parentage and bearing a typical Japanese name, I
> was certain that I would be attacked because the Filipino people
> despised the Japanese. And I didn't blame them. But a Filipino boy
> said to me, "You're Japanese, but from Hawaii. That's different." He
> and I were good friends after that.

U.S. military officials saw to it that Fujii was protected with a bodyguard: "Everybody took precautions and made sure that I had an escort wherever I
went. . . . When I went to town or anyplace, to the opera or anything, [there]
was [always a male soldier] sitting in a jeep with a gun. . . . If I was called at
night to take dictation, they'd send a jeep over to pick me up and take me
wherever I was supposed to go. . . . I'd have a jeep driver and a soldier sitting
in front with a gun."

On February 12, 1946, after spending eleven months in the Philippines,
Fujii received orders to report to the China theater. She spent two weeks in
Shanghai before traveling with a special group of Wacs assigned to Nanking.
Everyone she was assigned with in Asia seemed to get along: "Everybody
treated me well. My officers and fellow servicemen and women, we always
did things together; I got to go all over the place." The living conditions in
the Philippines, however, were somewhat less than desirable: "We had no

sheets; only army cots, army blankets, and that's it. . . . And then when I went to China, it was different. We had service—linen tablecloths, . . . and all because the Wacs were living in the same building as the [male] officers, only on a different floor."

The other two Hawaiian Nisei women I interviewed, Alice Kono and Hisako Yamashita, had attended clerk school at Fort Des Moinet l as Fujii did. Unlike Fujii, however, they were assigned to the Military Intelligence Service Language School at Fort Snelling for training in the Japanese language. In contrast to other military installations where Wacs were assigned, Fort Snelling had a majority of Nisei among its Wacs.

From Fort Snelling, Kono and Yamashita were sent to Camp Ritchie, Maryland, to translate Japanese documents confiscated by American soldiers. Yamashita recalled:

> Camp Ritchie was where all the captured manuscripts were. There
> was a Japanese document center and a German document center
> too . . . I met some of the fellas that were doing German
> transcribing. . . . I remember that the Japanese were building air-
> planes. They weren't getting resources, so they were using
> wood. . . . The wings were wood instead of metal, the way American
> [planes] were, because we had all of the iron needed to build planes;
> they didn't. And so these manuscripts were telling about these
> things. . . . These were important things for Americans to find out.

The Military Intelligence Service Language School

The Military Intelligence Service Japanese Language School (MISJLS), the precursor to the MISLS, was established to train military men in Japanese language and culture. As early as spring 1941, U.S. military officials viewed war with Japan as imminent. They were concerned that there would not be a sufficient number of Japanese linguists to meet the army's needs in the event of war. On April 15, 1941, in responding to this need, the United States Army began planning for a Japanese-language school to train Japanese Americans as translators, interpreters, and interrogators in the field. Seven months later, fifty-nine Nisei men and one Caucasian began instruction in Japanese at the Fourth Army Intelligence School, at the Presidio of San Francisco.

As mentioned in chapter 1, the War Department's need for Japanese linguists superseded its policy of excluding Japanese Americans from military service. Five months after Japan's attack on Pearl Harbor, thirty-six enlisted men and two officers were graduated; all but ten enlisted men were deployed in small teams to combat zones. These ten men, all Kibei, "were kept as instructors at Camp Savage, Minnesota, where the school was forced to relocate because of exclusion orders prohibiting Nisei to remain on the West Coast."[19] Clifford Uyeda and Barry Saiki reported that the other Nisei graduates were shipped overseas: "[T]eam leader Yoshio Hotta led five Nisei linguists to Alaska. Team leader Mac Nagata and five others were sent to New Caledonia . . . Eight Nisei left for Australia."[20] Unbeknown to many, these Nisei soldiers were assigned military intelligence duties as early as May 1942, eight months before the War Department officially reinstated Nisei men to military service.

The army expanded the school's program in April 1942. As noted above, limited facilities at the Presidio and the evacuation of Japanese Americans forced the school to relocate to Camp Savage, Minnesota, (and later to Fort Snelling, Minnesota). During this time, the name was changed from the Military Intelligence Service Japanese Language School (MISJLS) to the Military Intelligence Service Language School (MISLS). On June 1, 1942, 193 Nisei men and seven Caucasians were enrolled. By December 15, 1942, the number of men enrolled had increased to 434, and the faculty was expanded to 15 civilians and 30 enlisted instructors. The civilian instructors were selected from among evacuees interned at relocation centers.

Given the urgent need for officers, a preparatory course for qualified Caucasian personnel was established at the University of Michigan in October 1942.[21] According to Colonel Kai Rasmussen's report, the school was given wide publicity and received many applicants; 148 of the best qualified were selected and were inducted voluntarily into the army with cadet status. By May 29, 1944, 34 officers and 234 enlisted men were enrolled in this intensive Japanese-language program under the supervision of Professor Joseph K. Yamagiwa of the University of Michigan and a staff of 35 Nisei assistants.

As noted above, in January 1943 the War Department began to seek qualified Nisei women to serve as linguists. A series of conferences was held from January 25 to January 30 to discuss the possibilities of procuring Nisei women for voluntary induction into the army.[22] Subsequently, WAAC officers were sent to the ten internment camps (in Utah, Arizona, Colorado, Wyoming, California, Idaho, and Arkansas) to ascertain Nisei women's interest in serving; several WAAC officers reported back that the Nisei women were enthusiastic about such service.

In June 1944 the War Department began making arrangements to replace trained Nisei males with Nisei Wacs at MISLS. The first Nisei Wacs were assigned to the MISLS at Fort Snelling, Minnesota, on November 8, 1944. Eight were attached to Headquarters Company and assigned clerical duties. A former hospital building was used as a WAC barracks, providing sleeping quarters, a day room, and a laundry room equipped with an electric washer and drying space. The number of women increased to 48 in May 1945; at that time, two WAC academic sections were activated to train women as translators and interpreters. Shortly thereafter the peak strength of 51 women was reached, consisting of three Caucasians, one Chinese American, 18 Japanese Americans from Hawaii, and 29 Nisei women from the mainland; some of the latter had been recruited from internment camps.[23]

These Wacs learned to read, write, translate, and interpret *heigo* (Japanese military and technical terms). They also learned Japanese geography and map reading, along with the sociopolitical and cultural background of Japan. In addition, *sosho* (Japanese cursive writing) and instructions on the battle order of the Japanese Army were part of the curriculum. The first three months of training consisted of Japanese grammar, reading, writing, and simple translations. In the fourth month and the first half of the fifth month, students learned military terminology, military interpreting, geography, translation of newspapers, and Japanese writing style. In the latter half of the fifth month, lectures were given on Japanese history, politics, culture, and the military. Students also were instructed in Japanese operations and tactics and in American military tactics. Finally, in the sixth month, the entire class was separated into translating and interpreting teams for practical exercises. Table 4 displays the MISLS curriculum.

Nishikaichi recalls that, although she spoke Japanese at home with her parents, there was much about the language that she did not know before studying at the MISLS. For example, she learned words for "parts of a plane and the Japanese vocabulary for army [organizational] terms like *commander* and *battalion*." The study of geography, according to Nishikaichi, did not involve "the tourist places that we heard about. [It consisted of] naval bases and so forth. . . . We were being trained to be translators." Florence Toshiko Kaneshiro of Hawaii, described the work at MISLS as "confining," and as requiring "long hours of study."[24]

The language school was separated according to proficiency level: beginning, intermediate, and advanced. Like the other students, Nishikaichi was required to take an entrance examination to determine the level to which she would be assigned:

> I didn't think I would even pass the exam, but I found myself in the top class. And when I got into class, they had been in session for several weeks. I looked at the books, and I said, "oh my God!" The only language I used with my parents was Japanese, and I could not believe that I had forgotten that much Japanese in less than a year. They taught us Japanese vocabulary for military terms . . . the breakdown of how the army is set up . . . where the naval bases

Table 4
Military Intelligence Service Language School Courses

Course Title	Content
Naganuma reader	Reading and translation
Heigo (military) readers	Introductory course
Sakuson Yomurei (field service reg.)	Reading and translation
Cyo Senjutso (applied tactics)	Reading and translation
Interrogation and interpretation	Military procedures
Captured documents	Military procedures
Grammar, Japanese	Colloquial
Grammar, Japanese	Literary
Grammar, English	Basic course for those requiring it
Sosho (Japanese fluid grass writing)	A form of shorthand
Kanji	Characters and dictation
Japanese geography	Basic geography
Heigo (military)	Lectures in English and Japanese
American military terms	Reading and interpretation
Conversation, Japanese	Basic course for those requiring it
Japanese-English and English-Japanese translation	Reading and translation
Radio monitoring	Military procedures
Interception of messages	Military procedures
Lectures on Japanese society	History, politics, military, etc.

Source: Report by Colonel Kai E. Rasmussen, "History and Description of the Military Intelligence Service Language School," RG 319, Box 1 of 1, Ft. Snelling, Minn., National Archives, College Park, Md.

were. . . . The people in the lowest level could hardly say "How are you?" One of the girls in the lowest class was told by a faculty member, "Your mother's going to be sad. She's going to cry." And he was saying it in Japanese, but the girl didn't understand a word he was saying. I'm sure her parents never spoke to her in Japanese.

Nishikaichi did well at the MISLS, receiving a promotion at the end of each semester: " I was a private when I first got there, after a couple weeks I was already a PFC, and then the next semester I was a corporal." When she graduated, Nishikaichi had attained the rank of staff sergeant and was retained at the school to teach.

As noted earlier, Nishikaichi entered the WAC purposely to attend the MISLS. She realized that many people did not have the ability to serve as a linguist and that she possessed a much-needed skill. Yet although Nishikaichi was proficient in the Japanese language and also was motivated to work as a linguist, she knew that her military assignment would be limited because of her gender: "After I graduated they assigned me to the faculty. . . . I was teaching the beginners' class of the Wacs. . . . Most of us did very little as far as military intelligence is concerned because we were allowed into the service so late." More than half of the Wacs graduating from language school went to the East Coast; the rest remained at Fort Snelling. Nishikaichi was among those who stayed behind: "I was assigned to the faculty . . . I also did typing, and as soon as the war was over the faculty was assigned to translate the civil service code."

Harada, assigned as a clerk at Fort Benjamin Harrison before attending the MISLS, described the school as very challenging:

> The classes at Fort Snelling started at 9 A.M. and lasted until four in the afternoon; but we had to get up at 5 A.M. to do our exercises and clean our barracks for inspection. And then we had to go across a big field to have our meals with a [male] company that we were attached to. And then we would have to go back to our barracks, get into formation, and march to classes by nine. We'd study until four, and then marched back to our barracks. We had dinner at five and then had to go back to classes from seven until nine at night. And then we studied until lights out, which was 11 P.M.

The weekends were reserved for chores. "On Friday nights," said Harada, "we cleaned up the whole barracks for Saturday morning's white-glove inspection. After the inspection was over . . . and if we passed, we had the weekend off. If we didn't, . . . we were confined to the barracks."

The men assigned to the MISLS were mostly of Japanese descent. As Harada observed, "There were a few Caucasians, but they had to be quite fluent in Japanese to be there." Initially the women were not accepted by their male counterparts. When Harada and the other women first arrived, "the men thought we were terrible to even go into the military." However, as Harada later observed, the more men and women of the school came into contact with each other, the more they learned to respect each other: "Since we had to all study and work together we just got along fine there."

The men and women assigned to the school had plenty of opportunities to socialize after work. As Harada recalled:

> There was a club where we could go in the evenings for dancing and to socialize. It wasn't far from our detachment. That's where I met my husband—at a dance in the so-called "field house," a big auditorium. We were married before he was shipped overseas. I was very reluctant because I hadn't known him very long. But we talked to my parents and they just thought that he was a wonderful person and that I shouldn't let him go. I suggested that we just become engaged, but they said no. We went ahead and got married in a very short while because he had already received orders to go overseas.

Although the men and women at the school generally got along fairly well, there was a noticeable double standard, not only in occupational assignments but also in social privileges. The men assigned to MISLS had company dances, said Nishikaichi, "in which a fellow could bring in two and three girls, but we couldn't take in two men." This double standard caused some friction between the servicemen and the Wacs: "We put up a big fuss about [gender] discrimination" explained Nishikaichi. "If the guys could bring in more than one date, why couldn't the girls bring in more than one date?" This double standard was more or less accepted by the women, however, and did not affect their morale.

Rosenthal did well in her studies at the MISLS. "I don't know how I ever got into the top of the class," she said, "but I think it was because of my proficiency in English. I could write very well." She was given an entrance examination that required her to translate Japanese into English: "I knew enough Japanese characters to fudge it. Just like taking French—if you know the Latin of it, you can kind of guess it out." Rosenthal liked her assignment at the MISLS:

> I enjoyed it all the time I was there. I didn't have to do KP, and we didn't have to cook or anything. I didn't buzz around with Japanese American men like the rest of the Japanese American women. My friends were white. I remember one fellow; he was white, and he was an officer. I told him, "You're not supposed to associate with me because you're white and you're an officer." He said, "I'll just come and pick you up, and who's gonna know what we do off post?" The only reason I went with him anywhere was that I had just got there and he was leaving in about a week and a half. He had graduated and was being sent overseas. I felt sorry for him, I guess, so I went out with him. Japanese men never knew who I dated or whether I dated. And they said that I was a "kutonk"—you know, a snob; a mainland snob. I never dated Japanese guys.

During an interview, Lieutenant Colonel Marion Nestor, the former WAC commander at the MISLS, told me that WAC commander was an additional duty; her primary duty was as the intelligence officer for the school, "and . . . I only had a total of 53 women, of which two were Caucasian and one was Chinese, and the rest were Japanese Americans." Nestor recalled, "The school started in San Francisco before we even got into the war. It started to train Japanese Americans in the techniques of interrogation and translation of military information." Nestor was assigned to the school in September 1943: "I was with the school when it moved from Fort Savage to Fort Snelling, and from Fort Snelling to Monterey. . . . My whole career during the war was with the school."[25]

Colonel Nestor viewed the Nisei Wacs in her command as remarkable: "The Japanese Americans were in a terrible position; their whole families were in concentration camps. And . . . not only that, but the women had to fight the Japanese male macho, if I can use the word *macho* with the Japanese Americans. So for [these women] to come into the military was a double-barrel thing." According to Nestor, the Nisei Wacs at the MISLS were an outstanding group: "I was their commanding officer for not quite two years, and I never had a disciplinary problem. There might have been a few little things happen that eventually I heard of, but they took care of it; they didn't let anybody get out of line. . . . They were at school and then they had compulsory study hall at night. They didn't have too much time to get into trouble."[26]

Thirty-four Wacs were graduated from the regular course on November 17, 1945. Three of these women remained at the school as instructors, Staff Sergeants Isonaga!±nd Segawa of Hawaii, and Yanomoto of Los Angeles. In January 1946, for the first time in the history of the MISLS, Wacs—these Wacs—began teaching Japanese to male soldiers, most of Japanese descent.

Most of the other women who demonstrated proficiency in the Japanese language were assigned first to Camp Ritchie, Maryland, at the Pacific Military Intelligence Research Section (PACMIRS), and later to a document center in Washington, D.C. These women worked with translators from allied countries (Britain, Australia, and Canada), translating Japanese diaries, journals, manuals, and books. Some were assigned to nonlanguage duties at the headquarters of the MISLS.

Some Nisei women attending MISLS were proficient in Japanese, others not. This was attributable to the variations in exposure of these women to the Japanese culture while growing up. Fuchida's parents had sent her and her siblings to Japanese-language school, "but we didn't take it seriously. We would cut classes, go to the lake, and play around because it really didn't mean that much to us. I'm sorry now." Women who had lived and studied in Japan (Kibei) and those from Hawaii were usually the most proficient in Japanese language and culture, and were most often assigned to the advanced tier.

Still, every woman I interviewed stated that the MISLS was difficult and challenging—even the Nisei Wacs from Hawaii, who allegedly had more knowledge of the Japanese language than had those from the mainland. Kono, who grew up in Molokai, found the school particularly tough. Although fluent in Japanese, she knew nothing about Japanese military language before studying it at Fort Snelling. Hisako Yamashita, who grew up on the island of Kauai, stated that the MISLS "was challenging, all right." Both Kono and Yamashita were stationed at Camp Ritchie after completing language school. Yamashita said, "We translated captured military documents. There were bags and bags of them for us to translate. I wasn't terribly good so I didn't get the very important ones."

As for morale, all of my informants expressed sentiments similar to Nishikaichi's:

> I think our morale was good because as a group we got along well. I think we had a pretty good idea that we were all in there for honorable reasons. So we respected each other, and we enjoyed each other's company. And we all worked hard and studied hard. We tried to do our best, and I think that in that sense our morale was high. The war ended while we were still in classes, and then we graduated. About two-thirds of us went back to the East Coast; the rest of us just remained there. Some of us were assigned to the faculty; those at the bottom of the class were assigned to clerical work, typing duties, and things like that

Still, regardless of a Wac's skills and achievements in the MISLS, her race as well as her gender put limitations on what she could do after she completed language training. As Irene Nishikaichi stated, "Most of us did very little as far as military intelligence is concerned because we were [not] allowed into the service [until] 'forty-three when they finally opened up to Nisei women."

Serving in Japan

After the war, in January 1946, thirteen Wacs left Fort Snelling for Japan. They were among the first class of women to graduate from the Military Intelligence Service Language School, and were assigned to work with Allied Forces as clerks, secretaries, and translators. Eleven were Nisei, and four of these were from Hawaii: T5 Harriett Hirakowa, Sgt. Funiko Segawa, T5 Matsuko Kido, and Sgt. Chito Isonaga. The other Nisei Wacs were from the mainland: Pfc. Michkey Minata, T5 Toyome Nakanishi, T5 Edith Kodama, T5 Shizuko Shinagawa, Sgt. Miwako Yanamoto, T5 Mary Nakamura, and Sgt. Atsuko Moriuchi. One Caucasian Wac, Sgt. Rhoda Knudsen, and a Wac of Chinese descent, Bertha Chin, also were assigned with the group. Chin was from Seattle and had stopped briefly in Japan on her way to Hong Kong before the war. Knudsen had been born in Tokyo to missionary parents and had graduated from a Japanese-American school there. According to newspaper articles, the women would be discharged from the army upon arrival in Japan, and would become civilian workers.

The Wacs were thrilled to go to Japan; most reported that their families were equally excited. Nishikaichi's mother had cautioned her not to volunteer for overseas duty when she joined the WAC, but was excited that she was being deployed to Japan: "When we finally got our orders to go overseas, right away she wanted me to look up this relative and that relative and so forth." In a newspaper interview Knudsen stated: "I have a long list of Japanese Christians to contact . . . That is my extra-curricular work. I will keep the Lutheran Board of Foreign Missions informed of those whom I meet. This may help them to plan the future mission program."[27] A Wac named Marie Minata stated that she looked forward to seeing her uncle, a practicing physician in Japan. Minata revealed that her uncle had been imprisoned during the war for not supporting the imperial conquest efforts.[28] Harada's husband was already serving with the U.S. intelligence service in Tokyo, and she was eager to reunite with him.

Many Nisei Wacs viewed themselves as ambassadors for democracy; this theme is best exemplified in an article written by Kathy Gorman for the *St. Paul Dispatch*. The headline included the words "Nisei to be Mannequins of Democracy." Gorman wrote, "To model feminine Americanism in the land of their ancestors 12 Nisei WACs will leave . . . for Japan. . . . These mannequins for democracy will be the first American born Japanese WACs to put their feet on Japan. And part of their job will be to show the Japanese how becoming to women the garb of Americanism can be."[29] Gorman cited one of the Nisei Wacs as declaring, "We have Japanese faces, but we are Americans. . . . By our example we will have to show them [the Japanese] what a woman of Japanese background can be like—how she acts—when she has lived in a democratic country and had the advantages offered by such a country. It's going to be a big job—but we all know it and we are going to do our best to be successful at it."[30] Similarly, the *Advertiser*, a Honolulu newspaper, contrasted the Wacs with the Issei women immigrants: "Eleven Japanese-American women, including four from Hawaii, arrived by Air Transport Command plane yesterday en route to the land of their ancestors—but in a totally different role than that of the traditionally down-trodden women of Nippon."[31]

Because so many military people were traveling during this period, it took the women a few weeks to fly to their destination. Nishikaichi recalled, "We went from Minneapolis to San Francisco, Hamilton Field. We were there about a week or ten days before we could catch a flight to go to Honolulu. We were in Honolulu for about twelve days because we were flying with low priority. We were at the bottom of the totem pole, and kept getting bumped." Many of the Wacs took leave in Hawaii. This was the first such opportunity for the Hawaiian Wacs traveling with the group; they had not been home since their induction. Two of the women were from islands other than Oahu; Florence Segawa was from Hilo, and Chito Koloa was from Kauai. They were given sufficient leave time to go home. From Hawaii the Wacs flew to Guam, where they remained for six days, having arrived, according to Nishikaichi, too late for the army to fly them to Tokyo, and finally were flown to Japan by the navy.

Although there were (white) women officers already in Japan on temporary duty (TDY), Japanese American Wacs were the first enlisted women to arrive.[32] When they finally reached Tokyo, the exhausted women were informed that they would have to travel to the Philippines and be discharged in Manila. According to Nishikaichi, "We were all the way across the ocean, and then they said they were going to send us to the Philippines to get discharged because they didn't have facilities to do that." To the women's delight, the plans were changed, and the Wacs were taken by car about forty miles from Tokyo, to Zama, where they were discharged. They were told that, if they did not want to stay, they could return to the States, but all opted to remain and work as civil servants. Harada recalled, "We had to sign up for one year in order to get our transportation back to the States paid for. So the original contract was for a year."

The women were immediately assigned as civil servants for the Allied Translator and Interpreter Section (ATIS) of the U.S. Army.[33] Harada explained, "We were working for General MacArthur. Some of these women were doing translation work because they were getting an awful lot of documents at that time; and the war trials were going on. We were all . . . doing different things, but mostly clerical work." Each woman was tested to determine her occupational assignment. Nishikaichi qualified as a translator, with a civil service rank of CAF–7, and was indeed assigned to do translation. She described her co-workers as members of a team.

Even though she had little difficulty translating printed words, Nishikaichi found handwritten material challenging. "If you cannot read a character, you count the strokes, and you look it up in one dictionary to find out how it's read. Then you go to the other dictionary to get the meaning. But if it's handwritten—you know how illegible handwriting can be—then how many strokes are there? . . . Did [the writer] drop a dot or something? Where I was working there were native Japanese, so I'd ask them to translate written words." On the other hand, Nishikaichi stated, there were Kibei working in her department who needed assistance with English and were stronger in Japanese than in English. Therefore, the translators worked in teams consisting of Kibei and Nisei. The Kibei could read the Japanese but their translation was sometimes faulty; the Nisei, often college-educated, would translate this translation into standard English.

Nishikaichi believed that she did "as well as could be expected," given the materials; she and her fellow workers translated war diary entries taken from a period of years:

You'd finish one day, . . . like January 4, 1933, and then hand that in.
The next day you'd be given something like December 6, 1940. It was
not continuous; there was no connection between the two dates. You
could have one day, and when you got through with that section, you
might be given a diary for three months later. So what happened in
between, . . . especially when you don't know the recent history of
Japan? These were political documents. I had a vague idea of what the
Japanese political system was, but it was very, very vague. We were
not trained in that. . . . We were doing translation in something we
were not trained in. We didn't even know how many representatives
[there were], how they were elected or anything. And we were
translating the diary of someone who was in a position like . . .
Kissinger or somebody like that. . . . [I]f you knew absolutely nothing
about the American political system or Congress, you'd have difficulty. And . . . someone eventually had to put it all together. I read
somewhere that somebody in Washington had to redo all of our work.
But I think that for the training we had and for the knowledge we
had, we did the best that we could under the circumstances.

Harada, on the other hand, had very limited knowledge of the Japanese
language:

I wasn't very strong in Japanese, coming from an area [Idaho] where
there were no Orientals. We just didn't speak the language. . . . And so,
when we were sent to Japan, I had an awful hard time working with
[Japanese] military terms. . . . Some of the girls from Hawaii used to
work as radio announcers in Japanese. They had a lot more training
and they could read and write [Japanese] fluently. At Fort Snelling, I
was in one of the lowest classes, just learning the basics of Japanese.

Harada was assigned clerical duties and worked in general headquarters
(GHQ). She explained, "That's where General MacArthur was. That was the
Daitchi Building: *Daitchi* means number one." Fuchida also knew very little
Japanese. She was assigned to work for a lieutenant colonel who was research-
ing Japanese history and had lived in Japan for many years. She recalled sitting in a room with the other Wacs when the lieutenant colonel announced
that he needed a bilingual secretary:

I wasn't bilingual by a long shot and I wasn't a secretary . . . he looked
at me and said, "What do you do?" And I said, "Not much of anything." And he said, "Well, then, I'll take you." So this is how I met
this Colonel Davis, who gave me away when I was married; he
became sort of a pseudo father to me.

Although it was not a major problem, some difficulties arose because the women were civil servants rather than Wacs. Wearing the U.S. military uniform, which they did while at work, reduced confusion about their national origin. Nishikaichi dated a Caucasian soldier while in civilian clothes, and was stopped by the military police (MPs) as well as Japanese police. In retrospect she stated, "I would have been better off if I spoke English. Whenever I tried to explain something, I would start out in Japanese and then naturally all the more they thought I was Japanese. . . . There was one incident when I got really fired up and went to the MP station and blew my top. The insinuation was that I was Japanese and shouldn't be with a Caucasian soldier."

In some ways, the American uniform was a shield against racial antagonism by white male soldiers. Nishikaichi also remembered difficulties with some white male soldiers stationed in Japan:

> In the beginning, we were in uniform, and then later we changed to civilian clothes, and some of the white soldiers thought we were Japanese. . . . At the very beginning, we would go to the Red Cross in uniform, and talk to men who were in combat with the Japanese. And they would talk to us and treat us like we were Americans. But the men who came later, who had not been in combat, and who had not been overseas during the war years, caused problems. They made racial slurs, especially if they were drinking in bars. In the bars we were more likely to experience those kinds of incidents. These were white soldiers; I don't recall running into too many of the black soldiers because I think they were more in supply [occupations]; they were much more segregated in World War II.

Nishikaichi added, however, that these racial incidents were isolated cases; most of her experiences "even with Caucasian GIs were very pleasant."

Because problems of identity were anticipated, the women were required to wear their uniforms to work. Harada said that, although they had been discharged from the WAC, they were not allowed to wear civilian clothing on duty: "We had to take everything off of our WAC uniforms, all the insignia and everything, and that's what we wore to work." The women had very little contact with natives, other than the native Japanese they worked with, in Tokyo. They worked in a secluded area of the city and billeted exclusively with Americans. Fuchida found that, when she did come into contact with Tokyo natives, "they just stared at us." She bought candy and other items from the post exchange and took them to church on Sundays so that they could be distributed to the native residents. "To watch the children scavenging in the garbage cans was . . . so hard. That part was hard."

According to Harada, "Japan was so wartorn that anything we could do was a help to [the native Japanese]. I was happy to be [in Tokyo] because I could see my husband. But I think overall it was sad because we never experienced anything like this, and no matter which way you turned there was war ravage; and there was nothing you could really do to help." The women described their encounters with children on the streets of Tokyo begging for something to eat. All of the interviewees stated that they always carried candy or other edibles in their pockets to give to these hungry children. As Harada remembered, "Even if you gave them one little piece of candy, why, you made somebody happy."

The women were welcomed by the few adults they encountered. According to Harada, "We were very welcomed there because we could speak the language. They would come to us and ask little questions, or they would ask for candy, or gum, or help with this and that. It was right after the war, and it is so hard to describe. They didn't have food, and everything was so wartorn that it was just a pathetic sight." Harada stayed in Japan with her husband and witnessed the beginning of reconstruction. She recalled, "As they began to build and as we stayed, because of my husband's work, the people of Tokyo started inviting us to their homes. They were mainly the more influential people of Japan, who had beautiful homes. They were much wealthier, and were in a better position to entertain."

Some of the women were able to visit family members in Japan. Nishikaichi had met all of her relatives before the war, having been in Japan as a child: "I was there for about two months. I was only seven, so I don't remember that much of it. But this particular uncle, my mother's brother, they corresponded until my mother died." Nishikaichi visited her uncle while in Japan: "Where my uncle lived was hard to get to. I had to ask one of the GIs to drive me out there; it was quite a trip. . . . I only visited him twice. One time I took a train and then I had to take a bus, and, it was very, very difficult." Transportation in Japan was limited after the war, and Americans were not familiar with the transportation system. Nishikaichi also spoke with a cousin while in Japan: "I don't think she knew my father, but my father before he married, had been sending money to her family. She told me that her younger brothers and sisters would not have any feelings or any memory of it but she remembered. She said that anytime they had problems and were in trouble, my father came through for them."

Fuchida, too, visited her uncle while in Japan: "I went to see my relatives down in Beppu. My mother's older brother and family were [there]. . . . We met all of her family that was left." Harada, on the other hand, was unable to visit her family on her initial tour in Japan, since her relatives lived in southern Japan; "At the time, we weren't allowed to travel that far." In later years, Harada's husband was stationed in Japan, and, Harada said "my uncle, my mother's youngest brother, came to see us in Tokyo, so he was the only one that I had met."

For the most part, the women I interviewed remembered that the cordial atmosphere of the military community made up for the challenges of living in wartorn Tokyo. The women lived in hotels with maid service; because they were somewhat secluded, they found ways of entertaining themselves. "We used to have our own private parties. At the beginning, some enlisted men's group might have a dance or something and invite civilian women or something like that. But, later on it was mostly private parties."

The women appreciated their overseas assignment. Fuchida, for example, enjoyed her work and the military community in Tokyo. She met her future husband, also a MISLS graduate, in General MacArthur's headquarters.

> I think I worked a lot better in Tokyo than anywhere else because it was so interesting—looking up things in the file and running all over the place. The servicemen were so happy to see all of us who could speak English. . . . I had this Japanese face, and a serviceman would bring out a picture of a blonde and say, "Oh, you remind me of my wife." They were really good to us. There was dancing every night in the officers' billets, and the Red Cross would have dances. They later started up a Japanese theater, ballet. All of this started up while we were there, and very early. I went over in 1946 and stayed two years. I loved it because everybody was so nice.

Harada was happy to be assigned to Japan, because her husband was stationed there.

> My husband was working in Nigata, which is quite a distance from Tokyo. Eventually he was transferred to the counterintelligence unit in Tokyo, and so he was there . . . we could see each other, but we couldn't live together at first because they didn't have living quarters for dependents. So he lived over there in the men's quarters and I lived in the women's quarters, and we would get together for dinner and little chats in the evenings. But most of the time we were pretty busy day and night. We received an apartment about a year after I arrived there. Our oldest son was born in Tokyo on April 7, 1947.

Although Nishikaichi had no regrets about serving in Japan, and stated that she "would not have traded that experience for anything," she felt anxious for most of her tour. Nishikaichi's parents had only recently been resettled after their stay in an internment camp, and she was concerned about them: "I didn't know what was going on with my parents. Mail service was very, very bad. They were working as domestics, and I did not get any letters from them for weeks. Being an only child, I had no other way of getting information as to how they [were], so my morale in that sense was very poor."

Similarities and Differences: Nisei Women and Other Women of Color

Up to this point, I have made comparisons between the military experiences of Nisei women and those of Nisei men and white women. Here, I focus on how their experiences of joining and serving in the military compare with those of other women of color.

African American women were the largest and arguably the most stigmatized racial minority in the United States before and during World War II. They were inducted into the WAAC at its inception, largely as a result of previous political struggle. African Americans campaigned for expanded opportunities in the U.S. military through the black press, letters to government officials, and political rallies. While the WAAC was still in its proposal stage, black political organizations requested that a nondiscriminatory clause be written into the resulting law. According to historian Ulysses Lee, "such an amendment was proposed in the Senate . . . and accepted."[34] The War Department, however, refused this amendment, arguing that black units in fact would be formed in the WAAC and that an amendment to include a nondiscriminatory clause was unnecessary. Similarly, black political organizations initially objected to Olveta Culp Hobby's appointment as director of the WAAC. The black community felt that Hobby, a Texan, would discriminate against African Americans. The political pressure ceased after Hobby appointed forty African American women as officer candidates in the first WAAC officer training class.

Although War Department officials opened the WAAC to African American women from the beginning, it imposed a racial quota of 10 percent and rigidly enforced a policy of racial segregation. African American women were forced to serve in segregated units. Accordingly, among the 440 women selected to attend officer training at Fort Des Moines in July 1942, 40 were African American. These women were segregated into an all-black platoon; they trained, dined, socialized, and were billeted in areas separate from their white counterparts. Many of these women were well educated and entered the military with professional skills. Yet, due to the stigma placed on their race, they were often assigned menial work.

For example, all of the African American enlisted women stationed at Camp Breckenridge, Kentucky, initially were assigned to clean and do laundry, simply because they were black. After these women rebelled, and a request was made that the commander of the WAAC Training Command launch an inspection, the women were reassigned according to their skills.[35]

Similarly, in 1945, four African American Wacs were court-martialed, convicted, and dishonorably discharged for refusing to obey a direct order to do orderly work at Lovell General Hospital, Fort Devens.[36] The court-martial was voided after Congressmen Emanuel Celler, Vito Marcantonio, and Adam Clayton Powell launched an investigation. Referring to the African American Wacs in this case, an article in the *Washington Post* stated:

> They felt, and with some justification, that they had been made
> victims of racial discrimination. They had been assigned to menial
> work as hospital orderlies. A colonel, one of them testified, had
> refused to let them perform more advanced duties to which white
> Wacs were assigned because "I don't want black Wacs as medical
> technicians in this hospital. I want them to scrub and do the dirty
> work." When along with 50 other colored girls, they refused to carry
> on their duties, General Miles personally ordered them back to their
> jobs. It was for refusal to obey this order that the four girls brought
> before the court-martial were sentenced to a year at hard labor and
> dishonorable discharge from the Army. . . . The disobedience in this
> instance stemmed from considerations involving the essential self-
> respect and human dignity of the four girls concerned.[37]

It was further stated in the article that morale in the Women's Army Corps would be strengthened "by a thorough investigation of the charges made against the colonel in command of the hospital at which the four Wacs served. There is no room for racial discrimination among the men and women who wear the uniform of the United States."[38]

The institutional racism directed against blacks in the military, such as the policy of racial segregation, created an atmosphere that encouraged individual acts of racial discrimination. The personal racism of the colonel at Lovell General Hospital in the incident described above is one of many documented examples of racism in the WAC during World War II.[39] Such examples were not the case for Nisei Wacs, because they were assigned to integrated units according to skill. This racially integrated military environment fostered equality of treatment.

To be sure, there were isolated acts of racism directed against Nisei Wacs. Among the women I interviewed, Ruth Fujii was discriminated against by the colonel she worked for at Camp Hood. In addition, Stacey Hirose documented that Sue Ogata Kato was a target of hostility by a Euro-American Wac whose brother died in combat against Japan. Further, Hirose documented that, during basic training, a Nisei woman was severely beaten by a group of women because of her Japanese heritage.[40] However, according to the statements of the women I interviewed, these isolated cases were the exception and not the norm.

The racial segregation policy in the WAAC/WAC was directed exclusively at African Americans. All other minority women, including Native American women and other women of Asian descent, were scattered through ordinary WAC units according to skill.[41] The only exception was a group of Puerto Ricbæ Wacs who were enlisted, trained, and assigned as a unit because they did not speak English. In Puerto Rico, the WAC was authorized to enlist up to two hundred women. On October 6, 1944, fifty-one enlisted Puerto Rican women traveled from the island to Miami, and were then transported to Fort Oglethorpe, Georgia, for basic training;[42] two weeks later, a second shipment of fifty Wacs from Puerto Rico traveled to the mainland. All other women of Hispanic descent, however, according to army historian Mattie Treadwell, served in racially integrated units with white Wacs.[43]

Although Nisei women were at first barred from serving in the U.S. military, such restrictions were not placed on women of other Asian groups. As mentioned above, the social status of other Asian Americans improved during World War II as Asian countries became allies of the United States. Some Chinese American women, such as Marietta (Chong) Eng, and Nymphia (Yok) Taliaferro, served in the navy as WAVES.[44] Japanese American women, by contrast, were not accepted into the navy at all during World War II. African American women were not accepted into the WAVES until November 1944, after political protest by blacks. By 1945, two African American officers and seventy-two enlisted women had joined the WAVES.[45]

Before the first Nisei woman was inducted into the WAC, Chinese American women such as Corporal Helen M. Lee, who joined in August 1943, served as Chinese translators at Lowry Army Air Field in California. Helen (Toy) Nakashima and Jit Wong served with the Army Air Force. At least two Chinese American women, Maggie Gee and Hazel (Ying) Lee, served as members of the Women Air Force Service Pilots (WASP), ferrying planes from factories to air bases.[46] Neither Japanese nor African American women were ever accepted into the WASP.

Filipino American women worked with the indigenous underground resistance movement to assist American forces in the Philippines throughout the war. They smuggled food and medicine to American prisoners of war, and provided intelligence to both the Filipino and the American forces.[47] Among these women was Florence (Ebersole) Smith Finch, who worked with the underground movement and was arrested and tortured by Japanese soldiers. She returned to the United States after being liberated by American forces, and joined the Coast Guard SPAR. Finch was the first SPAR to receive the Asian-Pacific Campaign ribbon, which she received for her service in the Philippines; after the war she was awarded the civilian United States Medal of Freedom. Another Filipino American woman, Josefina V. Geurrero, worked with the underground movement and also received a Medal of Freedom after the war.

Even though other Asian American women were not denied entry into the armed services, their representation in the active-duty armed services was low. There is no available documentation that reveals just how many Chinese, Korean, and Filipino women served in the military. At this point, one can only hypothesize that, given the burning desire to prove their loyalty to the United States, Japanese American women served in greater numbers than women of Chinese, Korean, or Filipino descent.

All Japanese American women serving in the WAC were of enlisted ranks; there were no officers among them. There is no historical document that reveals why this was the case. However, given the racial climate of the time, one can speculate that the War Department did not want to place Nisei Wacs in positions superordinate to white Wacs. By contrast, there were African American Wac officers specifically to lead black segregated units.

The only Nisei women officers in the military during World War II served in the Army Medical Corps.

Chapter 6

Commissions in the Army Medical Corps

The Army's obligation to care for the civilian populations caught up in the aftermath of the fighting was a new dimension of warfare. . . . They needed a medical team whose scientific specialty officers not only supported soldiers in combat but could enable the United States to prosecute the peace. Those officers were indispensable in providing medical support for refugees uprooted by combat action and for people in areas liberated from the Axis Powers.

—The History of the U.S.
Army Medical Service Corps[1]

WOMEN WHO SERVED as army nurses and physicians differed from those who served in the WAC: they were college graduates, entering the military from established civilian professions. All nurses and eventually all physicians received commissions (officer status) upon entering the armed services. Most American women serving in the medical field were nurses; in the 1940s few entered as doctors. Service as a military doctor during World War II was even more of a rarity for U.S. women. According to the Bureau of the Census, in 1940 there were approximately 165 thousand physicians and surgeons in the United States; only seven thousand (or 4.6 percent) were women.[2] Although some nine female physicians were serving with the WAAC in March 1943, women were not commissioned as medical doctors in the Army Medical Corps until April of that year.

The initial gender restriction on the assignment of female physicians and surgeons was heavily challenged, because women doctors were called to serve with military units without adequate compensation. Two bills were introduced in the House of Representatives to address this issue. New York Congressman Emanuel Celler introduced H.R. 824 to amend Public Law 252 with regard to the temporary appointment of officers in the army. Public Law 252 was a bill to authorize temporary appointments of officers in the Army of the United States. The War Department had interpreted the words *person* and *persons* in Public Law 252 to refer only to men. H.R. 824 proposed to change the words *person* and *persons*, wherever they appeared in the statute, to read *man and woman* and *men and women*, thereby authorizing the War Department to appoint female physicians as officers.

While H.R. 824 was being introduced, Alabama Congressman John J. Sparkman introduced H.R. 1857, proposing that licensed women physicians and surgeons be appointed in the medical departments of the army and navy. The Sparkman Bill proposed further that:

> Those appointments shall be commissioned in the Army of the
> United States or the Naval Reserve, and shall receive the same pay
> and allowances and be entitled to the same rights, privileges, and
> benefits as members of the Officers' Reserve Corps of the Army and
> the Naval Reserve of the Navy with the same grade and length of
> service: Provided, That female physicians and surgeons appointed
> under this Act shall only be assigned to duty in hospitals or other
> stations where female nurses are employed.[3]

In March 1943, the House of Representatives Subcommittee on Military Affairs held three days of hearings on these proposed bills. Among those who testified was a War Department official, Lieutenant Colonel C. J. Hauck of the Legislative and Liaison Division. Hauck testified that the War Department had no objections to assigning a woman physician to any duty for which she was professionally qualified. For administrative purposes, however, the War Department assigned those women to the Women's Army Auxiliary Corps (WAAC). Hauck stated that the nine women physicians serving in the military were accepted to work as contract surgeons before they were appointed to the WAAC. They had completed WAAC training at Fort Des Moines and subsequently were commissioned in the WAAC.

Many other points were made at the congressional hearings. Commission in the WAAC did not give a woman physician wartime rating. Additionally, in March 1943, female physicians employed by the U.S. military were not assigned to the Medical Corps and were not given the same classification as their male counterparts. Several testimonies illustrated the negative consequences of thus excluding female physicians. Congressman Celler pointed out that the niece of the Secretary of War, Dr. Barbara Stimson, was a distinguished physician whose application for commission as a doctor in the U.S. military was rejected because of the narrow interpretation of Public Law 252. Consequently she went to Great Britain, was accepted into the British armed services as a physician, and at the time of the hearings, was a major in the British army.

Dr. Emily Dunning Barringer was a fellow of the American College of Surgeons, a member of the House of Delegates of the American Medical Association, and chairperson of a special committee of the American Medical Women's Association, which was organized specifically to secure commissions for women physicians in the army and navy. In her sworn statement before the House subcommittee, Dr. Barringer spoke of a woman physician who had trained as an anesthetist and had been in practice for fifteen years before she was called by the War Department to work in a military camp (because there was a shortage of anesthetists at this camp). Dr. Barringer stated:

> In one of the military camps there was a shortage of anesthetists, and this physician was asked to give anesthesia. She was employed on a non–civil service basis, and was not even offered a contract surgeon appointment, but was classified as a special technician. . . . [She worked] a 48-hour week with a salary of $150 a month, out of which she must pay her own living expenses. She was allowed to buy her own gasoline at Army prices and pay for her own lunches in the officers' mess hall at 22 cents a day. In addition to giving anesthesia to the military patients, she was instructor to groups of corpsmen, who take a three months course in anesthesia. . . . As to insurance, she received only compensation insurance while on the grounds. She wears no uniform and has no rank. . . . If this woman physician were a member of the Medical Corps, she would undoubtedly be a major.[4]

Dr. Barringer stated further that female physicians did not receive any of the military benefits that their male counterparts enjoyed. Unlike male physicians assigned to the Army Medical Corps, female physicians working in the military did not receive military quarters, food, or medical benefits.

Dr. Frank Howard Lahey, chairman of the procurement and assignment division of the War Manpower Commission, was one of many to testify at these hearings. His agency was responsible for obtaining medical personnel for the armed forces. Dr. Lahey illustrated that women physicians, surgeons, and veterinarians were critically needed in the military:

> There are . . . 43,000 doctors in the Army now. . . . If we continue according to the Army tables of organization, which are one and

one-half doctors per thousand, one and one-half dentists, and 0.75 veterinarians, we would about use up our supply of active doctors. It seems to me that we will need women doctors, and we will need them, I believe, very seriously. We will get to a place where, I believe, if this goes on 2 or 3 years longer, we will really literally be scraping the bottom of the barrel for doctors.[5]

Shortly after these hearings, there was a change in the policy of excluding female physicians and surgeons from the medical corps. According to the U.S. Congressional Record, H.R. Bill 1857, the act providing for the appointment of female physicians and surgeons in the medical corps, reached joint resolution and became Public Law 38 on April 16, 1943. This law approved the appointment of female physicians in the Army and Navy Medical Corps for the duration of the war plus six months.[6] Dr. Margaret Craighill, dean of the Woman's Medical College in Philadelphia, was awarded the rank of major and became the first female officer in the Army Medical Corps.[7] According to an article published in the July 1943 issue of *The Military Surgeon*, Dr. Craighill was assigned to the Surgeon General's office with the responsibility of supervising the health care administered to the WAAC.[8]

As recorded in the notes of Surgeon General Raymond Bliss, and later in the journal *Military Medicine*, some 75 women physicians were serving with the Army Medical Corps before the end of the war.[9] This estimate is lower than that of Esther Lovejoy, who in 1957 documented that 180 female doctors served as officers in the Medical Corps of the United States Army and Navy, and more than 20 in the Public Health Service during the war. In any case, the representation of women in the Medical Corps was low.

These women physicians ranged in rank from first lieutenant to lieutenant colonel.[10] Four were assigned to the 239th General Hospital, an infectious hepatitis center in France, from 1944 to 1945. Captain Jessie Reid of New Jersey was the hospital's chief of general surgery. Captain Bronislava Reznik of Chicago worked in otolaryngology. A Captain Seno, a graduate of Wisconsin Medical Center without a specialty, was assigned to general ward duty. Lieutenant Colonel Clara Raven was assigned as chief of laboratory service.[11]

The massive mobilization by the United States for World War II placed an unprecedented demand on the army's medical department. Documents from the Center of Military History reveal that more than 11 million men and women served in the army during the war, with a peak of 8.3 million in 1945. Army personnel served in eleven theaters of operation, and often were exposed to disorders unknown to medical professionals in the United States. Diseases such as malaria, typhoid, jungle rot, hookworm, typhus, dysentery, smallpox, meningitis, tuberculosis, dengue fever, and Japanese encephalitis were breaking out in epidemic proportions. To meet the increasing medical needs, the Army Medical Department expanded its military and civilian personnel to approximately 800 thousand.[12]

Army nurses and physicians were among the medical professionals intensely sought by the War Department. Still, in spite of the shortage of personnel in these occupations, racial and gender restrictions placed limits on the involvement of Nisei women. During the first two years of the war, Nisei medical professionals were denied entry.

The Army Nurse Corps

The Army Nurse Corps (ANC) became a permanent part of the Medical Department under the Army Reorganization Act, passed by Congress in 1901. It reached its all-time peak strength of fifty-two thousand during World War II, while Colonel Florence A. Blanchfield was superintendent.[13] Although nurses were appointed in the regular army, they were given only relative rank—that is, they were not actually commissioned as army officers. They wore the insignia of their grade, but they were denied the pay associated with that grade, a decision made by the comptroller general—until 1944.[14]

Like the WAAC, the ANC segregated African American women, integrated most Asian American women, and temporarily excluded Nisei women. The ANC was still closed to African American women applicants in 1940; the few African American women who had served in the ANC during World War I were released immediately after the war. When questioned about the omission of African American nurses in 1940, Surgeon General of the U.S. Army Medical Corps James C. Magee stated that it was "impracticable" to employ them in time of peace.[15]

This sentiment was challenged politically by the National Association of Colored Graduate Nurses (NACGN). Political pressure, coupled with the growing need for African American nurses to staff racially segregated wards in military hospitals, forced the ANC to recruit African American women.[16] By the summer of 1941, twenty-two African American women had become members of the corps. They served in racially segregated wards at Fort Bragg, North Carolina; Camp Livingston, Louisiana; and Fort Huachuca, Arizona.

Some of these women were deployed overseas. Prudence Burns Burrell was assigned to the all-black 268th Station Hospital at Fort Huachuca, Arizona, and later was deployed to Australia with 14 other African American nurses. In a published interview, Burrell stated: "We sailed from San Francisco on the SS *Monterey* on October 15, 1943, without a convoy. For two days we were escorted by a Navy blimp and destroyer. After zig-zagging across the Pacific, we arrived in Sidney, Australia, eighteen days later. After orientations, the nurses were sent by train to a women's staging area (WACO) in Brisbane, while construction was underway on our hospital in Milne Bay, New Guinea."[17] Thirty African American nurses also were deployed to Liberia in 1943, to treat the African American male troops stationed there. The following year, some 63 African American nurses were assigned to the 168th Station Hospital in Warrington, England, and later to the 10th Station Hospital, where German prisoners of war were treated; Mary L. Petty of Chicago, who served at Fort Huachuca, Fort Bragg, and Tuskegee, Alabama, before being deployed to England, was the nurses' supervisor.[18] By August 1945, the number of African American nurses had increased to 479, or 1 percent of the entire ANC.[19]

In contrast to African American women, Chinese American women, though few in number, were eligible for appointment in the ANC without racial restrictions. Helen Pon Onyett, for example, a Chinese American woman from Connecticut, served in North Africa during the war.[20] The barring of Nisei women at the onset of the war, however, meant that those Nisei women who volunteered for the ANC in 1942 were rejected.

Mary Yamada is a case in point. After the United States declared war on Japan, she applied for the Army Nurse Corps. When she tried to join with the Bellevue group, she was rejected:

> I was serving as an afternoon supervisor of the entire building, and I
> was listening to what was happening in Pearl Harbor. . . . The
> following day I went to my alumni association office to volunteer.
> And that is when the whole thing started that I was not going to be
> joining the Bellevue group. . . . I never had any question in my mind;
> I just expected [that] if there was a war, that was part of my nursing
> career to serve and report for duty . . . I expected to go with the
> Bellevue unit to England, 'cause that was where they were stationed
> for World War II. . . . But I was still trying to get in [the ANC] when
> volunteers were [returning home from overseas duty].

In September 1942, Yamada wrote to the Office of the Surgeon General requesting admittance to the Army Nurse Corps. A few days later she received the following letter, signed by ANC superintendent Blanchfield, denying her entry:

> In reply to your letter of September 3, you are advised that we are
> sorry to inform you that nurses of Japanese parentage are not eligible
> for assignment with the Army Nurse Corps. Although your individual
> loyalty to the United States is not questioned, the War Department

does not permit a deviation from this policy. Your tender of service is sincerely appreciated, and it is regretted that circumstances preclude a more favorable reply.[21]

Thus Yamada initially was denied entry into the ANC solely because of her racial identity. Not accepting "no" for an answer:

I kept writing . . . The day after Pearl Harbor I expressed my desire to become a member of the Bellevue Hospital unit for overseas duty. It took over three years after that before I was commissioned a second lieutenant in the Army of the United States for assignment to the Army Nurse Corps. And during that time I wrote many letters to many people in offices. [After a negative reply] I wrote again, and to my letter of February 5, 1943, I received a letter dated February 11. "We regret very much that we have not received authority to assign nurses of Japanese heritage to duty in the Army Nurse Corps and we have placed your name on file and plan on if, . . . " and blah, blah like that.

On February 21, 1943, the Office of the Surgeon General informed Yamada that she was now eligible to apply for duty in the Army Nurse Corps. The letter, signed by Captain Pearl C. Fisher, stated:

Today we have received authority to assign qualified Japanese nurses who hold American Citizenship to duty in the Army Nurse Corps. We are enclosing the necessary blanks. Please fill them out very carefully and send them to the American Red Cross as instructed.[22]

Although Yamada had received authorization to apply to the ANC, she had not been scheduled to take a physical examination. "At that time" she said, "I was able to contact someone in the personnel division in New York City, and she gave me a letter of authority for a physical examination." Finally, on June 18, 1943, Yamada took her physical, but, as she explained, "I had to keep contacting different people to see where I stood. . . . I think it pays to do things because I noticed [that] when I had written something, about two weeks later I would get a reply."

At last, on February 12, 1945, Yamada received a letter from the Army Service Forces stating:

The report of your recent physical examination has been reviewed and although you have been found physically qualified for appointment to the Army Nurse Corps, an administrative delay in final processing is anticipated since certification of your professional qualifications has not as yet been received from the American Red Cross. Upon receipt of clearance by the American Red Cross, the form for your oath of office will be mailed to you and when it is returned to this office completely executed, the official notification of your appointment will be sent to you and orders placing you on active duty, on or about the date you have specified, will be issued.

Yamada remained vigilant and completed all of the forms necessary for her oath after she received clearance by the American Red Cross. As instructed, she returned all of the forms to the Army Service Forces on Governors Island, and awaited a reply. In March, just five months before the end of the war, she received notification that she had been appointed and commissioned a second lieutenant in the U.S. Army Nurse Corps:

> By direction of the President you are temporarily appointed and commissioned a Second Lieutenant in the Army of the United States, effective this date [March 27, 1945] for assignment to the Army Nurse Corps. . . . This commission will continue in force during the pleasure of the President of the United States for the time being, and for the duration of the war and six months thereafter unless sooner terminated. This letter should be retained by you as evidence of your appointment as no commissions will be issued during the war. By command of Major General Terry.[23]

"On March 28," Yamada recalled, "I received a telephone call to report to Whitehall Street in New York to take the oath. I was sworn in on March 30, 1945, and a press conference was arranged for April 5. . . . And so I finally got in. I went into the Army on May 1."

Yamada went to basic training at Tilton General Hospital at Fort Dix, New Jersey. Independent of the Women's Army Corps, the Army Nurse Corps established centers in which new army nurses were oriented to the military. The entire training lasted approximately four weeks and consisted of 144 hours of instruction. Like Wacs, army nurses were taught military customs and courtesy, and the care of military equipment and uniforms. Also like Wacs, army nurses were drilled and underwent physical training. In addition, they received training in military sanitation and ward management. A former army nurse, Retired Colonel Mary Sarnecky, reported that the training course later was expanded to include defense against chemical, air, parachute, and mechanized attacks. Army nurses also were eventually trained to "dig a fox hole, use camouflage, read maps, pitch tents, and advance under a barrage of enemy shell fire."[24]

After completing basic training, Yamada was assigned to Halloran General Hospital on Staten Island for permanent duty. She wanted to serve overseas, however:

Every time a piece of paper went up on the wall requesting volunteers for overseas duty, I signed up 'cause I wanted to go overseas. It didn't matter to me where I was going to go, I just wanted to go overseas. It just didn't seem fair to me that my friends could go from Hawaii to the U.S. [mainland] . . . and the furthest I got was to Staten Island.

Although few Nisei nurses were serving in the ANC, Yamada learned that another Nisei nurse was stationed at Halloran Hospital while she was there:

I was at Little Brook General Hospital. I went there after my basic training; at that time it was called Halloran General Hospital. I was on day duty, and there was a Japanese [American] nurse who was the night nurse. I don't remember the first thing about her because we had no time to talk. . . . I didn't see any Japanese outside of this person. Her name was Toshito Hirata. I was there on day duty, she was on night duty, so I didn't see her.

On January 22, 1946, Yamada was promoted to first lieutenant and was transferred from Halloran Hospital back to Fort Dix, where she had received her basic training a few months earlier.

I was an instructor in the medical training school. And at that time, I met another Japanese [American] nurse. . . . We were both teaching in the medical training school. Her name was Yae Togasaki, and then she married a Mr. Breightenbach. I remember that her family had many doctors. Her sister was a practicing physician.

After serving as an instructor at the medical technical training school, Yamada was assigned as the assistant director of the U.S. Senior Cadet Nurse School. The Cadet Nurse Corps had been organized in June 1943 in an effort to provide more nurses for the war effort. Frances Payne Bolton, congresswoman from Ohio, introduced the legislation authorizing the corps; President Roosevelt signed the bill into law on June 15, 1943.[25] The U.S. Public Health Service subsidized the educational expenses of enrolled student nurses, who in return made a nonbinding promise to serve in a military or civilian nursing role for the duration of the war.[26]

There were some Nisei women among the cadet nurses. Ruth Tanaka, for example, entered cadet training after leaving the Manzanar Relocation Center and received her initial training at Children's Hospital in Denver; in September 1945, she was assigned to Glockner Hospital in Colorado Springs.[27]

In the final analysis, Yamada stated, she did not go into the military for material gain. She was motivated by knowing that she was rendering a necessary service:

I went in with nothing special in mind—what this [was] going to do for me. I wasn't interested in promotions or ranks or anything like that. I didn't know the first thing about that. But looking over my records today, I notice what the colonel had written [then]. . . . He wrote that my abilities were excellent and whatever I did was excellent. So I know I did all right.

Yamada added that she went into the ANC "because to me it was just an extension of what I was doing every day. I never gave a second thought about going in. I went because I wanted to go."

One regret Yamada expressed about her active duty in the military is that she was not accepted for service earlier:

I'm sorry that I couldn't have gotten in earlier. I don't know who I might have helped. I remember talking with certain young men; one man had to have surgery. He had to have an amputation and he didn't want to. I remember consoling him, and thought that if I had been in service sooner I could have consoled more people maybe, or just listened to them if nothing else.

Perhaps another disappointment for Yamada was that she never received the overseas assignment she had hoped for:

I never got to go overseas. . . . I stayed at Fort Dix and was charge nurse of the medical ward. I was also assistant to the chief nurse, and I would make my rounds at Tilton General as well as at the hospital annex. . . . When we served night duty we served from seven to seven, thirty-one nights with no days off. So that was all I did during the war. I was still there at Fort Dix during VJ Day.

Although the exact number of Nisei women in the ANC is unknown, only a few served during the war. Like their Chinese American counterparts, Nisei women served in units with white nurses.

A Nisei Woman Physician Who Became a U.S. Army Captain

When Dr. Yoshike Togasaki set out to join the United Nations Relief and Rehabilitation Administration (UNRRA) toward the end of the war, she had no idea that she would soon become a captain in the U.S. Army. In an interview conducted by the Japanese American Historical Society in 1985, Togasaki stated:

I volunteered to go to the Rehabilitation Program for Refugees on the basis that with my experience of medical [practice], as well as with

persons in camps, I would be more effective and more useful to the
refugees there than another person just plucked out of a university
and sent over there, directly out of a middle class environment. . . .
When I went to Washington to volunteer, I didn't expect to be in
uniform because this is a civilian organization, but it seems that all
the medical staff from the United States specifically had to be military
or they could not serve.

The UNRRA was an international agency established in November 1943
to administer aid to populations in countries devastated by the war.[28] Mil-
lions of people throughout Europe and Asia had been displaced as war victims. Representatives of forty-four united and associated nations met at the
White House and signed an agreement to contribute funds and services to
the relief effort in Europe, China, other Far Eastern countries, and the islands
of the Pacific. The scope and functions of the agency were outlined as follows:

> UNRRA is a service agency, which is authorized by the member
> nations to operate during the military period specifically at the
> request of the military and when the military period is over, at the
> request of, and in agreement with, the national authorities of liber-
> ated nations. . . . All members whether or not they have been
> invaded, will contribute, in varying degree, to the administrative
> expenses of the organization.[29]

The UNRRA provided relief in the form of money, food, clothing and tex-
tiles, agricultural rehabilitation, medical supplies and services, and other
welfare services. Among the administration's many health services, an epi-
demiological center was established to assist the health services of liberated nations to prevent the spread of epidemics aggravated by the movement of
displaced persons back to their homelands.

The UNRRA Training Center was located on the campus of the University of Maryland at College Park. The basic training program was approximately six weeks long and was followed by an advanced program. The training
consisted of intensive work in language, regional study, UNRRA organization
and policy, policies and procedures in the field, and field planning and field
operation. A special orientation program was designed for thirty-five Chinese
technical experts selected by the U.S. government to work toward rehabili-
tating China by employing modern techniques in medicine, flood control, agriculture, and welfare.[30] Frances Berkeley Floore, a dietician at the UNRRA
Training Center in 1944, described her experience:

> I was the only dietician at the UNRRA Training Center although
> there were many nurses, doctors, engineers, sanitarians, and countless

numbers of welfare workers. The scope of our UNRRA work was far
more challenging than any of us had realized. There were twelve
million refugees to be fed, housed, clothed, and later resettled or
repatriated in whatever was left of their former homeland. Our
indoctrination, which had an intensity and seriousness never before
encountered in any classes I had attended, made us thoroughly
cognizant of the devastating aftermath of war. . . . It was a disquieting
experience, geared to take away any self-complacency we might have
felt and to weed out any who doubted their ability to withstand the
pressure.[31]

Togasaki was commissioned with the rank of captain before deploying to
Italy, where she served as a medical doctor in refugee camps with the UNRRA.
"By the time I left for Italy," she said, "Governor [Herbert] Lehman [of New
York] had finished his term and was the governor-general for UNRRA." The
agreement signed by the nations establishing the UNRRA called for a governing council. On November 11, 1943, the council opened its first session
in Atlantic City, New Jersey. Lehman was elected director general of the council and assumed office. Togasaki added, "Because the war was still going on
and we were going into war territory. . . . I had to accept a commission in the
United States Public Health Service . . . [W]ithin six weeks or so, that shifted
from U.S. Public Health Service into full Army, and so I was commissioned
as a captain in the U.S. Army and then sent over[seas]."[32]

Togasaki was deployed to Europe in a Liberty Ship convoy, which took
twenty-eight days to reach Italy:

Just about the time we passed Gibraltar, V-E Day was declared. And so
when we landed in Naples, the European war was over. . . . There was
no longer any activity of war in Italy. . . They were rapidly dissolving
prisoner of war camps, especially in south Italy, and using the facilities
for the refugees. . . . They were housing these people in what is known
as villas that the Italians had down in these little seaside resorts."

Togasaki recalled further:

By the time I was there the group known as the Southern Italian
group consisted of six different displaced persons camps with headquarters in this province of Lecce, which was the southernmost
province in the heel of Italy, across from Greece and Albania,
Yugoslavia, etc. At the beginning there were all varieties of refugees—
Yugoslavs, Hungarians, Austrians, etc. Very quickly the various
nationals were sent back to their homes as they requested, and what
was left were central European refugees who were from Poland,
Germany, Austria, Hungary, Yugoslavia, and there were Jewish

[refugees]. . . . Later on, within two or three months, carloads . . . of concentration camp people were sent down to us.[33]

At the beginning of her tour, Togasaki was a medical officer, assistant to the chief. There were only two American medical doctors and a few American nurses, as well as doctors and nurses from other countries. According to Togasaki, "It was a polygot, I assure you. You couldn't even have a staff meeting because it was a matter of eight or nine languages." Togasaki revealed that one of the European doctors:

> was so offended that a woman was in charge that he refused to make rounds when I got there. I decided, when you get these macho men, it's no use to argue with them, they are going to retaliate in one form or another. The more you do, the more they do. The best thing to do is to ignore them, so I would go around and see the patients to make sure everything was okay.[34]

Togasaki also spoke of a shortage of qualified physicians. A Belgian psychiatrist was working in one of the refugee camps, which was directed by an American sergeant:

> The sergeant was excellent, but . . . this guy . . . was a psychiatrist, and he was giving psychiatric therapy, which was extremely necessary, very helpful, but [when] a little baby [was] dying of diarrhea, dehydrated, it [psychiatry] was no use. Or to a young girl . . . [whose lungs were filling up with fluid], also no good. The parents would worry all night. . . . and I would see these problems. When [I was] there, it was fine. But I would get into those camps at the most three times a week. . . . So when the chief colonel came down from Rome I said, "Look, I understand why you people send these medical directors down to these places, but I can't be responsible for the patients if these are the kinds of people you send me." Lo and behold, on his next visit, [he fired the psychiatrist]. I was getting it in the neck from the population because this wonderful psychiatrist was no longer there.[35]

Togasaki left Italy at the end of October, 1945, and reached California in November: "I went down to the State Department of Public Health, and I was offered a job then and there to start the next day."

Togasaki was one of the most senior ranking Nisei woman in uniform at that time. None of the Nisei Wacs were officers, and Nisei nurses were assigned the rank of lieutenant. The highest-ranking Nisei women in uniform were medical doctors, but the number of Nisei women who served in this capacity during the war remains unknown.

Chapter 7   The Postwar Years

*After I got out of the military I went back to work at Del
Monte; they gave me leave while I was in the service.
When I returned, my boss told me that he needed a
secretary and told me to get a degree. I went to business
school in Honolulu, got a degree, and worked at Del
Monte for twenty-nine and a half years.*

—Alice Kono

IN THEORY, war has the ability to reorder society. Cynthia Enloe argued that,
during periods of war, nations often call upon the services of groups ordinarily
excluded from full participation in society due to ethnic difference.[1] In a similar way, war affects gender relations by changing the role of women.[2] In their
article "The Social Impact of War," John Modell and Timothy Haggerty asserted that service in World War II provided many soldiers with the basis for
transforming their civilian roles, by providing large numbers with experiences
in organizational roles they otherwise would not have:[3]

> Not only must new members for the military (with particular skills or
> capacities) be secured from the civilian population, but new . . . paths
> must be devised within the military for filling critical roles that
> cannot be filled laterally from the civilian population. Recruitment,
> training, transfer, and promotion within the military, as well as
> changes in war itself, are highly consequential for the structuring of
> military forces and military careers, and thus for the impact war will
> have when hostilities are over.[4]

Throughout this book, I have discussed the implications of historical events on the lives of Nisei servicewomen. In this chapter, I focus on the effects on their lives of military service. I employ a life course analysis, more specifically the concept of "subjective turning points," to guide my discussion.[5] Glen Elder Jr., Cynthia Gimbel, and Rachel Ivie have defined turning points in the following way: "Dramatic changes in life histories represent turning points that separate the past from the future; people refer to themselves in terms of who they were before and after the event."[6] These authors have listed ten reasons that military service was a turning point for men in their study. In order of nomination frequency, these reasons were: maturity, education, travel and adventure, independence, altered view of life, life disruption, [meeting of] spouse, altered view of death, career, and leadership.[7]

What were some global changes in society following World War II, and how did these changes affect Nisei servicewomen? Did military service help the Nisei to achieve citizenship rights? Do Nisei women veterans now perceive the military to have been a turning point in their lives? If so, are the reasons they give similar to those found by the men in Elder, Gimbel, and Ivie's study? These questions are addressed below.

Race and Gender Changes Affecting the Lives of Nisei Women Veterans

No discussion about the effects of military service on Nisei women's postwar lives would be complete without considering the changes taking place in America's gender and racial climate at the time; just as in the prewar years, Nisei women's life chances were affected by both gender and racial trends. For women, the wartime emergency lowered traditional barriers and altered their role as homemaker. Women, including many who were married, found themselves outside the home, working in heavy manufacturing plants, earning more money, and exercising more freedom than in the past. Although most of these female beneficiaries of higher wages were Caucasian, some African American women were able to enter jobs in manufacturing for the first time. Still, as Maureen Honey observed, "women found themselves at the end of the war in nearly the same discriminatory situation they had faced prior to Pearl Harbor."[8] Thousands of civilian women who had made enormous occupational gains during the wartime labor shortage were laid off after the war.

As men retired their uniforms and returned to their civilian occupations, women were expected to relinquish these jobs willingly and return to their previous lives as mothers and housewives. Federally funded daycare facilities were discontinued, as were the grocery stores, beauty shops, and shoe repair facilities that some employers had established for the convenience of their women workers.[9] Women who remained in the workforce were forced to exchange their nontraditional roles in industry, construction work, and shipbuilding for lower-paying female-dominated jobs. Many of these women expressed dissatisfaction with being laid off.[10]

The loss in occupational opportunity experienced by women working in war industry, however, does not generally reflect the occupational changes experienced by military women in the postwar years. I would argue that the scenario was somewhat different for the women veterans, particularly those of color. Unlike women who had remained on the homefront and had worked in jobs traditionally held by men, most women in the armed services were assigned to female-dominated occupations. Thus at the end of the war, when many civilian working women found their occupational gains dismantled, military women entering the postwar labor force were being hired (and in some cases rehired) in occupations that had always been dominated by women.

Postwar changes in race relations are also important in explaining the opportunities that surfaced for Nisei women veterans. If Caucasian women's roles were disrupted by the wartime emergency, the roles of Japanese American women as wife, worker, and mother were upset even more seriously by mass evacuation. Nisei women could not gain entry into industrial plants during the war. Many welcomed the opportunity to enter female-dominated occupational positions after the war because such jobs often had been closed to them before. As mentioned in some of the testimonies above, domestic work was virtually the only job that Nisei women could find during the war. Grace Harada, for example, joined the WAC because she was tired of working as a domestic. Therefore, Nisei women veterans often viewed traditional female occupations as jobs with status.

The postwar years introduced an entirely new economic, social, and political context for the Nisei. Although some Japanese American stores, restaurants, and professionals catered to the Japanese American community, there was no longer the strong network of Japanese Americans working in agriculture or other services that had existed on the West Coast during the prewar years.[11] Many Japanese American farmers had lost their land during the mass evacuation; as a result wholesale and retail operations declined after the war. Not only did Japanese Americans' farm ownership decrease; so did their workforce, especially the unpaid family labor in which many Nisei women were employed before the war. Thus, in the years following World War II, Nisei women and men who had worked before the war in Japanese American–owned businesses began to move into skilled and semiskilled occupations in the general economy; they were absorbed by private as well as public agencies, particularly in civil service positions.[12]

In addition, the military services of both Nisei women and Nisei men helped to reduce the prejudice, stereotypes, and racial antagonism directed toward them in previous years. Postwar economic prosperity provided Nisei women veterans with occupational, educational, and family choices that had not existed for them before. A salient theme that runs through all of these women's testimonies is that their military service facilitated their goal of attaining the American dream. As was true of other racial and ethnic minorities of the postwar era, Nisei women veterans wanted to be a part of the American mainstream; some remained in the military after the war; most, however, reentered civilian society to pursue education, career goals, or marriage.

Moving toward Mainstream America

EDUCATION

Miwako Rosenthal left the military after she graduated from the Military Intelligence Service Language School. She immediately took advantage of the GI Bill and eventually earned bachelor's, master's, and doctoral degrees in biochemistry and microbiology from the Illinois Institute of Technology (IIT). While studying at IIT, Rosenthal met her husband, a Jewish student who later became a physician engaged in medical research. Although she had always been an excellent student, she found physical chemistry quite challenging:

> I was number three in science. I went to school with five thousand
> [students]; most of them were veterans. I was the only girl, but [the
> male students] treated me just like one of them. It was tough, I tell
> you . . . I would have failed P Chem [physical chemistry] if my
> husband wasn't there to tutor me because I'd never had that kind of
> math. It's beyond organic chemistry; physical chemistry is very
> hard . . . you have to know calculus. I never had calculus, so I was
> getting tutored by my husband on calculus and all the problems and
> everything. It's all calculus. I don't know how I ever got through it.

Irene Nishikaichi used the GI Bill for advanced education immediately after returning to the United States from Japan; she enrolled in advanced secretarial studies and completed training as a stenotype reporter. Later, Nishikaichi secured a job as a court reporter. She explained that her military experience was indeed a crucial point in her life: "The military was a turning point in my life because it enabled me to get my training as a reporter on the GI Bill. I don't think I could have afforded that, especially with the evacuation and all that. And as a reporter, I was able to make more money than I would have simply as a secretary, even a legal secretary. [The military] helped me to do better economically."

Similarly, Cherry Shiozawa claimed that her military service "was the best thing I ever did. . . . Later I made use of California's veterans loans, and the GI Bill for education."[13] Shiozawa enrolled in the social service program at the University of California at Berkeley and received a certificate qualifying her for employment in the social services department as a counselor.

Hisako Yamashita also took advantage of the educational benefits offered by the GI Bill:

> I enrolled in Columbia University and graduated with a four year degree. I [did] substitute teaching after I graduated college. . . . and then I signed up to be a teacher for a year. I taught courses in English [and] history for seventh and eighth graders and hated it; I had no free time. . . . I said, "This isn't for me." Then I remembered that I had an English professor at the university. She liked me and my friends and used to invite us to her home, and talked to us about doing library work. . . . After deciding that I didn't like teaching, I decided to enroll in Columbia's graduate program to become a librarian. I used the GI Bill to get my master's; that's how I became a librarian.

Each of these women was able to advance economically through the use of the GI Bill. Indirectly, the U.S. military was an avenue of upward mobility for them. For those who had attained high levels of education before the war, there was now the opportunity to work in occupations commensurate with their education.

WORK

Some of the women interviewed for this study went directly into the labor force after completing their military commitments. Many who entered the military from Hawaii returned to the jobs they had held before being inducted. Alice Kono resumed her employment at Del Monte, a manufacturing company in Hawaii. She stated, "They gave me leave while I was in the service, so I came back and continued working for them." The company needed a secretary and gave Kono additional leave to attend business school under the GI Bill in Honolulu. Later, she was transferred to San Francisco and worked there for Del Monte for nearly thirty years, until she retired.

Similarly, Ruth Fujii's secretarial position at the McKinley School in Honolulu was held for her while she served in the WAC. She never used the GI Bill, "because I had to go back to work." Fujii worked at the school for slightly over two years before being transferred to the office of the state superintendent of education.

This was not the case on the United States mainland, where Nisei women veterans usually started new careers after the war. Mary Yamada, who had been commissioned in the Army as a nurse, abandoned her hopes of becoming a physician when she returned to civilian society:

> I got my appointment with the Board of Education here [in New York City.] I had my mother then, and I had to spend months trying to find an apartment for us, I couldn't go in the direction I was chiefly interested in. . . . so that was what happened to me. I got out of the Army and then I wrote my letter of resignation to the Department of Hospitals and accepted the assignment to the Board of Education. . . . That was in teaching. The examination for guidance counselor came up later. I got my second master's in 1962, twenty years after my first one. . . . I took the examination and passed it and became a guidance counselor.

Dr. Yoshiye Togasaki returned to California in October 1945: "I went to the State Department of Public Health and was offered a job then and there." She worked as a medical officer establishing maternal and child care services. Later, Togasaki attended Harvard University and earned an advanced degree in public health. She was subsequently assigned to maternal and child health care services in Contra Costa County, California. Reflecting on her postwar work experiences, she concluded:

> Everything went smoothly because professionals are professionals; they are doing their work. So many of the people I worked closely with were classmates of my sisters or myself and friends of previous years—enough of a nucleus to support me as I was going through. Interns that I had trained in Los Angeles were in practice up there in Chico and Oroville. . . . There was no outspoken antagonism at the time, and yet I knew all along that around Loomis and Penryn and throughout that area, there were a lot of strong [anti-Japanese] expressions, such as burning of barns and throwing of incendiary bombs into houses . . . of servicemen who had returned. . . . All of these outlying areas were terribly in need of [health] service. The nurses and the families were very happy to have me. I didn't do the service myself— the specialists did—but I was responsible to see that things were moving. With it all we managed very well.[14]

Some Nisei women attributed their success in finding jobs directly to their military veteran status. Irene Nishikaichi, for example, claimed that her service facilitated her efforts in securing employment, not only because she was able to use the GI Bill to finance her education (see above), but also because she was able to use the veteran "point" system:

My veteran's points helped me to get the job. Veteran points, both
with the city and the state, made a big difference. I trained, and then I
took the civil service exam. Eventually, many years after that, I
obtained a license as a CSR: certified shorthand reporter. I had been
working for quite a number of years before I got that. It wasn't
necessary for the jobs that I got. If I went into the courts, it would
have been necessary.

Nishikaichi worked for the Los Angeles Police Department for fourteen years
before moving to the State Unemployment Insurance Board; there she worked
for nineteen years as a court reporter: "With the police department I was also
taking statements of witnesses, suspects and victims and . . . other things like
that." Nishikaichi worked as a state employee until she retired.

Similarly, Cherry Shiozawa secured gainful employment in addition to
educational benefits. She worked in the welfare department of Highland Hospital, Oakland, California, before moving on to supervise a children's program.
In 1989, when Shiozawa was interviewed by the National Japanese American Historical Society, she claimed that she was enjoying the life of a retiree.
She was involved in a senior citizens' companion program, and was still living in a house purchased with her veteran's home loan.

FAMILY

For the majority of American women in the 1940s, family roles were central:
"more of them married, they married at younger ages, and they had more children [than women in the previous decade]."[15] As historian D'Ann Campbell
stated accurately in *Women at War with America*, "The housewife, not the Wac
or the riveter, was the modal woman."[16] Citing statistics from the Roper-
Fortune Poll, collected in 1943 in Williamstown, Massachusetts, Campbell
reported that 75 percent of American women "preferred the [role of]
housewife . . . over being single with a successful career (6.5 percent) or com-
bining marriage and career (19 percent)."[17] Indeed, the average American
woman of the 1940s identified strongly with the roles accompanying marriage
and family.

Some of the Nisei Wacs married soldiers while still on active duty, and
announcements of their wedding vows were published in local newspapers.
Corporal Mildred Tamashiro, for example, married Corporal Steve Uetake
while both were stationed in Minnesota. Tamashiro was a student at the
MISLS; Uetake was an instructor there. After exchanging vows in Septem-
ber 1945, they honeymooned in Chicago for a week and then returned to Fort
Snelling for duty.[18] An announcement of their marriage was published in the
Honolulu Star-Bulletin. Similarly, in December 1945 the *Honolulu Star-Bulletin*

announced the engagement of Corporal Misue Nouichi, a medical Wac stationed at Fort Des Moines, to Walter Kitagawa of Honolulu, who recently had been discharged from the 100th infantry.[19]

Some of the women I interviewed also married while on active duty or shortly thereafter. After completing her tour with the WAC, Grace Kutaka married a Nisei serviceman assigned to the 442nd RCT. They subsequently had three daughters, one of whom served in the U.S. Air Force for four years. Similarly, Grace Harada and her husband were both assigned to the MISLS when they married; Harada was a student at the school; her husband was a Nisei officer assigned there. After the war, both were assigned to duty in Japan. Ellen Fuchida and her husband, also a Nisei officer, were married in Tokyo.

Both Harada and Fuchida married career army officers and spent most of their adult years as wives of active-duty officers. Fuchida's husband was assigned to the military intelligence office in Tokyo, where the couple lived for three tours. Fuchida worked part-time while living in Japan: "The first time I went [to Japan], I was a civil service worker. The second time we went to Tokyo, I worked in the security group, G–2. And at that time they asked me to look at the newspapers every day and cut out articles for the analysts and look in the file for different things that they needed. It was an interesting job, and I was promoted to a GS–7."

Fuchida and her husband started their family in Japan: "I had three children over there on three different tours of duty with my husband. Before we left from there the first time, I had my first daughter. And then I went back the second time and I had a son. Then I went back the third time and had a daughter. And then I went back the fourth time and came home with no more." Fuchida did not have an opportunity to take advantage of the GI Bill: "I never had time to go back to school because I was so busy having babies." Her husband was on active duty for twenty-six years, and she recalled that the role of an officer's wife was very demanding:

> I had to entertain a lot most of the time at the house. There would
> usually be about thirty or forty people. I've done a lot of volunteer
> work, mostly in the Red Cross. And I worked in a hospital unit at
> Camp Drake [in Japan] during the Vietnam War. I worked with the
> Girl Scouts, the Boy Scouts, and all that sort of thing. I went through
> the Brownie course twice, with my oldest and my youngest. Then I
> had the Cub Scouts in Hawaii, when we were stationed in Hawaii
> after my husband got out of the service. He was still working with the
> Army, with the same group. . . . I started up my own Girl Scout troop
> because I heard that Hawaii is supposed to be a melting pot. But it
> really isn't because all the Japanese are here, and all the Chinese are

here, and all the Portuguese are here, and all the Caucasians are here. So I decided to start my own troop and [ethnically] mix up the whole bunch. I was only there for three years.

Harada's husband, too, was an officer assigned to the military intelligence office in Japan. Harada returned to the United States in February 1951, two years after her oldest son was born, only to return to Japan just months later. Harada suffered a miscarriage during her second pregnancy and returned home to the United States during her third: "During my third pregnancy the Korean War broke out and the doctors were busy and couldn't care for the dependents anymore. They suggested that I go home."

Like Fuchida, Harada did not take advantage of the GI Bill; she was "busy raising a family and being a serviceman's wife." Also like Fuchida, she recalled that the role of a military wife was a major commitment:

> I had too many military duties. My husband being an officer, required me to do certain things. I had to join the women's club and had to carry on certain duties. I never worked [outside the home] because, trying to take care of a family and getting involved in all this other work, I didn't have time. I did an awful lot of volunteer work. I did a lot of Red Cross work in the hospital. I was determined to get into the medical field, so I worked for seven or eight years doing volunteer work at a hospital.

Both of Harada's sons completed college; her older son also served in Vietnam. "As a matter of fact," said Harada, "my husband and son both were over there at the same time." Harada's younger son owns a business in Houston; he received his B.A. from San Francisco State University and then went on to Purdue University for his master's degree.

Fuchida and Harada personified the military wife as described in the social science literature. Sociologist Morris Janowitz has observed that the military wife of the World War II era had duties far beyond child rearing. She was responsible for participating in the welfare and recreational activities of the military community.[20] As stated by Janowitz:

> Many of the welfare and recreational activities of the military community—to assist newcomers, to help sick wives and children, etc.—involved active participation of the military wife. She had a role outside of the household, short of employment in the labor market. The role may have been limited, formalized, and dull by standards of "gracious living," but it was a recognized and accepted part of the military style of life.[21]

Doreen Drewry Lehr has described the roles of military wives as part of "the gendered pattern of U.S. military culture" fostering a double standard.[22] She argues that the labor of wives has been exploited by the military:

> The public's lack of knowledge about military culture allowed the military to maintain the traditional role of the military wife well beyond the time when women in the larger society were expanding their professional horizons. From the 1960s to the 1990s, while their civilian sisters were renegotiating their gender roles, relationships, and boundaries, military wives were providing volunteer labor for the benefit of the military, frequently against their will.[23]

To some degree the sentiments articulated by Lehr are reflected in Harada's statement, "I had too many military duties." Both Fuchida and Harada described their family roles as extending beyond their individual households. However, they accepted these roles as their duty as wives of military officers. These women may well have even internalized the values of military honor and have helped to transmit the military tradition to their children. This seems particularly likely when we consider that Fuchida's oldest daughter married a military man, and Harada's oldest son served on active duty in Vietnam at the same time as her husband.

Miwako Rosenthal also married a military man; they lived in Chicago for many years. In contrast to Fuchida and Harada, Rosenthal herself was a professional. She worked with the army as a civilian, while her husband was a regular army officer. ("He was a doctor and I went with him to a lot of conferences.") Both Rosenthal and her husband were veterans who had gone on reserve duty. After completing medical school, her husband returned to active duty and was stationed at Walter Reed Hospital. During this time, Rosenthal worked on military projects: "I did projects at Fort Dedrich, which is Camp David now."

Rosenthal was temporarily assigned after the war to work in Tokyo on a scientific mission: "I went to Hiroshima after the bombing as a DAC or defined army civilian, and my husband was regular Army. He was consultant to the surgeon general. . . . We rode pretty high in the scientific circles, and of course I still am involved with that. In a couple of weeks I have to go to San Diego: I have to present an award for a society that is doing critical research in nutrition that I sponsored about ten or thirteen years ago."

Rosenthal's husband died in the 1970s. "We had no children and he has no family," she noted. "And I have just my brother and sister, but I don't have much to do with them, since we lived such different lives. I've been taking care of all the things that we had. So, everything is geared to the Army for me still."

Unlike my other informants, Rosenthal married interracially. Speaking about her husband, she stated :

I didn't know what a Jew was until I went to school in Chicago and met my husband. He was Jewish. I never had experience with Jews my whole life. I have a lot of interesting tales about our relationship and all the things that he and I had to put up with, all the things I learned. The biggest compliment I got was when one of the judges' wives said to me, "You're one of us." And then another compliment I got was when I had my Hanukkah dinner and was told that I was a "fantastic Jewish cook."

Although Ruth Fujii never married and did not have any children of her own, she feels that family was a big part of her life in the postwar years. In those years, Fujii spent much time caring for family members, and was involved in extended-family activities:

When my kid sister got sick, we decided that I would take care of her. She was a sophomore in college. She got tuberculosis and had to be put in a sanitarium. I had to take care of all of her needs . . . and when she died I was there in the hospital. . . . And then my mother got bad and my sister called me. . . . I was there the last two weeks of her days on earth. She was almost 97 when she died. . . . And the lady who brought me up [Mrs. Coby] lived alone. She said she couldn't manage and asked me if I would come home. So I went back and stayed with her until she died.

Fujii also helped care for her brother's children and one of her sister's children, who she says were like her own children. She spoke of a family life with her nieces and nephews:

I have a nephew here. When he was a little boy, nine years old, I used to take him out to school during the summer. And then he would stay with me all day. And I used to take him to all of the ball games. Well, he finished college, got a good job and all, and now he has retired. He buys season tickets for the university games, picks me up, takes me to dinner, and takes me to the game. I'm really glad; all of the kids are like that. My nephews and nieces and grandnieces and nephews are taking good care of me. Most of them live on the mainland. And when I had my cancer problem, about three years ago, they used to come down and they'd call me and I'd say, "I'm fine." And they'd say, "No, no, we gotta see ya." And they would come to Hawaii—fly over, stay with me, and then go back. . . . Even to this day I get calls from them.

Military Service and Citizenship Rights

As stated in chapter 1, since the Revolutionary War, military service has been certification of citizenship in the United States. The United States' definition of citizenship is rooted in the English notion of obligations as well as rights.[24] The concept of citizenship, as it is used here, is taken from the writings of T. H. Marshall, who separated the definition of citizenship into three conceptual parts: civil, political, and social. "The civil element is composed of the rights necessary for individual freedom—liberty of the person, freedom of speech, thought and faith, the right to own property and to conclude valid contracts, and the right to justice."[25] By the political element Marshall meant "the right to participate in the exercise of political power, as a member of a body invested with political authority or as an elector of the members of such a body."[26] Finally, Marshall defined the social element as the range of social liberties including "a modicum of economic welfare and security" and living the "life of a civilized being according to the standards prevailing in the society."[27]

Two of the women interviewed for this study claimed that service in the Women's Army Corps helped to pave the way for full citizenship rights for Japanese Americans. Irene Nishikaichi, for example, stated that her military service helped to legitimize the right of her parents and other Issei to become naturalized citizens. Nishikaichi told of her mother declaring, "My daughter went into the service, I gave a child to the service, and certainly we're going to become citizens." Unfortunately her mother died of cancer before she could even apply for citizenship. Nishikaichi's father, on the other hand, went through the entire process and indeed became an American citizen. Nishikaichi recalled, "He was a very conscientious citizen, and voted in every election."

Similarly, Hisako Yamashita felt that her military service weighed positively in the federal government's decision to convert Hawaii from a U.S. territory to a state:

> After the war there began lobbying [on behalf of the residents of Hawaii] for statehood. . . . I went before a congressional commission that was in Hawaii at the time interviewing the public on the matter. My friends thought that since I was an ex-Wac I should make an impression on the commission, so I went and I said, "I want statehood." I said I was a Wac and I served the country. And they were impressed. I said, "I just wanted to put that in to be sure that we get statehood." And we got statehood.

For racial minorities and women, citizenship rights have come as a result of a process of removing social, economic, and political barriers. The Nisei servicewoman's military service helped to remove some of these barriers for Japanese Americans. The legislative process of removing such barriers for Japanese Americans began after World War II. In 1948 the Evacuation Claims Act was passed, awarding Japanese American internees approximately $37 million as restitution for their losses during the mass evacuation.[28] In 1988, Congress passed a bill stating that both citizens and resident aliens of Japanese ancestry were gravely mistreated during the war. The bill further stated that the mass evacuation of Japanese Americans was a result of "racial prejudice, wartime hysteria, and a failure of political leadership,"[29] and provided for a tax-free payment of twenty thousand dollars to each of the more than sixty thousand surviving detainees. As a result of an individual action, Gordon Hirabayashi won a court case in 1986 in which the court ruled false the government's claim that people of Japanese ancestry had been a threat to national security.[30] These political gains, as insufficient as they may be, are nonetheless steps in the direction of positive social change.

Reflections

Most of the women interviewed for this study believed that their military service contributed to their upward mobility in the postwar years. Miwako Rosenthal stated that the military was the turning point in her life because, ever since she joined the WAC, she had known nothing but the army; being a veteran, she said:

> has wonderful benefits for me, even now. We never have to stand in line; we can always say we're veterans and be first in line. And we don't have to pay for admittance to museums or the California Academy of Sciences [where she was also a trustee]. I belong to the American Legion, and . . . the WAC Veterans Association. I belong to the officers' clubs and I get discounts.

Ellen Fuchida said she would not have traded her experiences for anything: "I just enjoyed meeting all the people." She viewed her experience in the military and as an officer's wife as positive:

> I met people from all over, and in that way I think it's been good. And it has been good for my children. My oldest daughter went to about fifteen to seventeen schools before she graduated because we moved so much. She's able to get out and meet everybody. And they're doing very well now. My oldest daughter is married to a retired military man . . . and she's working for a packaging engineer and doing really well. I have a son that is working with the Corps of Engineers up in

Oregon, and he's one of the top civilians up there. . . . And then my youngest daughter is working in Texas as a computer analyst.

Ruth Fujii stated that her military service did not help her so much in her career as a secretary; she had obtained that position before entering the Women's Army Corps. For her, the greatest advantage of military service was the opportunity to "meet so many wonderful people, and . . . to see the world. I wouldn't have been able to travel that much if I had not gone into the military." Fujii added that she could think of no real disadvantages of military service: "Not having sheets to sleep on, and not having enough water to take a shower in the Philippines you take with the circumstances; these inconveniences were just part of the territory." Fujii reflected:

My oldest brother used to call me an old maid ever since I was a kid. I had to have things just so. And I never griped if I didn't get anything. And whatever I got all my life I earned it. And maybe that's the reason why I'm doing okay. . . . I belong to the WIMSA [Women in Military Service for America] and the Women's Army Corp Veterans Association.

Alice Kono said that her military service did not much help her advance economically, "but when I look back, I think it was great." Kono said that, in addition to the GI Bill, which she used for advanced education, she had the benefit of traveling in the military; "I guess I got my travel bug from being in service." She joined the American Legion after she left the WAC, and was an active member for six years.

Irene Nishikaichi spoke about long-lasting friendships: "The friendships I made in the service mean a great deal to me and have influenced the kind of person I am now. . . . Just to be able to say that I am a veteran, that I was in the service during World War II, gives me more . . . self-confidence."

Although the women in this study made gains probably unthinkable for their mothers, they acknowledged that these positions were not in the same league as those of women in military service today. Nishikaichi gives much credit to women in today's armed services for "doing things almost the same as the men. . . . We were never expected to do what the women do today. The physical demand on the women now is more than double. Those of us who were in the service then had a piece of cake compared to what they do now."

Similarly, Fuchida recognized that her military experience during World War II was quite different from that of women who served later:

At the time that I was a WAC we weren't expected to go out and bear arms or anything. It was quite a sheltered vocation really. All we were supposed to do was take the jobs of the men so they could be freed for frontline duty. That's what [the War Department officials] were telling us. [Women in today's military] probably wouldn't be satisfied with the kind of existence we had at that time because they want to be at the forefront. We weren't so liberated, and so I think we were very satisfied with where they put us.

For Grace Harada, the personal benefits of joining the WAC surfaced immediately after she was inducted:

I was very, very unhappy before I went into the service because there was so much discrimination. We couldn't do anything; we couldn't even walk the streets, and when my father lost his job with the railroad nobody would rent us a home. And my parents had to live in a car for almost a month. Some lady introduced them to some Greek family with a little house, and they rented a house to my parents.

Life as a member of the WAC was dramatically different; in Harada's words:

In the military, I felt so much happier because I could do more as I pleased . . . we could talk more freely and express our opinions and have friends. My morale was always high in the military. I got along all right with everybody and always kept myself busy and found everything interesting because it was my first time away from home. I just wanted to know a little bit more about everybody and everything.

Grace Kutaka stated that to this day she is proud of her military service. Above all, she said, "I am so proud to be an American."

Striving to Assimilate

Echoed in the statements throughout this book is an assimilation theme, the adaptation of an ethnic group to the values and norms of the dominant core group in society at the expense of the ethnic group's cultural distinctiveness. Like white racial minorities in the United States during the World War II era, the Nisei strove to assimilate in American society, and to be absorbed into the mainstream, as assimilation was a prerequisite for citizenship rights. For racial/ethnic groups that could not blend into the proverbial "melting pot," the penalties were great: unemployment, social isolation, and the resultant hunger, family disruption, and lack of medical care.

According to Milton Gordon's conceptual framework, assimilation occurs in seven stages: cultural, structural, marital, identificational, attitude receptional, behavior receptional, and civic.[31] Using Gordon's theory, several studies have shown that during and immediately following World War II, Japanese Americans were assimilating culturally, structurally (penetrating cliques and associations of the core society at the primary-group level), in terms of intermarriage, and identificationally.[32] Analyzing data from the Japanese American Research Project (JARP) and the U.S. Bureau of the Census before and after World War II, Eric Woodrum found that, in the years following the war: significantly fewer Issei and Nisei lived in mostly Japanese American neighborhoods; three times as many Nisei (as their parents) identified with Judeo-Christian religions; and Nisei had fewer arranged marriages.[33] Similarly, while the Issei rarely had white friends or belonged to primarily white volunteer organizations, the Nisei began integrating at the friendship and organizational level, and the majority of their children (the Sansei) reported friends and membership in predominantly non-Japanese American voluntary organizations.[34] Many studies have confirmed that the rate of interracial marriage among Japanese Americans, primarily with Caucasians, has increased significantly in the postwar years.[35]

The Nisei's movement toward full assimilation into American society was accelerated by the events of World War II; indeed, this movement was nurtured by the patriotic fervor of the time. However, the cost of assimilation was great, creating a generational cleavage between the Nisei and their parents, a growing issue among some Nisei even before the war ended. A vivid account of the Nisei/Issei relationship was offered by Corporal George Morimitsu in an editorial, "These Are Our Parents," published in internment camp newspapers in 1944.[36] Morimitsu described how the Issei sweated and slaved with Oriental stoicism to give their children a better than adequate American education, and how that education widened the gap between the two generations "to the point where Nisei looked with disdain upon their [parents'] Japanese ways." Morimitsu said he knew little of his parents' past:

> My only connecting link with it would be through the language we
> supposedly speak in common. But this we lack and have always lacked
> since we children started learning English in grade school. The
> culture of my parents' homeland ended with the songs we heard and
> the foods we ate and the holidays my parents observed.[37]

This concern is also reflected in the following statement by Miwako Rosenthal regarding World War II veterans (Nisei) and their children (Sansei):

> The Japanese people don't tell their children anything they did.
> Children don't even know what their parents did in the war. . . . I
> have five nephews . . . [four] married to Caucasians and one . . .
> married to a Japanese girl, and that's because of their parents. . . .
> Their children are a mixture of Japanese and Caucasian, right? And if
> the wife is Caucasian and they have girls, they're going to lose their

Japanese identity because they'll marry into another Caucasian name. . . . The only person [to carry on the heritage] will be the son . . . he will bear the Japanese name, but he will be half and half. . . . My nephews' children don't look Japanese at all. . . . One of them graduated from the University of Minnesota. He opted to go into the Army. . . . He's six feet tall. . . . He doesn't look Japanese at all. His mother is Caucasian.

Similarly, Mary Yamada stated that she never identified with her Japanese heritage, yet she displays mixed feelings about not knowing the Japanese language:

I know I'm a Japanese [American] and I'll support the Japanese Americans, but I really don't have many Japanese [American] friends . . . so I never thought of myself as being with them or not with them. . . . I always felt that I was more on the periphery when it came to the Japanese because I wasn't living among them. . . . I don't seem to feel that close to Japan. I'm not ashamed that I'm a Japanese. I know a little bit about Japan, and I still don't know the language. I feel that, if I knew language, I would know more about the country. . . . But I'm an American, as my father said. . . . So we never spoke Japanese in the house, we spoke English. . . . I think maybe in a way it was wiser for those parents who would not let their children speak English in the home. They had to speak Japanese, so they ended up knowing both Japanese and English. . . I didn't learn [any Japanese] and I don't remember my father ever speaking Japanese to us.

What Morimitsu and so many others observed during World War II, and Rosenthal, Yamada, and so many others observe today, is a process of assimilation—a break from the Japanese culture and absorption into the American way of life.

In recent years, there has been a renewed interest in Japanese culture, particularly among the Sansei; while there is some evidence of a persistent ethnic culture, the evidence of assimilation is far more compelling. Given the increasing trend of outmarriage among the Sansei, it remains to be seen whether the Japanese American ethnic community will be maintained in future generations.

Conclusion

The military was a turning point in the lives of many servicewomen, as it helped to redefine their social, economic, and political roles in society. Certainly, some of the changes in race and gender relations in the United

States following the war were global, affecting military veterans and civilians alike. However, as indicated by the above statements, the military service also represented subjective turning points in the lives of Nisei servicewomen. Like those of military veterans in Elder, Gimbel, and Ivie's study "Turning Points in Life: The Case of Military Service and War," the lives of Nisei servicewomen were enhanced by travel, education, independence, and marriage.

The Japanese American women interviewed for this study revealed that their military service benefited them socially, economically, and politically in later years. Further, their voices help to dispel the nativistic view of Japanese Americans as foreigners to the United States, and challenge the race and gender stereotypes of Japanese American women. Contrary to the docile, subservient image portrayed in the media, the women interviewed for this study were both assertive and determined to take charge of their lives. Serving on active duty facilitated their objective to be recognized as American citizens, and provided them the benefits to achieve personal goals.

Through their service, Nisei women helped to lay the foundation for the journey toward full citizenship rights for Japanese American men and women, and, while full rights have not yet been achieved, there has been considerable progress. By supporting the American ideal of democracy, Nisei servicewomen helped to secure the social, political, and economic status enjoyed by Japanese Americans today.

Appendix

Wacs Who Entered the Army from Hawaii, December 1944

HEADQUARTERS CENTRAL PACIFIC BASE COMMAND
Office of the Commanding General
APO 958

AG 326.22   18 December 1944

SUBJECT: Orders to report for Active Duty.
TO: Women's Army Corps Recruits.

1. The following named enlisted women /ERC are recalled to active duty and will report to the CO Casual WAC Detachment, Territorial Guard Armory, South Hotel and Miller Sts., Honolulu, T. H. by 1100 27 December 1944:

Pvt. Marian H. Rapoza, A-50-000

Pvt. Haruko Oda, A-50-001

Pvt. Unoyo Kojima, A-50-002

Pvt. Frances E. Alsebrook, A-50-003

Pvt. Bernalda N. Paragoso, A-50-004

Pvt. Hannah M. Kawaihau, A-50-005

Pvt. Helen A. Bechert, A-50-006

Pvt. Hideko Kanda, A-50-007

Pvt. Shizuye Furuheshi, A-50-008

Pvt. Rectina D. Eilers, A-50-009

Pvt. Yacko Misawa, A-50-010

Pvt. Julie H.K. Maertens, A-50-011

Pvt. Edwina C. Cluney, A-50-012

Pvt. OK Yum Shinn, A-50-013

Pvt. Hung Ngow Choy, A-50-014

Pvt. Toshiko Kanashiro, A-50-015

Pvt. Julia Larm, A-50-040

Pvt. Tetsuko Kono, A-50-041

Pvt. Harriet K. H. Lum, A-50-042

Pvt. Chito Isonaga, A-50-043

Pvt. Mitsue Nouchi, A-50-044

Pvt. Bernice Naukana, A-50-045

Pvt. Kyu Sung L. Jones, A-50-046

Pvt. Hatsu S. Kitayama, A-50-047

Pvt. Reiko Hanashiro, A-50-048

Pvt. Veronica E. Smith, A-50-049

Pvt. Iwa M. Hussey, A-50-050

Pvt. Fumiko Segawa, A-50-051

Pvt. Rachel E. Holloway, A-50-060

Pvt. Hattie C.H. Pang, A-50-061

Pvt. Lillian G. Mott-Smith, A-50-062

Pvt. Marion E. King, A-50-063

Pvt. Laurentia R. Torres, A-50-016   Pvt. Hisako Yamashita, A-50-064
Pvt. Matsuko Kido, A-50-017   Pvt. Emma L. Drake, A-50-065
Pvt. Evaline R. Gunderson, A-50-018   Pvt. Beatrice Bender, A-50-066
Pvt. Eunice K. Kapuniai, A-50-019   Pvt. Dorothy Yamagami, A-50-067
Pvt. Toshiko Nakasato, A-50-020   Pvt. Alice W. H. Chow, A-50-068
Pvt. Maude E. Conant, A-50-021   Pvt. Marjorie Y. Hade, A-50-070
Pvt. Emily J. Kaalehua, A-50-022   Pvt. Charlotte Chow, A-50-031
Pvt. Emily B. Johnson, A-50-023   Pvt. Agnes L. Wilhelm, A-50-032
Pvt. Linda Y. Tanaka, A-50-024   Pvt. Genevieve M. L. Hoe, A-50-033
Pvt. Ruth Y. Fujii, A-50-025   Pvt. Hisako Hirakawa, A-50-034
Pvt. Fujiko (Grace) Kutaka,   Pvt. Eileen K. Malterre, A-50-035
Pvt. Irma P. Cosca, A-50-027   Pvt. Jeanne C. Stevens, A-50-036
Pvt. Tamayo Tamashiro, A-50-028   Pvt. Margaret K. C. Yang, A-50-037
Pvt. Mitsuyo Oshiro, A-50-029   Pvt. Anna Kim, A-50-038
Pvt. Sachiko Shichina, A-50-030   Pvt. Toshiko Kawamura, A-50-039

2. Equipment for travel will be accordance with information sheets furnished
   you at time of enlistment.
3. Air Transportation authorized, where necessary.
   By command of Major General BURGIN:

> HARRY L. EHRENERG,
> Captain, A. G. D.,
> Ass't. Adjutant Gen.

Notes

Preface and Acknowledgments

1. Admiral Isoroku Yamamoto, commander in chief of the Japanese Imperial Navy, planned the surprise aerial attack.
2. See Michael J. Lyons, *World War II: A Short History* (1989; reprint, Englewood Cliffs, N.J.: Prentice Hall, 1994), 147–149.
3. See for example, Thomas St. John Arnold, *Buffalo Soldiers: The 92nd Division and Reinforcements in World War II, 1942–1945* (Manhattan, Kans.: Sunflower University Press, 1990); Bradley Biggs, *The Triple Nickles: America's First All-Black Paratroop Unit* (Hamden, Conn: Archon Books, 1986); Martha Putney, *When the Nation Was in Need: Blacks in the Women's Army Corps during World War II* (Metuchen, N.J.: Scarecrow Press, 1992); Brenda L. Moore, *To Serve My Country, To Serve My Race: The Story of the Only African American Wacs Stationed Overseas during World War II* (New York: New York University Press, 1996).
4. Bill Hosokawa, *Nisei: The Quiet Americans* (New York: William Morrow and Co., 1969), 398.
5. See Masayo Umezawa Duss, *Unlikely Liberators: The Men of the 100th and 442nd*, translated by Peter Duus (Honolulu: University of Hawaii Press, 1987); see also Donald Teruo Hata, Dominguez Hills, and Nadine Ishitani Hata, *Japanese Americans and World War II* (Wheeling, Ill.: Harlan Davidson, 1995).
6. Members of the most decorated unit in U.S. military history, the 442nd, initially were awarded a Congressional Medal of Honor (MOH), 52 Distinguished Service Crosses, 342 Silver Stars, 810 Bronze Stars, and 3,000 Purple Hearts, with 500 Oak Leaf Clusters. In April 2000, the Military Intelligence Service received a Presidential Unit Citation for extraordinary heroism in military operations against an armed enemy (from May 1, 1942, to September 2, 1946). In May 2000, twelve former members of the 442nd RCT and seven former members of the 100th Battalion were awarded the Congressional Medal of Honor; most of these awards were given posthumously.
7. See U.S. Committee on Interior and Insular Affairs. *Personal Justice Denied* (Washington, D.C.: U.S. Government Printing Office, 1992), 258; Hosokawa, *Nisei*, 405.
8. In July 1943, the Women's Army Auxiliary Corps (WAAC) was converted to the Women's Army Corps (WAC) through Public Law 78–110. Under this new law, members of the WAC would receive the same benefits and pay allowances as men in equivalent ranks, and were subject to the same disciplinary code. See Bettie Morden, *The Women's Army Corps, 1945–1978* (Washington, D.C.: Center of Military History, United States Army, 1990), 12–13; also Mattie Treadwell,

United States Army in World War II: Special Studies: The Women's Army Corps
(Washington, D.C.: U.S. Government Printing Office, 1954), 220–221.

Chapter 1   *Introduction*

1. "All-Out Victory," *The Rafu Shimpo*, Los Angeles, 10 December 1941, p. 1.
2. Morris Janowitz, "The All-Volunteer Military as a Sociopolitical Problem," *Social Problems* 22 (February 1975): 435.
3. See David Segal, *Recruiting for Uncle Sam: Citizenship and Military Manpower Policy* (Lawrence, Ks.: University Press of Kansas, 1989), 108.
4. John Hope Franklin, *From Slavery to Freedom: A History of Negro Americans*, 6th ed. (New York: Alfred Knopf, 1988), 310–313.
5. President Roosevelt signed the Servicemen's Readjustment Act into law in 1944. For a thorough discussion of the bill, see Keith W. Olson, *The G.I. Bill, the Veterans, and the Colleges* (Lexington: University Press of Kentucky, 1974). Several sociological studies have found that, since World War II, military service has increased the earning potential of racial-minority males. Some have argued that the military provides a "bridging" environment, enhancing the human capital of minorities. See, for example: Harley Browning, Sally Lopreato, and Dudley Poston, "Income and Veterans Status: Variation among Mexican Americans, Blacks, and Anglos," *American Sociological Review* 38 (1973): 74–85; see also Sally Lopreato and Dudley Poston, "Differences in Earnings and Earnings Ability between Black Veterans and Nonveterans in the United States," *Social Science Quarterly* 57 (1977): 750–766. Others emphasize that the military provides a level playing field which virtually eliminates social barriers to upward mobility. See Charles C. Moskos, "From Citizens' Army to Social Laboratory," *Wilson Quarterly* 27 (1993): 83–94; Charles Moskos and John Butler, *All That We Can Be: Black Leadership and Racial Integration the Army Way* (New York: Basic Books, 1996), 73–74.
6. See Stacey Yukari Hirose, "Japanese American Women and the Women's Army Corps, 1935–1950" (M.A. thesis, University of California Los Angeles, 1993); Cynthia Neverton-Morton, "Securing the 'Double V': African-American and Japanese-American Women in the Military during World War II," *A Woman's War Too: U.S. Women in the Military in World War II*, ed. Paula Nassen Poulos (Washington, D.C.: National Archives and Record Administration, 1996), 327–354; Brenda L. Moore, "Reflections of Society: The Intersection of Race and Gender in the U.S. Army in World War II," in *Beyond Zero Tolerance: Discrimination in Military Culture*, ed. Mary Fainsod Katzenstein and Judith Reppy (Boulder, Colo.: Rowman and Littlefield, 1999), 125–142.
7. Clifford Uyeda and Barry Saiki, eds., *The Pacific War and Peace: Americans of Japanese Ancestry in Military Intelligence Service, 1941 to 1952* (San Francisco.: National Japanese American Historical Society, 1991), 13.
8. This nomenclature has been used by scholars to locate Asian Americans in the black/white paradigm. See Gary Y. Okihiro, *Margins and Mainstreams: Asians in American History and Culture* (Seattle: University of Washington Press, 1994), 33. See also James W. Loewen, *The Mississippi Chinese: Between Black and White* (Cambridge, Mass.: Harvard University Press, 1971).
9. See Michael Omi and Howard Winant, *Racial Formation in the United States: From the 1960s to the 1990s* (New York: Routledge, 1994); Juan Perea, "The Black/White Binary Paradigm of Race: The Normal Science of American Racial Thought," *California Law Review* 85 (1997): 1213, 1215; Robert Chang, "Toward an Asian American Legal Scholarship: Critical Race Theory, Post-Structuralism, and Narrative Space," *Asian Law Review* 1 (1994): 27.

10. Angelo N. Ancheta, *Race, Rights, and the Asian American Experience* (New Brunswick, N.J.: Rutgers University Press, 1998), 64.
11. See Ulysses Lee, *United States Army in World War II: Special Studies: The Employment of Negro Troops* (Washington, D.C.: U.S. Government Printing Office, 1966), 73–76; Brenda L. Moore, *To Serve My Country, To Serve My Race: The Story of the Only African American Wacs Stationed Overseas during World War II* (New York: New York University Press, 1996), 29.
12. That informal agreement was confirmed by a letter from the Secretary of War, dated 17 June 1942 and addressed to General Hershey, then director of the Selective Service System. See memorandum for the Assistant Chief of Staff, 31 July 1945, RG 165, Box 441, Folder 291.2, National Archives, College Park, Md..
13. Hawaii Nikkei History Editorial Board, *Japanese Eyes, American Heart: Personal Reflections of Hawaii's World War II Nisei Soldiers* (Honolulu: Tendai Educational Foundation, 1998), 315–320.
14. Dorothy Thomas and Richard Nishimoto, *The Spoilage: Japanese-American Evacuation and Resettlement during World War II* (Berkeley and Los Angeles: University of California Press, 1969), 56 n.6.
15. Allan Beekman, *The Niihau Incident* (Detroit: Harlo Press, 1982), 77.
16. See Uyeda and Saiki, *The Pacific War and Peace*, 13; Bill Hosokawa, *Nisei: The Quiet Americans* (New York: William Morrow and Co., 1969), 398.
17. Edna Bonacich and John Modell, *The Economic Basis of Ethnic Solidarity: Small Business in the Japanese American Community* (Berkeley and Los Angeles: University of California Press, 1980).
18. Historian Roger Daniels links discrimination against Japanese Americans to the "anti-Orientalism" that surfaced in 1849 when Chinese immigration to the United States began. See Roger Daniels, *Concentration Camps: North America* (Malabar, Fla.: Krieger Publishing Co., 1981), 2.
19. Jacobus tenBroek, Edward N. Barnhart, and Floyd Matson, *Prejudice, War, and the Constitution: Causes and Consequences of the Evacuation of the Japanese Americans in World War II* (Berkeley and Los Angeles: University of California Press, 1954), 69.
20. Ibid., 70.
21. *The Rafu Shimpo*, Los Angeles, editorial comment "Rumors, Rumors . . . " 28 March 1942, p.1.
22. William Manchester, *The Glory and the Dream: A Narrative History of America, 1932–1972*, (New York: Bantam Books, 1973), 297; U.S. Commission on Wartime Relocation and Internment of Civilians Report, *Personal Justice Denied* (Washington, D.C.: U.S. Government Printing Office, March 1992), 117.
23. Dennis M. Ogawa, *From Japs to Japanese* (Berkeley, Calif.: McCutchan, 1971), 11.
24. Manchester, *The Glory and the Dream*, 297.
25. Ibid., 298.
26. Executive Order 9066 was ambiguous and left the decision of mass evacuation to the discretion of the secretary of war and his designated commander. The order authorized the secretary of war and designated commanders to prescribe military areas from which any or all persons might be excluded, and with respect to which the right of any person to enter, remain in, or leave would be subject to whatever restriction the secretary "or appropriate Military Commander may impose in his discretion." See Thomas and Nishimoto, *The Spoilage*, 9.
27. Yoshiye Togasaki, unpublished interview, National Japanese American Historical Society, San Francisco, 10 August 1985.

28. These statistics are reported in Thomas and Nishimoto, *The Spoilage*, 13.
29. Roger Daniels, *Prisoners without Trial: Japanese Americans in World War II* (New York: Hill and Wang, 1993), 26.
30. U.S. Commission on Wartime Relocation and Internment of Civilians Report, *Personal Justice Denied* (Washington, D.C.: U.S. Government Printing Office, March 1992), 51. The Commission was citing from a brief for the United States, *Hirabayashi v. United States*, No. 870, Oct. Term 1942, pp. 16–17, as well as from a proposal for coordination of the FBI, ONI, and MID, June 5, 1940, approved and signed by Louis Johnson, Acting Secretary of War, on June 28, 1940.
31. See Mady Wechsler Segal, "Women's Military Roles Cross-Nationally: Past, Present, and Future." *Gender and Society* 9 (1995): 757–775; Margaret Higonnet, Jane Jenson, Sonya Michel, and Margaret Weitz, *Behind the Lines: Gender and the Two World Wars* (New Haven, Conn.: Yale University Press, 1987); D'Ann Campbell, *Women at War with America: Private Lives in a Patriotic Era* (Cambridge, Mass.: Harvard University Press).
32. Mattie Treadwell, *United States Army in World War II: Special Studies: The Women's Army Corps* (Washington, D.C.: U.S. Government Printing Office, 1954), 24.
33. Ibid., 16.
34. Ibid., 20.
35. For more details about the 1942 congressional debate over whether women should serve in the military, see Treadwell, *The Women's Army Corps*, chapters 1 and 2; Bettie J. Morden, *The Women's Army Corps, 1945–1978* (Washington, D.C.: U.S. Government Printing Office, 1990), chapter 1; Leisa D. Meyer, *Creating GI Jane: Sexuality and Power in the Women's Army Corps during World War II* (New York: Columbia University Press, 1996), 11–16.
36. The Rogers bill was approved by the Senate, 38–27, on May 14, 1942, and the president of the United States signed Public Law 554 the following day. See Treadwell, *Women's Army Corps*, 45.
37. Morden, *Women's Army Corps 1945–1978*, 5.
38. Moore, *To Serve My Country*; Lee, *The Employment of Negro Troops*.
39. For a detailed discussion about African American Waacs/Wacs, see Moore, *To Serve My Country*; Martha Putney, *When the Nation Was in Need: Blacks in the Women's Army Corps during World War II* (Metuchen, N.J.: Scarecrow Press, 1992); and Charity Adams Earley, *One Woman's Army: A Black Officer Remembers the WAC* (College Station, Tex.: Texas A & M University Press, 1989).
40. Treadwell, *The Women's Army Corps*, 18.
41. Morden, *Women's Army Corps, 1945–1978*, 12.
42. Richard Nishimoto, Lane Ryo Hirabayashi (eds.), *Inside an American Concentration Camp: Japanese American Resistance at Poston* (Tucson: University of Arizona Press, 1995), 235.
43. *Personal Justice Denied*, 188; Donald E. Collins, *Native American Aliens: Disloyalty and the Renunciation of Citizenship by Japanese Americans during World War II* (Westport, Conn.: Greenwood Press, 1985), 23; Bill Hosokawa, *JACL: In Quest of Justice* (New York: William Morrow and Co., 1982), 197–201, 209–211.
44. The Daughters of the American Revolution was founded on October 11, 1890, and was incorporated by an act of Congress in 1896.
45. See letter to Secretary of War Stimson from Mrs. Lilliebell Falck of the Daughters of the American Revolution, Golden Spike Chapter, Ogden, Utah, RG 407, Box 4282, Folder 291.3, National Archives, Washington, D.C.
46. Two registration forms were prepared in Washington, D.C. to be administered to persons age seventeen or older of Japanese ancestry: one for Japanese-American

male citizens (Nisei), the other for Nisei women and Issei men and women. See Thomas and Nishimoto, *The Spoilage*, 57–59.

47. Before a Japanese American or a Japanese national was cleared for induction, the provost marshal reviewed files of the Federal Bureau of Investigation, the Office of Naval Intelligence Service, the War Department General Staff, the Japanese American Branch of the Provost Marshal General's Office, and the Civil Affairs Division of the Western Defense Command.

48. See: Memorandum for the Adjutant General, Appointment and Induction Branch, Attention Colonel Sailor, 5 January 1943, signed by Martha E. Eskridge, Second Officer, WAAC, Chief Recruiting Branch, Personnel Division, RG 407, Army AG Project, Decimal File 1940–1945, Box 4297, Folder 341, National Archives, Washington, D.C.

49. See transcribed conversation between the WAAC director, Oveta Culp Hobby, and Assistant Secretary of War John J. McCloy, RG 407, Army AG Project, Decimal File 1940–45, Box 4297, Folder 341, National Archives, Washington, D.C.

50. On July 25, 1944, the pre-induction screening function, until then performed by the assistant chief of staff, G–2, was transferred to the provost marshal general, Army Service Forces. See Memorandum for the Assistant Chief of Staff, RG 165, Box 441, Folder 291.2, National Archives, College Park, Md.

51. "Only 3,771 Enemy Aliens Interned in U.S. Camps," *New York Times*, 3 November 1943, p.1.

52. See letter to: Commanding General of the Eighth Service Command, from Manice M. Hill, Second Officer, WAAC, Subject: "Investigation of Attitude of Women in Rohwer Relocation Center toward the Women's Army Auxiliary Corps," 4 March 1943, RG 407, Box 4282, Folder 291.3, National Archives, Washington, D.C.

53. See letter to: Assistant Chief of Staff, G–2, from Brigadier General Hayes A. Kroner, Chief, Military Intelligence Service, 14 April 1943, RG 165, Box 441, Folder 291.2, National Archives, College Park, Md.

54. See letter to commanding generals: from Oveta Culp Hobby, Director of WAC: "Enlistment in WAC of Women Citizens of U.S. of Japanese Ancestry," 23 July 1943, RG 407, File 1940–1945, Box 4300, Folder 341.1, 342.05, National Archives, Washington, D.C.

55. John O'Donnell, "Capitol Stuff," *New York Daily News*, 8 June1943.

56. Treadwell, *The Women's Army Corps*, 191–217; Morden, *Women's Army Corps, 1945–1978*, 10–11. For a graphic account of slander against Wacs in the media, see Meyer, *Creating GI Jane*, 47–51.

57. Treadwell, *Women's Army Corps*, 231.

58. See intra-office Memorandum to WAAC director: "Enrollment of American Women of Japanese Extraction," with a report of T. O. Busse attached, 1 February 1943, RG 165, Box 441, Folder 291.2, National Archives, College Park, Md.

59. Frank Wu speaks of racial groups being conceived as "white, black, honorary whites, or constructive blacks." For Wu, honorary connotes privilege and constructive connotes oppression. See Frank Wu, "Neither Black nor White: Asian Americans and Affirmative Action," *Boston College Third World Law Journal* 15 (summer 1995): 225, 226.

60. See letter: to Henry L. Stimson, Secretary of War, from Allen C. Blaisdell, Director of the International House at the University of California at Berkeley, 28 January 1943, RG 407, Box 4282, Folder 291.3, National Archives, Washington, D.C.

61. See memorandum prepared for: Assistant Secretary of War, attention Lieutenant

Joseph D. Hughes, March 12, 1943, RG 165, Box 441, folder 291.2, National Archives, College Park, Md.

62. See: Memorandum to the Assistant Secretary of War from Oveta Culp Hoby, 7 April 1943; and Memorandum to the Assistant Chief of Staff, G–1: "Admission of Female Citizens of Japanese Ancestry into the WAAC," 10 April 1943, both documents in RG 165, Box 441, Folder 291.2, National Archives, College Park, Md.

63. Moore, *To Serve My Country*, chapters 3 and 4.

64. This is not to suggest that there were not gender differences and dual standards. There still existed a double standard in occupational assignment, promotion, and rank. Norms of sexuality also differed for servicewomen and men. It has been reported that unlike their male counterparts, servicewomen who contracted venereal disease were often found guilty of "conduct unbecoming" or of "reflecting discredit on the Corps." Meyer in *Creating GI Jane* discusses the double standard in how the army defined sexual misconduct during World War II.

65. "Three Japanese Americans Inducted into Women's Army," *Pacific Citizen*, 18 December 1943.

66. See letter to Dillon S. Myer, Director of the War Relocation Authority, from Harry Tarvin, 13 December 1943, RG 165, Box 441, Folder 291.2, National Archives, College Park, Md.

67. "Nisei Girls and WACs," *Pacific Citizen*, 13 November 1943.

68. See letter to Headquarters Ninth Command, WAAC Branch, Washington, D.C., from Henriette Horak, Second Officer of the WAAC Recruiting Office, Los Angeles, 7 March 1943, RG 165, National Archives, Washington, D.C.

69. Thomas and Nishimoto, *Spoilage*, 70.

70. Tomotsu Shibutani, *The Derelicts of Company K: A Sociological Study of Demoralization* (Berkeley and Los Angeles: University of California Press, 1978).

71. Eric L. Muller, *Free to Die for Their Country: The Story of the Japanese American Draft Resisters in World War II* (Chicago: University of Chicago, Press, 2001); see also John Okada, *NO-NO BOY* (Seattle and London: University of Washington Press, 1976).

72. *Denson (Ark.) Tribune*, vol. 2, no. 10, 4 February 1944, p. 1, found in Wason Film 8676, Japanese Camp Papers, Reels 1–5, Kroch Library, Cornell University, Ithaca, N.Y.

73. Thomas and Nishimoto, *Spoilage*, 68.

74. Ibid.

75. *Pacific Citizen*, "Three Utah Nisei Girls Train for Wacs at Des Moines: Get Send-Off from Friends, Relatives in Salt Lake City," 19 February 1944, p. 3.

76. *Pacific Citizen*, "Japanese American Girl Will Be Inducted in Wac," 4 December 1943.

77. *Denson (Ark.) Tribune*, vol. 1, no. 85, found in Wason Film 8676, Japanese Camp Papers, Reels 1–5, Kroch Library, Cornell University, Ithaca, N.Y., 21 December 1943, pp. 1, 6.

78. This is an excerpt from an interview conducted in September 1943 as part of the Japanese American Evacuation and Resettlement Study; see Dorothy Swaine Thomas, *The Salvage* (Berkeley and Los Angeles: University of California Press, 1952), 318–320.

79. Yoshiye Togasaki, unpublished interview, 10 August 1985.

80. Mary T. Sarnecky, *A History of the U.S. Army Nurse Corps* (Philadelphia: University of Pennsylvania Press, 1999), 270; Pauline E. Maxwell, *History of the Army Nurse Corps* (Washington, D.C.: U.S. Center of Military History, 1976), 26.

Chapter 2 Before the War

1. Ruth Benedict highlights the Meiji reform in Japan in *The Chrysanthemum and the Sword: Patterns of Japanese Culture* (1946; reprint, New York: New America Library, 1974), 76–97.

2. Ronald Takaki, *Iron Cages: Race and Culture in Nineteenth Century America* (New York: Oxford University Press, 1990), 258.

3. Eileen H. Tamura, *Americanization, Acculturation, and Ethnic Identity: The Nisei Generation in Hawaii* (Urbana and Chicago: University of Illinois Press, 1994), 9–21.

4. Yuji Ichioka, *The Issei: The World of the First Generation Japanese Immigrants, 1885–1924* (New York: Free Press, 1988); Robert A. Wilson and Bill Hosokawa, *East to America: A History of the Japanese in the United States* (New York: William Morrow and Co., 1980).

5. Ichioka, *The Issei*.

6. According to a Japanese law first enacted in 1873, men aged seventeen to forty were eligible for the military draft. Deferments were granted to students studying abroad. See Ichioka, *The Issei*, 13.

7. In exile these Japanese immigrants enjoyed freedom of speech, assembly, and press. See Ichioka, *The Issei*, 16.

8. Ibid.

9. Yoshiye Togasaki, unpublished interview, National Japanese American Historical Society, San Francisco, 10 August 1985.

10. Ibid.

11. Ichioka, *The Issei*.

12. Linda Tamura, *The Hood River Issei: An Oral History of Japanese Settlers in Oregon's Hood River Valley* (Urbana and Chicago: University of Illinois Press, 1993), 19.

13. Ichioka, *The Issei*, 28–39.

14. Arthur Golden, *Memoirs of a Geisha* (New York: Alfred A. Knopf, 1997).

15. Ibid.

16. Yoshiye Togasaki, interview, 10 August 1985.

17. Ibid.

18. Ibid.

19. Hawaii was discovered in 1778 by Captain James Cook, who named it the Sandwich Islands in honor of his patron, the Earl of Sandwich. It was ruled by native monarchs until 1898, when it was ceded to the United States.

20. Wilson and Hosokawa, *East to America*, 141.

21. Ibid., 143.

22. Ibid., 153.

23. This figure is taken from Joe R. Feagin and Clairece Booher Feagin, *Racial and Ethnic Relations*, 6th ed. (Upper Saddle River, N.J.: Prentice Hall, 1999), 383.

24. In 1907, the Japanese government agreed with the United States to end direct immigration of Japanese laborers to the United States under the so-called "Gentlemen's Agreement." This agreement provided that Japan would issue passports only to nonlaborers, laborers who sought to join a close relative in the United States, or persons who had already engaged in a farming enterprise located in the United States. See Ichioka, *The Issei*, 71–72. These figures are taken from Thomas, *The Salvage*, 7.

25. Ruth Benedict, *The Chrysanthemum and the Sword*, 53–54.

26. Harry H. L. Kitano, *Japanese Americans: The Evolution of a Subculture* (Englewood Cliffs, N.J.: Prentice Hall, 1969), 63.

27. Kitano, *Japanese Americans*, 63.
28. Tamura, *The Hood River Issei*, 46.
29. Tamura, *Americanization, Acculturation, and Ethnic Identity*, 25.
30. Yoshiye Togasaki, interview, 10 August 1985.
31. Thomas, *The Salvage*, 9.
32. Ibid., 13.
33. J. S. Chambers, "The Japanese Invasion," *Annals of the American Academy of Political and Social Science* (January 1921): 36.
34. U.S. Committee on Interior and Insular Affairs, *Personal Justice Denied* (Washington, D.C.: U.S. Government Printing Office, 1992), 38.
35. Stanley Lieberson, *A Piece of the Pie: Black and White Immigrants since 1880* (Berkeley and Los Angeles: University of California Press, 1980), 380–381.
36. Donald E. Collins, *Native American Aliens: Disloyalty and Renunciation of Citizenship by Japanese Americans during World War II* (Westport, Conn.: Greenwood Press, 1985), 72, 151.
37. For a thorough discussion of Japanese culture, see Minako K. Maykovich, *Japanese American Identity Dilemma* (Tokyo: Waseda University Press, 1972), 25–40.
38. Kitano, *Japanese Americans*, 66.
39. Kerrily J. Kitano and Harry H. L. Kitano, "The Japanese-American Family," *Ethnic Families in America: Patterns and Variations*, 4th ed., ed. Charles Mindel, Robert Habenstein, and Roosevelt Wright Jr. (Upper Saddle River, N.J.: Prentice Hall, 1998), 312.
40. Mei Nakano, *Japanese American Women: Three Generations, 1890–1990* (Berkeley, Calif.: Mina Press, 1990), 33.
41. Japan is still a male-dominated society. The recent trial of Mitsuko Yamada, who admitted to killing another woman's two-year-old daughter, raises questions about Japan's patriarchal society. According to an article published by the Associated Press in Tokyo, the trial suggests that Japanese housewives "are trapped in dull routines and overly preoccupied with the achievements of their children." See *The Honolulu Advertiser*, "Tot's Murder Shifts Focus onto Japan Wives," 7 March 2000, p. A8.
42. As part of this socialization process, according to Maykovich, a male child was "even permitted to attack and beat his mother." See Maykovich, *Japanese American Identity Dilemma*, 30–31.
43. Benedict, *The Chrysanthemum and the Sword*, 51–53.
44. See John W. Connor, "Acculturation and Family Continuities in Three Generations of Japanese Americans," *Journal of Marriage and the Family* (February 1974): 159–165.
45. Erwin Johnson, "The Emergence of a Self-Conscious Entrepreneurial Class in Rural Japan," in *Japanese Culture: Its Development and Characteristics*, ed. Robert J. Smith and Richard K. Beardsley (Chicago: Aldine, 1962), 91–99.
46. Tamura, *Hood River Issei*, 97.
47. Angela Y. Davis, *Women, Race, and Class* (New York: Random House, 1981); Alfreda M. Duster, *Crusade for Justice: The Autobiography of Ida B. Wells* (Chicago: University o f Chicago Press, 1970).
48. Louise Littleton, "Worse Than Slaves," *San Francisco Chronicle*, 1 October 1893, p. 2. Reprinted in Judy Yung, *Unbound Voices: A Documentary History of Chinese Women in San Francisco* (Berkeley and Los Angeles: University of California Press, 1999), 164–170.
49. See Evelyn Nakano Glenn, *Issei, Nisei, War Bride: Three Generations of Japanese American Women in Domestic Service* (Philadelphia: Temple University Press, 1986), 109–122.

50. Tamura, *Americanization, Acculturation, and Ethnic Identity*, 3.
51. Ibid., 4.
52. Andrew Lind, *Hawaii's Japanese: An Experiment in Democracy* (Princeton, N.J.: Princeton University Press, 1946), 11.
53. Ibid., 17.
54. Ibid., 12.
55. See *Rafu Shimpo*, 18 December 1993, p. 12.
56. Moore, *To Serve My Country*, 94.
57. Ibid.
58. Cherry Shiozawa, unpublished interview by Chizu Iiyama, tape recording, Japanese National American Historical Society, 21 February 1989, San Francisco.
59. Nakano, *Japanese American Women*.
60. Kitano, *Japanese Americans*, 65–66.
61. Nakano, *Japanese American Women*, 105, 198
62. Kitano, *Japanese Americans*, 66.
63. Evelyn Nakano Glenn, *Issei, Nisei, War Bride: Three Generations of Japanese American Women in Domestic Service* (Philadelphia: Temple University Press, 1986), 205.
64. Yoshiye Togasaki, interview, 10 August 1985.
65. Edward K. Strong, *The Second-Generation Japanese Problem* (Stanford, Calif.: Stanford University Press, 1934), 207. For a detailed discussion on the Kibei, see Minoru Kiyota, *Beyond Loyalty: The Story of a Kibei* (Honolulu: University of Hawaii Press, 1997).
66. War Relocation Authority, *Japanese Americans Educated in Japan* (Community Analysis Section Report No. 8, 28 January 1944), Confidential files, A1989:006, Box 12, fd. 8, University of Hawaii, Romanzo Adams Social Research Laboratory.
67. See John Modell, "Tradition and Opportunity: The Japanese Immigrant in America," *Pacific Historical Review* 40 (May 1971): 163–182.
68. Kitano, *Japanese Americans*, 25.
69. Richard Bell, *Public School Education of Second Generation Japanese in California* (Stanford, Calif.: Stanford University Press, 1935).
70. Roger Daniels, *Prisoners Without Trial: Japanese Americans in World War II* (New York: Hill and Wang, 1993), 19.
71. Yoshiye Togasaki, interview, 10 August 1985.
72. Ibid.
73. Tamura, *Americanization, Acculturation, and Ethnic Identity*, 101.
74. Ibid.
75. Ibid.
76. See Lane Ryo Hirabayashi's introduction of Richard S. Nishimoto, *Inside an American Concentration Camp* (Tucson: University of Arizona Press, 1995), xxxi.
77. Sucheng Chan, *Asian Americans: An Interpretive History* (New York: Twayne Publishers, 1991), 39.
78. Ibid.
79. Thomas, *The Salvage*, 23.
80. Ibid.
81. Wilson and Hosokawa, *East to America*, 224.
82. Edna Bonacich and John Modell, *The Economic Basis of Ethnic Solidarity: Small Business in Japanese American Community* (Berkeley and Los Angeles: University of California Press, 1980), 38; W. T. Kataoka, "Occupation of Japanese in Los Angeles," *Sociology and Social Research* 14 (September–October 1929): 53–58.
83. Leonard Bloom and Ruth Riemer, *Removal and Return: The Socio-Economic Effects*

of the War on Japanese Americans (Berkeley and Los Angeles: University of California Press, 1949).

84. Bonacich and Modell, *The Economic Basis of Ethnic Solidarity*, 67.

85. Ibid.; H. A. Millis, *The Japanese Problem in the United States* (New York: Macmillan, 1915); Jacobus ten Broek, Edward Barnhart, and Floyd W. Matson, *Prejudice, War, and the Constitution* (Berkeley and Los Angeles: University of California Press, 1954).

86. Bonacich and Modell, *The Economic Basis of Ethnic Solidarity*, 65.

87. Ibid., 78.

88. Daniels, *Prisoners without Trial*.

89. Ibid.; Bonacich and Modell, *The Economic Basis of Ethnic Solidarity*.

90. This work stoppage resulted from a disagreement between the Honolulu Rapid Transit Company and the Amalgamated Association of Street, Electric Railway, and Motor Coach Employees of American, Local 1,173. See William Norwood, "Racial Issues in Hawaii Stirred by Unions' Drive," *Christian Science Monitor*, 21 August 1943.

91. For a discussion about the theory of internal colonialism, see Robert [Bob] Blauner, *Still the Big News: Racial Oppression in America* (Philadelphia: Temple University Press, 2001); *Racial Oppression in America* (New York: Harper and Row, 1972).

Chapter 3   **Contradictions and Paradoxes**

1. "Editorial," *Rafu Shimpo*, 18 December 1941, p. 5.

2. In 1899 Secretary of State John Hay formulated the Open Door Policy to protect United States access to the China market.

3. For a detailed discussion of the Tripartite Pact and its effects on relations between the United States and Japan, see William L. Langer and S. Everett Gleason, *The Undeclared War, 1940–1941* (New York: Harper, 1953), 1–33.

4. Allan Beekman, *The Niihau Incident* (Honolulu: Heritage Press of the Pacific, 1982); Stephen Ambrose, *Rise to Globalism: American Foreign Policy since 1938* (New York: Penguin, 1983).

5. Ambrose, *Rise to Globalism*, 40–42; Robert A. Dallek, *Franklin D. Roosevelt and American Policy, 1932–1945* (New York: Oxford University Press, 1979).

6. Japan expected these negotiations to lead to a resolution before October 15. Fumimaro Konoye resigned as premier on that date after negotiations failed, and was replaced by General Hideki Tojo. Japan set a new deadline of November 29 to reach an agreement with the United States. See Michael J. Lyons, *World War II: A Short History* (Englewood Cliffs, N.J.: Prentice Hall, 1994), 143–147.

7. Langer and Gleason, *The Undeclared War*.

8. Ambrose, *Rise to Globalism*, 40

9. Roger Daniels, *Prisoners without Trial: Japanese Americans in World War II* (New York: Hill and Wang, 1993), 10.

10. Edna Bonacich, "A Theory of Ethnic Antagonism: The Split Labor Market," *American Sociological Review* 47 (1972): 547–559.

11. Takeshi Nakayama, "Mama Wore Combat Boots: Nisei women joined WACs to help shorten World War II," *Rafu Shimpo*, 18 December 1993, A14.

12. Ibid., A13.

13. Timothy Holian reports that Ludecke was sent personally to the United States by Adolf Hitler. See Timothy Holian, *The German-Americans and World War II: An Ethnic Experience* (New York: P. Lang, 1966), 17.

14. Ibid., 53.

15. U.S. Commission on Wartime Relocation and Internment of Civilians Report, *Personal Justice Denied* (Washington, D.C.: U.S. Government Printing Office, March 1992), 283; Samuel Eliot Morison, *The Battle of the Atlantic*, (Boston: Little, Brown and Co., 1947), 131–135.

16. Morison, *Battle of the Atlantic*, 131–35.

17. U.S. Commission on Wartime Relocation, *Personal Justice Denied*, 290.

18. Frederick C. Luebke, *Bonds of Loyalty: German-Americans and World War I* (De Kalb: Northern Illinois University Press, 1974), 255.

19. Ibid., 290.

20. Ibid., 291.

21. Ibid.

22. Holian, *The German-Americans and World War II*, 96.

23. George E. Pozzetta, "My Children Are My Jewels: Italian-American Generations during World War II," *The Home-Front War: World War II and American Society*, ed. Kenneth Paul O'Brien and Lynn Hudson Parsons (Westport, Conn.: Greenwood Press, 1995), 67.

24. This is a salient theme in the writings of Roger Daniels. See, for example, *Prisoners Without Trial* and *Concentration Camps*. This argument is also made by Donald Collins in *Native American Aliens: Disloyalty and Renunciation of Citizenship by Japanese Americans during World War II* (Westport, Conn.: Greenwood Press, 1985).

25. U.S. Defense Equal Opportunity Management Institute. *Asian and Pacific Islander–American Heritage Month 2000* (Patrick Air Force Base, Fla: Defense Equal Opportunity Management Institute, 2000), 16.

26. Ibid., 17.

27. See Charles Wagley and Marvin Harris, *Minorities in the New World* (New York: Columbia University Press, 1958), 256–263.

28. Ibid.; see also Donald Noel, "A Theory of the Origin of Ethnic Stratification," *Social Problems* 16 (fall 1968): 161.

29. Cecil Hengy Coggins, "Japanese Americans in Hawaii," *Harper's Magazine*, Pasadena, Calif., July 1943.

30. William Norwood, "Anti-Japanese Upsurge Now Evident in Hawaii," In *Christian Science Monitor*, 20 August 1943.

31. Editorial, "Racial Identity," *Rafu Shimpo*, 22 December 1941, p.1.

32. Commission on Wartime Relocation, *Personal Justice Denied*, 292.

33. Ibid., 292.

34. Pozzetta, "My Children Are My Jewels," 78 n.19; the Naturalization Act of 1790 provided for naturalization of any free white person. After the Civil War, in the 1878 decision by Circuit Judge Sawyer, the Naturalization Act prohibited Chinese immigrants from becoming American citizens. Finally, the 1922 Supreme Court ruling in *Ozawa v. United States* found the statute prohibited the naturalization of anyone of Asian descent.

35. See "Fellow American Scouts," *Rafu Shimpo*, 21 December 1941, p. 3.

36. Warren Tsuneishi, "Nisei's Greatest Failure," *Rafu Shimpo* 21 December 1941, pp. 10, 14.

37. The U.S. Senate's vote in favor of war was unanimous (82–0), and the House of Representatives voted 338–1; the only dissenting vote was cast by Representative Jeanne Rankin (R) of Montana.

38. *Rafu Shimpo*, 9 December 1941, pp.1–4; see also excerpts of Saburo Kido's speech to JACL in Bill Hosokawa, *JACL: In Quest of Justice* (New York: William and Morrow, 1982), 155–156.

39. *Rafu Shimpo*, 10 December 1941, p. 1.

40. Ibid.
41. Ibid., 19 December 1941, p.1.
42. Ibid., 17 December 1941, p.1.
43. Ibid., 11 December 1941, p.5.
44. Cherry Shiozawa, interview by Chizu Iiyama, tape recording, Japanese National American Historical Society 21 February 1989, San Francisco.
45. Richard Nishimoto, *Inside an American Concentration Camp: Japanese American Resistance at Poston*, ed. Lane Ryo Hirabayashi (Tucson: University of Arizona Press, 1995).
46. Ibid.
47. Ibid.
48. Ibid.
49. Ibid.
50. For a conceptualization of word racialization, see Michael Omi and Howard Winant, *Racial Formation in the United States: From the 1960s to the 1980s* (New York: Routledge, 1986), 64.
51. Nishimoto, *Inside an American Concentration Camp*, xxvi–xxvii.
52. Andrew W. Lind, *Hawaii's Japanese: An Experiment in Democracy* (Princeton, N.J.: Princeton University Press, 1946), 73.
53. Ibid.
54. Ibid.
55. Ibid., 74.
56. Commission on Wartime Relocation, *Personal Justice Denied*, 17.
57. Ibid., 16.
58. Stephen E. Ambrose, "Blacks in the Army in Two World Wars," *The Military in American Society*, ed. Stephen E. Ambrose and James A. Barber Jr. (N.Y.: Free Press, 1972), 178–179.
59. Dorothy S. Thomas and Richard Nishimoto, *The Spoilage: Japanese American Evacuation and Resettlement during World War II* (Berkeley and Los Angeles: University of California Press, 1969), 64.
60. Ibid., 65.
61. Ibid., 68.
62. Collins, *Native American Aliens*, 32.
63. See Thomas and Nishimoto, *The Spoilage*, 84–112; Collins, *Native American Aliens*, 23–34; Dorothy Swaine Thomas, Charles Kikuchi, and James Sakoda, *The Salvage: Japanese American Evacuation and Resettlement* (Berkeley and Los Angeles: University of California Press, 1952), 93–94.
64. United States Department of the Interior, War Relocation Authority, *The Evacuated People: A Quantitative Description* (U.S. Government Printing Office, Washington, D.C. 1946), 169.
65. Thomas and Nishimoto, *The Spoilage*, 363–365.
66. See Nasumi Tokeuchi's letter to the President of the United States, 6 September 1944, RG 165, Box 444, Folder 291.2, Japanese 1 September 1944 to 31 December 1944, National Archives, College Park, Md.
67. Collins, *Native American Aliens*, 121.
68. Ibid.
69. Daniels, *Prisoners without Trial*, 77.
70. Nishimoto, *Inside an American Concentration Camp*, 171.
71. Collins, *Native American Aliens*, 84.
72. Thomas and Nishimoto, *The Spoilage*, 93; The authors obtained this information from the War Relocation Authority, Community Analysis Section.

73. Daniels, *Prisoners without Trial*, 86.

74. Nishimoto, *Inside an American Concentration Camp*,179–181.

75. See Larry Tajiri, "The Profits in Racism," *The Pacific Citizen*, 22 July 1944, p. 4.

76. Ibid.

77. This was the Supreme Court ruling in the Endo case. See Commission on War-time Relocation, *Personal Justice Denied*, 231; Daniels, *Prisoners without Trial*, 81.

78. United States Department of the Interior, *The Relocation Program* (New York: AMS Press, 1975 [reprint of the 1946 edition published by the U.S. Government Printing Office, Washington.])

79. Eileen H. Tamura, *Americanization, Acculturation, and Ethnic Identity: The Nisei Generation in Hawaii* (Urbana and Chicago: University of Illinois Press, 1994), 188.

80. This editorial, "Jim Crow Deplored," was published in the *Pacific Citizen* and reprinted in the *Gila (Ariz.) News-Courier*, Arizona, 8 January 1944, p. 2.

81. Ibid.

82. Department of the Interior. *The Relocation Program*, 21.

83. See "Japanese in College Accepted as Americans," *Chicago Sunday Tribune*, reprinted in *Gila (Ariz.) News-Courier*, 23 May 1944, p. 4.

84. Larry Tajiri, "Undoing the Evacuation," *Pacific Citizen*, 13 January 1945, p. 4.

85. Ibid.

86. Ibid.

87. Commission on Wartime Relocation, *Personal Justice Denied*, 3.

88. See Yen Le Espirutu, *Asian American Women and Men* (Thousand Oaks: Sage Publications, 1997); Harry Kitano, *Japanese Americans: The Evolution of a Subculture* (Englewood Cliffs, N.J.: Prentice Hall).

89. Daisuke Kitagawa, *Issei and Nisei: The Internment Years* (New York: Seabury Press, 1967), 89.

90. Thomas and Nishimoto, *The Spoilage*, 39.

91. See Valerie Matsumoto, "Japanese American Women during World War II," *Frontiers* 8 (1984): 1.

92. Leslie Ito, "Japanese American Women and the Student Relocation Movement, 1942–1945," *Frontiers* 21 (2000): 12.

Chapter 4 *Women's Army Corps Recruitment of Nisei Women*

1. "Urge Japanese American Girls to Join Women's Army Corps: Pvt. Shinagawa Recruits Nisei Volunteers in Denver Area," *Pacific Citizen*, 27 May 1944, p. 3.

2. The languages were listed in order of the number of translators needed: Spanish, Portuguese, Chinese, Japanese, Russian, French, German, and Italian. See WAAC memo to commands from Martha E. Eskridge, Second Officer, 5 January 1943, RG 407, File 1940–1945, Box 4297, Folder 341, National Archives, College Park, Md.

3. See letter to Oveta Culp Hobby from E. M. Rovall, Acting Director of the War Relocation Authority, 26 January 1943, RG 165, SPWA 291.2, National Archives, Washington, D.C.

4. See letter to Secretary of War Henry L. Stimson from Allen C. Blaisdale, 28 January 1943, RG 407, Folder 291.3, Box 4282, National Archives, Washington, D.C..

5. See letter to Secretary of War Henry L. Stimson from President of the United States Franklin D. Roosevelt, 1 February 1943, RG 389, Box 1728, National Archives, Washington, D.C.

6. See War Department intra-office memorandum to WAAC Director Oveta Culp

Hobby, initialed H. P. T., including a report by Third Officer Busse on a series of conferences that she and Second Officer Ruth Fowler attended to investigate the possibility of procuring six thousand Nisei men for voluntary induction into the army, 1 February 1943, SPWA 291.2, National Archives, Washington, D.C.

7. See letter to Headquarters Ninth Command, WAAC Branch, Washington, D.C., from Henriette Horak, Second Officer, of the WAAC Recruiting Office, Los Angeles, 7 March 1943, RG 165, National Archives, Washington, D.C..

8. Officer Horak recommended that enrollment of Japanese women should begin quickly, because many of the women had job clearances. She reported that in responses made by 258 Nisei women on the WRA–126 Rev (War Relocation Authority, Application for Leave Clearance), 29 percent answered that they were willing to serve in the Army Nurse Corps or the WAAC if the opportunity presented itself (question 27). Most of these women were between twenty-one and thirty years of age and had no dependents. See letter to Headquarters Ninth Command, WAAC Branch, Washington, D.C., from Henriette Horak, Second Officer, of the WAAC Recruiting Office, Los Angeles, 11 March 1943, RG 165, National Archives, Washington, D.C..

9. Ibid.

10. Ibid.

11. See letter to Commanding General, Ninth Command, Fort Douglas, Utah, from Margaret E. Deane, Third Officer, WAAC, Headquarters Utah Recruiting and Induction District, Salt Lake, Utah, 8 March 1943, RG 165, National Archives, Washington, D.C..

12. See letter to Commanding General, Ninth Service Command, Fort Douglas, Utah, from Joyce Burton, Second Officer, WAAC, of Headquarters Montana Recruiting and Induction District, 11 March 1943, RG 165, National Archives, Washington, D.C..

13. Ibid.

14. The WAC Bill passed the Senate on 28 June 1943 and was signed into law by the president of the United States on 1 July 1943. The law gave the Army ninety days to dissolve the WAAC. By September 30, the WAAC ceased to exist.

15. "First Group of Nisei WACS Enter Training at Des Moines," *Pacific Citizen*, vol. 17, no. 26, 1 January 1944, p.8.

16. "Three Utah Nisei Girls Train for WACs at Des Moines: Get Send-off from Friends, Relatives in Salt Lake City," *Pacific Citizen*, vol. 18, no. 7, 19 February 1944, p. 3.

17. "Pvt. Michiyo Mukai Named Editor of WAC Newspaper," *Pacific Citizen*, vol. 19, no. 1, 8 July 1944, p. 1.

18. "Former Welfare Girl WAC," *Poston Chronicle*, vol. 17, no. 4, Poston, Arizona, 9 March 1944, p. 1.

19. See letter to Secretary of War from Oveta Culp Hobby on the enlistment of Japanese American Women in the Women's Army Corps, National Archives, RG 165, SPWA 291.2 File, 17 February 1944, College Park, Md..

20. See "Women's Army Corps Offers Opportunity for Nisei Girls," *Pacific Citizen*, 19 February 1944, p. 7.

21. "Urge Japanese American Girls to Join Women's Army Corps: Pvt. Shinagawa Recruits Nisei Volunteers in Denver Area," *Pacific Citizen*, 27 May 1944, p.3.

22. "Nisei Sisters Become WACs in Illinois," *Pacific Citizen*, 1 April 1944, p.1.

23. "Nisei Girl Leaves WRA Job to Enlist in Women's Army," *Pacific Citizen*, 1 April 1, 1944, p. 3.

24. "First Nisei Girl from Wyoming Enlists In WAC," *Pacific Citizen*, 8 April 1944, p. 1.

25. "Philadelphia Girl Leaves for Training In Women's Army," *Pacific Citizen*, 14 October 1944, p. 3.
26. "Pismo Beach Girl Enlists in WACs," *Pacific Citizen*, 28 December 1944, p.16.
27. Cherry Shiozawa, interview by Chizu Iiyama, tape recording, Japanese National American Historical Society, San Francisco, 21 February 1989.
28. "Nisei Wac Pays Tribute to U.S. Citizenship Rights," *Pacific Citizen*, 26 August 1944, p. 2.
29. "Yagi Nisei Girl Becomes WAC," *Gila (Ariz.) News-Courier*, 7 October 1944.
30. "Nisei Girl Joins WAC," *Gila (Ariz.) News-Courier*, 27 January 1945, p. 4.
31. "Sixth Nisei Girl From Poston Joins Women's Army Corps," *Pacific Citizen*, 11 November 1944, p. 2.
32. "Newswriter Joins Women's Army Corps," *Pacific Citizen*, 2 December 1944.
33. "Vest-Pocket Nisei WAC Joins Pharmacy Staff of Army Hospital," *Pacific Citizen*, 10 February 1945, p. 3.
34. Ibid.
35. "Nisei Anthropologist Volunteers for Service in WAC," *Pacific Citizen*, 18 November 1944, p. 7.
36. "Nisei Wacs Start Training as Army Hospital Technicians," *Pacific Citizen*, 10 March 1945, p. 5.
37. Ibid.
38. Ibid.
39. "Tanaka Joins Wacs in Des Moines, Ia.," *Manzanar Free Press*, 9 June 1945, p. 4.
40. "Nisei in Rochester WRA Office Leaves for WAC Training," *Pacific Citizen*, 12 May 1945, p. 6.
41. "Former Gilan Becomes WAC," *Gila (Ariz.) News-Courier*, 22 August 1945, p. 2.
42. Laurie Johnston, "Isle Girls Answer Call to Arms; Would-be GI Janes Entangled in Manpower Red Tape," *Honolulu Advertiser*, 3 October 1944.
43. Ibid.
44. Marion Narvis, "Hawaii Women Line up in Armory as Applicants for Duty with WACs," *Honolulu Advertiser*, 3 October 1944
45. Ibid.
46. Ibid.
47. Ibid.
48. Ibid.
49. Johnston, "Isle Girls Answer Call to Arms."
50. "First Hawaii WACs Are Honored at Review before Going to Mainland," *Honolulu Star-Bulletin*, 1 January 1945.
51. See letter from commanding general of Headquarters U.S. Army Forces, Pacific Ocean Areas, and replies, 9 December 1944, RG 407, Army AG Project, Decimal File 1940–45, Folder 353 WAC Training, Box 4302, National Archives, College Park, Md..
52. "Hawaii's WAC, Carrying Ukes, Head Overseas for Mainland," *Honolulu Star-Bulletin*, 2 January 1945.
53. The United Service Organization was founded on February 4, 1941, to serve members of the armed forces and defense industries. In 1942 the USO began to sponsor entertainment tours for celebrities to visit and entertain U.S. soldiers all over the world. Among the many celebrities who entertained with these touring companies were Bob Hope, Bing Crosby, Jack Benny, and Josephine Baker.
54. "Hawaiian WACs Find a Friend between Trains in Amarillo," *Amarillo Daily News*, January 1945.
55. Ibid.

56. See article in Memphis newspaper [title unknown], "Hawaii's WACs Hula Their Way to Memphis," 20 January 1945.

57. There were five WAAC/WAC basic training centers during World War II. The first was at Fort Des Moines, Iowa; the second in Daytona Beach, Florida; the third at Fort Oglethorpe, Georgia (activated on January 1, 1943); the fourth at Fort Devens, Massachusetts; and the fifth with three locations at Camp Monticello, Arkansas, Camp Polk, Louisiana, and Camp Ruston, Louisiana.

58. Women met the prerequisite for technical jobs in the AAF because they usually scored higher on the aptitude test (AGCT) than did men. See Mattie Treadwell, *United States Army in World War II: Special Studies: The Women's Army Corps* (Washington, D.C.: U.S. Government Printing Office, 1954), p. 289.

59. Treadwell, *The Women's Army Corps*, 281–295.

60. "Nakagawara Nisei Girl Now Air WAC," *Gila News-Courier*, 22 January 1944, p. 1.

61. "Girl Inducted into Air-WACs," *Pacific Citizen*, 5 February 1944, p. 3.

62. "Poston Girl Joins Air WAC," *Poston Chronicle*, 26 February 1944, p. 1.

63. "First Hawaii-Born Nisei Girl Joins Air Corps WACs," *Pacific Citizen*, 6 May 1944, p. 1.

64. "WACs Unsegregated," *Pacific Citizen*, 15 January 1944, p. 4.

Chapter 5   Service in the Women's Army Corps

1. Mattie Treadwell, *United States Army in World War II: Special Studies: The Women's Army Corps* (Washington, D.C.: U.S. Government Printing Office, 1954), 66; Bettie Morden, *The Women's Army Corps, 1945–1978* (Washington, D.C.: Center of Military History, United States Army, 1990), 8.

2. Brenda L. Moore, *To Serve My Country, To Serve My Race: The Story of the Only African American Wacs Stationed Overseas during World War II* (New York: New York University Press, 1996).

3. "Number 1" was the War Department's code for Caucasian. Moore, *To Serve My Country*, 75.

4. Laurie Johnson, "I'm Coming Back, Is Message of Island Wac," *Honolulu Advertiser*, 18 April 1945, p.1.

5. Lillian Mott-Smith, "Island Girl Describes Assignment in Georgia," *Honolulu Star Bulletin*, January 1945.

6. Ibid.

7. "Hawaiian Nisei Soldiers Meet New Wacs from Home Islands: Earl Finch Throws Party for Hawaiian Trainees in Deep South," *Pacific Citizen*, 3 March 1945, p. 6.

8. Editorial, *Honolulu Advertiser*, 18 April 1945, p. 4.

9. Treadwell, *The Women's Army Corps*, 41, 147, 148; Morden, *The Women's Army Corps, 1945–1978*, 18–19.

10. A manning document for a combat or combat-related unit was called a table of organization. Women were assigned only as noncombatants during World War II.

11. Morden, *Women's Army Corps, 1945–1978*, 19.

12. "Japanese American WAC Aids Chaplain at Kentucky Camp," *Pacific Citizen*, 17 February 1945, p. 2.

13. Editorial, *Honolulu Star Bulletin*, 5 November 1945.

14. "Vest-Pocket Nisei WAC Joins Pharmacy Staff of Army Hospital," *Pacific Citizen*, 10 February 1945, p. 3.

15. See Lillian Mott-Smith, "Hawaii WAC, Mitsue Nouichi, Is Engaged to Walter Kitagawa," *Honolulu Star Bulletin*, 24 December 1945.

16. "Nisei WAC Talks on Japan before Hospital Group," *Pacific Citizen*, 4 November 1944, p. 6

17. See "Enlistment of Japanese-American Women for Duty with the Medical Department," in Army AG, Project Decimal File, 1940–45, Box 4292, Memo 30 Jan 45, National Archives, College Park, Md..

18. Treadwell, *The Women's Army Corps*, 325.

19. Clifford Uyeda and Barry Saiki, *The Pacific War and Peace: Americans of Japanese Ancestry in Military Intelligence Service, 1941 to 1952* (San Francisco: National Japanese Historical Society, 1991), 17.

20. Ibid.

21. The course was known as the Army Intensive Japanese Language Course. Those accepted into the program were Caucasian officers who possessed some knowledge of Japanese or who demonstrated general linguistic ability. Subsequently the school became even more selective: candidates were required to have six months of academic training in Japanese, or the equivalent. See Colonel Kai E. Rasmussen, "History and Description of the Military Intelligence Service Language School," RG 319, Box 1 of 1, Ft. Snelling, Minnesota, National Archives, College Park, Md.

22. Memorandum to Commanding General, "Enrollment of linguists in WAAC," 7 January 1943, RG 407, Box 4297, Folder 341, National Archives, College Park, Md.

23. Uyeda and Saiki, *The Pacific War and Peace*, 23.

24. Lillian Mott-Smith, "With Hawaii WACS," *Honolulu Star Bulletin*, 11 September 1945.

25. Marion Nestor, interview by Brenda L. Moore, 6 April 1995.

26. Ibid.

27. "WACs Bound for Tokyo Include 4 from Territory," *Honolulu Star Bulletin*, 29 January 1946.

28. "11 Nisei WACs Leave for Tokyo," *Rafu Shimpo*, 23 January 1946, p. 1.

29. Kathy Gorman, "Yank WAC, 12 of Nippon Descent to Leave for Japan—Nisei to Be Mannequins of Democracy," *St. Paul Dispatch*, 18 January 1946, pp.1, 2.

30. Ibid., 2; one of the Wacs deployed with the group was Sgt. Rhoda Knudsen, a Caucasian woman who was born in Japan of missionary parents and lived in Tokyo until she was almost eighteen years old.

31. "Nisei Wacs Stop Here en Route to Japan for Interpreter Duty," *Honolulu Advertiser*, 29 January 1946.

32. Two WAC detachments were activated in Japan during 1946; the 8000th WAC Battalion in Yokohama, and the 8225th WAC Battalion in Tokyo. The former consisted of approximately 150 women who worked in the offices of Headquarters, 8th Army, and lived in a quonset hut compound. The latter comprised of four hundred enlisted women who worked in General Headquarters (GHQ), U.S. Army Forces, Far East, (USAFFE), and lived in a multistory converted office building formerly owned by the Mitsubishi Corporation; see Morden, *Women's Army Corps, 1945–1978*, 47.

33. Uyeda and Saiki, *Pacific War and Peace*, 23.

34. See Ulysses Lee, *United States Army in World War II: Special Studies: The Employment of Negro Troops* (Washington, D.C.: U.S. Government Printing Office, 1966), 422.

35. Moore, *To Serve My Country, To Serve My Race*, 20–21.

36. "4 Negro Wacs Convicted—NAACP Calls It Fair," *New York Post*, 21 March 1945; "Army Court Convicts 4 Negro Wacs of Disobeying Superior," *Washington Post*, 21 March 1945; "3 Congressmen Ask Probe of Wac Trials," *Washington Post*, 23 March 1945.

37. "Negro Wacs," *Washington Post*, 12 April 1945.
38. Ibid.
39. See Moore, *To Serve My Country*.
40. See Stacey Yukari Hirose, *Japanese American Women and the Women's Army Corps, 1935–1950*, M.A. thesis (Los Angeles: University of California Los Angeles, 1993), 44.
41. Treadwell, *The Women's Army Corps*, 589.
42. See letter to Commanding General, Fourth Service Command, on the shipment of women enlisted in the WAC in the Antilles Department, 14 October 1944, WAC File, National Archives, College Park, Md.
43. Treadwell, *The Women's Army Corps*, 589.
44. WAVES (Women Accepted for Volunteer Emergency Service) was the Navy's service organization for women.
45. Judy Barrett Litof and David C. Smith, "The Wartime History of the WAVES, SPARS, Women Marines, Army and Navy Nurses, and WASPS," *A Woman's War, Too: U.S. Women in the Military in World War II*, ed. Paula Nassen Poulos (Washington, D.C.: National Archives and Records Administration, 1996), 56.
46. Hazel Lee was one of thirty-eight WASPs to die in the line of duty. She and another pilot received identical instructions from an air traffic controller on their approach to Great Falls Air Force Base in Montana and consequently crashed. See Judy Yung, *Chinese Women of America: A Pictorial History* (Seattle: University of Washington Press, 1986); Judith Bellafaire, *Asian-Pacific American Servicewomen in Defense of a Nation* (Arlington, Va.: Women In Military Service for America Memorial, 1999).
47. Bellafaire, *Asian-Pacific American Servicewomen*.

Chapter 6   *Commissions in the Army Medical Corps*

1. Richard V. N. Ginn, *The History of the U.S. Army Medical Service Corps* (Washington, D.C.: Center of Military History, 1997), 186.
2. U.S. Department of Commerce, Bureau of the Census, *Statistical Abstract of the United States, 1949* (Washington, D.C.: U.S. Government Printing Office, 1949), Table 210.
3. Hearings before Subcommittee No. 3 of the Committee on Military Affairs, House of Representatives, Seventy-Eighth Congress, Appointment of Female Physicians and Surgeons in the Medical Corps of the Army and Navy (Washington, D.C.: U.S. Government Printing Office, 1943), 2.
4. Ibid., 18.
5. Ibid., 48.
6. "Commissioning of Female Doctors, U.S. Army," *Army Medical Bulletin* 68 (July 1943): 217; Mary T. Sarnecky, "Women, Medicine, and War," *A Woman's War, Too: U.S. Women in the Military in World War II*, ed. Paula Nassen Poulos (Washington, D.C.: National Archives and Records Administration, 1996), 71–81.
7. Esther P. Lovejoy, *Women Doctors of the World* (New York: Macmillan, 1957), 366; *The Military Surgeon: Journal of the Association of Military Surgeons of the United States* 93 (1943): 91 and (July 1943): 99; Sarnecky. "Women, Medicine, and War," 71–81.
8. *The Military Surgeon* (July 1943): 99
9. Brig. Gen. Raymond W. Bliss, MC, a physician who served as chief of operations under Surgeon General Norman T. Kirk, and would later (from 1947–1951) succeed Kirk as surgeon general. See Ginn. *History of the U.S. Army Medical Service*

Corps, 121–122, 191 n.37, 199; Clara Raven, "Achievements of Women in Medicine, Past and Present–Women in the Medical Corps of the Army," Military Medicine: Official Publication of the Association of Military Surgeons of the United States 125 (February 1960): 105–111.

10. Lovejoy, Women Doctors of the World, 367.

11. Raven, "Achievements of Women in Medicine, Past and Present," 109

12. Ginn, History of the U.S. Army Medical Service Corps, 119.

13. Colonel Julia O. Flikke, superintendent of the corps from June 1937 to June 1943, was succeeded by Colonel Florence A. Blanchfield, who held the position from July 1943 to December 1947.

14. Carolyn M. Feller and Deborah R. Cox, eds., Highlights in the History of the Army Nurse Corps (Washington, D.C.: U.S. Army Center of Military History, 2001).

15. Barbara Brooks Tomblin, G.I. Nightingales: The Army Nurse Corps in World War II (Lexington: University Press of Kentucky, 1996), 11; Darlene Clark-Hine, Black Women in White: Racial Conflict and Cooperation in the Nursing Profession, 1890–1950 (Bloomington: Indiana University Press, 1989), 170.

16. Clark-Hine. Black Women in White, 171.

17. Prudence Burns Burrell, "Serving My Country," in Negro History Bulletin 51–57 (1993): 47–50.

18. Pittsburgh Courier. "Commander Lauds Skill of Our Nurses in ETO." (Pittsburgh, Pa.: 1944).

19. Sarnecky, A History of the U.S. Army Nurse Corps (Philadelphia: University of Pennsylvania Press, 1999) 171–76; U.S. Department of Defense, Black Americans in Defense of Our Nation (Washington, D.C.: Government Printing Office, 1985), 101; Tomblin. G.I. Nightingales, 11, 21.

20. Judy Yung, Chinese Women of America: A Pictorial History. (Seattle: University of Washington Press, 1986), 66.

21. Letter from the War Department, Services of Supply, Office of the Surgeon General, Washington, D.C., addressed to Miss Masako Mary Yamado, 21 February 1943. From the private collection of Masako Mara Yamada, New York, N.Y.

22. Letter from the War Department, Services of Supply, Office of the Surgeon General, Washington, D.C., addressed to Miss Masaka Mary Yamada, 21February 1943. From the private collection of Masako Mary Yamada, New York, N.Y.

23. Letter from Army Service Forces, Governors Island, New York, addressed to Second Lieutenant. Masako M. Yamada, ANC, 27 March 1945. From the private collection of Masako Mary Yamada, New York, N.Y.

24. Sarnecky, A History of the U.S. Army Nurse Corps, 275.

25. Ibid., 270–71.

26. Ibid.

27. Manzanar Free Press (Manzanar, Calif., 1 September 1945), 2. In the Wason collection, Film 8676, Japanese Camp Papers, Reel 10, Kroch Library, Cornell University, Ithaca, N.Y.

28. For detailed information about the UNRRA, see United Nations Relief and Rehabilitation Administration; UNRRA: Organization Aims Progress (Washington, D.C.: U.S. Government Printing Office, 1945).

29. Ibid., 3, 7.

30. Ibid., 22.

31. Frances Berkeley Floore, The Bread of the Oppressed: An American Woman's Experiences in War-Disrupted Countries (Hicksville, N.Y.: Exposition Press, 1975), 27–28.

32. Yoshiye Togasaki, unpublished audiotaped interview, National Japanese American Historical Society, San Francisco, 10 August 1985, [transcript page] 46.

33. Ibid., 47.
34. Ibid., 48.
35. Ibid., 48.

Chapter 7   The Postwar Years

1. Cynthia Enloe, *Ethnic Soldiers: State Security in Divided Societies* (Athens: University of Georgia Press, 1980).
2. Margaret Higonnet, Jane Jenson, Sonya Michel, and Margaret Weitz, *Behind the Lines: Gender and the Two World Wars* (New Haven, Conn.: Yale University Press, 1987); D'Ann Campbell, *Women at War with America: Private Lives in a Patriotic Era* (Cambridge, Mass.: Harvard University Press, 1984).
3. John Modell and Timothy Haggerty, "The Social Impact of War," *Annual Review of Sociology* 17 (1991): 205–224.
4. Ibid., 220.
5. The life course perspective is a major paradigm in the study of human lives and a changing society. Among the numerous contributions to life course studies are these works of Glen H. Elder Jr.: "Time, Human Agency, and Social Change: Perspectives on the Life Course," *Social Psychology Quarterly* 57 (1994): 4–15; "War Mobilization and the Life Course: A Cohort of World War II Veterans," *Sociological Forum* 2 (1987): 449–472; *Life Course Dynamics: Trajectories and Transitions, 1968–1980* (Ithaca, N.Y.: Cornell University Press, 1985); *Children of the Great Depression: Social Change in Life Experience* (Chicago: University of Chicago, 1974). Other major contributions include: Glen H. Elder Jr. and Janet Z. Giele, *Methods of Life Course Research: Qualitative and Quantitative Approaches* (Thousand Oaks, Calif.: Sage, 1998); John Modell, Marc Goulden, and Sigurdur Magnusson, "World War II in the Lives of Black Americans: Some Findings and an Interpretation," *Journal of American History* 76 (1989): 830–848.
6. See Glen H. Elder Jr., Cynthia Gimbel, and Rachel Ivie, "Turning Points in Life: The Case of Military Service and War," *Military Psychology* 3 (1991): 215–231.
7. Ibid., 223.
8. Maureen Honey, *Creating Rosie the Riveter: Class, Gender, and Propaganda during World War II* (Amherst, Mass.: University of Massacusetts Press, 1984), 23.
9. Kay Deaux and Joseph C. Ullman, *Women of Steel: Female Blue-Collar Workers in the Basic Steel Industry* (New York: Praeger, 1983), 1–10.
10. Deaux and Ullman cite an intensive study conducted by the Women's Bureau of the U.S. Department of Labor in 1944–1945. The study revealed that 75 percent of the women who had been working during World War II expected to continue to work, and most wanted to continue in the nontraditional jobs they were filling during the war rather than return to jobs held before the war. See Deaux and Ullman, *Women of Steel*, 9; the same study is cited in Maureen Honey. Honey also cited another study published by the Women's Bureau of the U.S. Department of Labor, *A Preview as to Women Workers in Transition from War to Peace*, as evidence of dissatisfaction among women being laid off. See Honey, *Creating Rosie the Riveter*, 23, 227.
11. Edward H. Spicer, Aseal T. Hansen, Katherine Luomala, and Marvin K. Opler, *Impounded People* (Tucson: University of Arizona Press, 1969).
12. Leonard Bloom and Ruth Riemer, *Removal and Return: The Socio-Economic Effects of the War on Japanese Americans* (Berkeley and Los Angeles: University of California Press, 1949); U.S. War Agency Liquidation Unit, *People in Motion: The*

Postwar Adjustment of Evacuated Japanese Americans (Washington, D.C.: U.S. Government Printing Office, 1947).

13. Cherry Shiozawa, interview by Chizu Iiyama, tape recording, Japanese National American Historical Society, San Francisco, 21 February 1989, [transcript page] 50.

14. Yoshiye Togasaki, audio-taped interview, National Japanese American Historical Society, San Francisco, 10 August 1985, 46.

15. D'Ann Campbell, *Women at War with America*, 225.

16. Ibid., 224.

17. Ibid., 225.

18. Lillian G. Mott-Smith, "Hawaii Interpreter Weds Hawaii WAC at Fort Snelling, Minnesota," *Honolulu Star-Bulletin* (November 1945).

19. Lillian G. Mott-Smith, "Hawaii WAC, Mitsue Nouichi, Is Engaged to Walter Kitagawa," *Honolulu Star-Bulletin* (24 December 1945).

20. Morris Janowitz, *The Professional Soldier: A Social and Political Portrait* (New York: Free Press, 1971), 189.

21. Ibid., 189.

22. Doreen Drewry Lehr, "Military Wives: Breaking the Silence," in *Gender Camouflage: Women and the U.S. Military*, ed. Francine D'Amico and Laurie Weinstein. (New York: New York University Press, 1999), 117.

23. Ibid., 125.

24. Morris Janowitz, *Reconstruction of Patriotism: Education for Civic Consciousness* (Chicago: University of Chicago Press, 1983), 1–3; David R. Segal, *Recruiting for Uncle Sam: Citizenship and Military Manpower Policy* (Lawrence: University Press of Kansas, 1989), 97–99.

25. T. H. Marshall, *Class, Citizenship, and Social Development* (Chicago: University of Chicago Press, 1963), 78.

26. Ibid.

27. Ibid.

28. See Sandra C. Taylor, "Evacuation and Economic Loss: Questions and Perspectives," *Japanese Americans: From Relocation to Redress*, ed. Roger Daniels, Sandra C. Taylor, and Harry H. Kitano (Seattle: University of Washington Press, 1991), 163–167.

29. Daniels, Taylor, and Kitano, *Japanese Americans*, 226.

30. U.S. Commission on Wartime Relocation and Internment of Civilians Report, *Personal Justice Denied* (Washington, D.C.: U.S. Government Printing Office, March 1992), 7.

31. Milton M. Gordon, *Assimilation in American Life: The Role of Race, Religion, and National Origin* (New York: Oxford University Press, 1964), 70–71.

32. See for example Eileen Tamura, *Americanization, Acculturation, and Ethnic Identity: The Nisei Generation in Hawaii* (Urbana and Chicago: University of Illinois Press, 1994); Edna Bonacich and John Modell, *The Economic Basis of Ethnic Solidarity: Small Business in the Japanese American Community* (Berkeley and Los Angeles: University of California Press, 1980); Harry H. L. Kitano, *Japanese Americans: The Evolution of a Subculture* (Englewood Cliffs, N.J.: Prentice Hall, 1969).

33. Eric Woodrum, "An Assessment of Japanese American Assimilation, Pluralism, and Subordination," *American Journal of Sociology* 87 (1981), 157–169.

34. Ibid., 160.

35. For example, see John N. Tinker, "Intermarriage and Ethnic Boundaries: The

Japanese American Case," *Journal of Social Issues* 29 (1973), 49–66, and Akemi Kikumura and Harry Kitano, "Interracial Marriage: A Picture of the Japanese Americans," *Journal of Social Issues* 29 (1973), 67–81.

36. See "Nisei Writes of Issei Parents," *Gila (Ariz.) News Courier*, 24 February 1944, 2. Found in Wason Film 8676, Japanese Camp Papers, Reel 8, Kroch Library, Cornell University, Ithaca, N.Y.

37. Ibid.

Glossary

ANC: Army Nurse Corps

ASF: Army Service Forces

commission: Officer status in the armed services. Commissioned officers may be viewed as the managers.

crude birth rate: The number of live births in a given year for each thousand persons in an entire population. It is calculated by dividing the number of live births in a year by a society's total population and multiplying the results by one thousand. It is an indicator of a society's overall fertility.

DAC: Defined Army Civilian

enlisted: members of the armed services who are subordinate to officers. Enlisted members may be viewed as the workers.

ethnic group: Narrowly defined in sociology as one distinguished primarily on the basis of cultural or natural-origin characteristics

gannen mono: Japanese contract laborers

heigo: Japanese military and technical terms

ideal-type: A sociological term referring to an analytical construct that allows social scientists to measure similarities and differences in concrete cases; it is an abstract of the essential characteristics of any social phenomenon. The term was coined by the prominent German scholar Max Weber.

issei: the first generation of Japanese immigrants, having immigrated to the United States

JACL: Japanese American Citizens League

kibei: a Nisei sent by his or her parents at a young age to be educated in Japan

Meiji Era: the period 1868 to1912, when Emperor Meiji ruled. This period designates the end of the feudal era and the beginning of the modern era in Japan.

MISLS: Military Intelligence Service Language School

nisei: a child of Issei, born in the United States; second-generation Japanese American

PACMIRS: Pacific Military Intelligence Research Section

on: Deep obligation to superiors

racial group: Narrowly defined in sociology as a group composed of persons who share biologically transmitted traits considered by societal members to be socially significant

racism: Defined in sociology as a belief that one racial category is innately superior or inferior to another

RCT: Regimental Combat Team

sansei: third generation Japanese American

sosho: Japanese cursive writing

SPAR: women in the Coast Guard. The term is taken from the Coast Guard motto, *Semper Paratus* (always ready)

SWPA: Southwest Pacific Area

tanomoshi: rotating credit associations

TDY: temporary duty

WAAC: Women's Army Auxiliary Corps

Waac: member of the Women's Army Auxiliary Corps

WAC: Women's Army Corps

Wac: member of the Women's Army Corps

WAVES: Women Accepted for Volunteer Emergency Service, the Navy organization for women

WCCA: Wartime Civil Control Authority, a unit created within the Western Defense Command to take charge of civilian affairs. The WCCA was in charge of the forced evacuation of Japanese Americans.

Bibliography

Ambrose, Stephen. *Rise to Globalism: American Foreign Policy since 1938.* New York: Penguin, 1983.

Ancheta, Angelo N. *Race, Rights, and the Asian American Experience.* New Brunswick, N.J.: Rutgers University Press, 1998.

Arnold, Thomas St. John. *Buffalo Soldiers: The 92nd Division and Reinforcements in World War II, 1942–1945.* Manhattan, Kans.: Sunflower University Press, 1990.

Beekman, Allan. *The Niihau Incident.* Detroit: Harlo Press, 1982.

Bell, Richard. *Public School Education of Second-Generation Japanese in California.* Stanford, Calif.: Stanford University Press, 1935.

Bellafaire, Judith. *Asian-Pacific American Servicewomen in Defense of a Nation.* Arlington, Va.: Women in Military Service for America Memorial, 1999.

Benedict, Ruth. *Chrysanthemum and the Sword: Patterns of Japanese Culture.* New York: New American Library, [1946, 1967] 1974.

Biggs, Bradley. *The Triple Nickles: America's First All-Black Paratroop Unit.* Hamden, Conn.: Archon Books, 1986.

Blauner, Robert [Bob]. *Still the Big News: Racial Oppression in America.* Philadelphia: Temple University Press, 2001.

Bloom, Leonard, and Ruth Riemer. *Removal and Return: The Socio-Economic Effects of the War on Japanese Americans.* Berkeley and Los Angeles: University of California Press, 1949.

Bonacich, Edna, and John Modell. *The Economic Basis of Ethnic Solidarity: Small Business in the Japanese American Community.* Berkeley and Los Angeles: University of California Press, 1980.

Browning, Harley, Sally Lopreato, and Dudley Poston. "Income and Veterans Status: Variations among Mexican Americans, Blacks, and Anglos." *American Sociological Review* 38 (1973): 74–85.

Burrell, Prudence Burns. "Serving My Country." *Negro History Bulletin* 51–57, Nos. 1–12 1993): 47–50.

Campbell, D'Ann. *Women at War with America: Private Lives in a Patriotic Era.* Cambridge, Mass.: Harvard University Press.

Center of Military History. *American Armies and Battlefields in Europe.* Washington, D.C.: United States Army, 1992.

Chambers, J. S. "The Japanese Invasion." *Annals of the American Academy of Political and Social Science* (January 1921): 36.

Chan, Sucheng. *Asian Americans: An Interpretive History.* New York: Twayne Publishers, 1991.

Chang, Robert. "Toward an Asian American Legal Scholarship: Critical Race Theory, Post-Structuralism, and Narrative Space." *Asian Law Review* 1 (1994): 27.

Clark-Hine, Darlene. *Black Women in White: Racial Conflict and Cooperation in the Nursing Profession, 1890–1950*. Bloomington: Indiana University Press, 1989.

Coggins, Cecil H. "Japanese Americans in Hawaii." *Harper's Magazine* (July 1943).

Collins, Donald E. *Native American Aliens: Disloyalty and Renunciation of Citizenship by Japanese Americans during World War II*. Westport, Conn.: Greenwood Press, 1985.

"Commissioning of Female Doctors, U.S. Army." *Army Medical Bulletin* 68 (July 1943).

Connor, John W. "Acculturation and Family Continuities in Three Generations of Japanese Americans." *Journal of Marriage and the Family* (February 1974): 159–165.

Dallek, Robert A. *Franklin D. Roosevelt and American Policy, 1932–1945*. New York: Oxford University Press, 1979.

Daniels, Roger. *Concentration Camps: North America*. Malabar, Fla.: Krieger, 1981.

———. *Prisoners Without Trial: Japanese Americans in World War II*. New York: Hill and Wang, 1993.

Daniels, Roger, Sandra C. Taylor, and Harry H. Kitano, eds. *Japanese Americans: From Relocation to Redress*. Seattle: University of Washington Press, 1991.

Davis, Angela Y. *Women, Race, and Class*. New York: Random House, 1981.

Deaux, Kay, and Joseph C. Ullman. *Women of Steel: Female Blue-Collar Workers in the Basic Steel Industry*. New York: Praeger, 1983.

Duster, Alfreda M. *Crusade for Justice: The Autobiography of Ida B. Wells*. Chicago: University of Chicago Press, 1970.

Duus, Masayo Umezawa. *Unlikely Liberators: The Men of the 100th and 442nd*. Translated by Peter Duus. Honolulu: University of Hawaii Press, 1987.

Earley, Charity Adams. *One Woman's Army: A Black Officer Remembers the WAC*. College Station, Tex.: Texas A & M University Press, 1989.

Elder, Glen H. Jr. *Children of the Great Depression: Social Change in Life Experience*. Chicago: University of Chicago, 1974.

———. *Life Course Dynamics: Trajectories and Transitions, 1968–1980*. Ithaca, N.Y.: Cornell University Press, 1985.

———. "Time, Human Agency, and Social Change: Perspectives on the Life Course." *Social Psychology Quarterly* 57 (1994): 4–15.

———. "War Mobilization and the Life Course: A Cohort of World War II Veterans." *Sociological Forum* 2 (1987): 449–472.

Elder, Glen H. Jr., and Janet Z. Giele. *Methods of Life Course Research: Qualitative and Quantitative Approaches*. Thousand Oaks, Calif.: Sage, 1998.

Elder, Glen H. Jr., Cynthia Gimbel, and Rachel Ivie. "Turning Points in Life: The Case of Military Service and War." *Military Psychology* 3 (1991): 215–231.

Enloe, Cynthia. *Ethnic Soldiers: State Security in Divided Societies*. Athens: University of Georgia Press, 1980.

Espiritu, Yen Le. *Asian American Panethnicity: Bridging Institutions and Identities*. Philadelphia: Temple University Press, 1992.

———. *The Gender Lens: Asian American Women and Men*. Thousand Oaks, Calif.: Sage, 1997.

Feagin, Joe R., and Clairece Booher Feagin. *Racial and Ethnic Relations*. 6th edition. Upper Saddle River, N.J.: Prentice Hall, 1999.

Feller, Carolyn M., and Deborah R. Cox, eds. *Highlights in the History of the Army Nurse Corps*. Washington, D.C.: U.S. Army Center of Military History, 2001.

Floore, Frances Berkeley. *The Bread of the Oppressed: An American Woman's Experiences in War-Disrupted Countries*. Hicksville, N.Y.: Exposition Press, 1975.

Franklin, John Hope, and Alfred A. Moss Jr. *From Slavery to Freedom: A History of Negro Americans*. 6th edition. New York: Alfred A. Knopf, 1988.

Ginn, Richard V. N. *The History of the U.S. Army Medical Service Corps.* Washington, D.C.: Center of Military History, 1977.

Glen, Evelyn Nakano. *Issei, Nisei, War Bride: Three Generations of Japanese American Women in Domestic Service.* Philadelphia: Temple University Press, 1986.

Golden, Arthur. *Memoirs of a Geisha.* New York: Alfred A. Knopf, 1997.

Gordon, Milton M. *Assimilation in American Life: The Role of Race, Religion, and National Origin.* New York: New York University Press, 1964.

Gorman, Kathy. In *St. Paul Dispatch,* 18 January 1946.

Hata, Donald Teruo, Dominguez Hills, and Nadine Ishitani Hata. *Japanese Americans and World War II.* Wheeling, Ill.: Harlan Davidson, 1995.

Hawaii's Nikkei History Editorial Board. *Japanese Eyes, American Heart: Personal Reflections of Hawaii's World War II Nisei Soldiers.* Honolulu: Tendai Educational Foundation, 1998.

Higonnet, Margaret, Jane Jenson, Sonya Michel, and Margaret Weitz, *Behind the Lines: Gender and the Two World Wars.* New Haven, Conn.: Yale University Press, 1987.

Hirose, Stacey Yukari. "Japanese American Women and the Women's Army Corps, 1935–1950." Master's thesis. University of California Los Angeles, 1993.

Holian, Timothy J. *The German-Americans and World War II: An Ethnic Experience.* New York: P. Lang, 1966.

Honey, Maureen. *Creating Rosie the Riveter: Class, Gender, and Propaganda during World War II.* Amherst: University of Massachusetts Press, 1984.

Hosokawa, Bill. *JACL: In Quest of Justice.* New York: William Morrow and Co., 1982.

———. *Nisei: The Quiet Americans.* New York: William Morrow and Co., 1969.

Ichioka, Yuji. *The Issei: The World of the First Generation Japanese Immigrants, 1885–1924.* New York: Free Press, 1988.

Ito, Leslie. "Japanese American Women and the Student Relocation Movement, 1942–1945." *Frontiers* 21 (2000): 1–24.

Janowitz, Morris. "The All-Volunteer Military as a Sociopolitical Problem." *Social Problems* 22 (February 1975): 435.

———. *The Professional Soldier: A Social and Political Portrait.* New York: The Free Press, 1971.

———. *Reconstruction of Patriotism: Education for Civic Consciousness.* Chicago: University of Chicago Press, 1983.

Japanese National American Historical Society, San Francisco. Unpublished interview with Cherry Shiozawa by Chizu Iiyama, tape recording, 21 February 1989. Unpublished interview with Yoshiye Togasaki, audio-taped, 10 August 1985.

Johnson, Erwin. "The Emergence of a Self-Conscious Entrepreneurial Class in Rural Japan." In *Japanese Culture: Its Development and Characteristics,* ed. Robert J. Smith and Richard K. Beardsley, 91–99. Chicago: Aldine, 1962.

Kataoka, W. T. "Occupation of Japanese in Los Angeles." *Sociology and Social Research* 14 (September–October 1929): 53–58.

Katzenstein, Mary Fainsod, and Judith Reppy, eds. *Military Culture,* 125–142. 1999.

Kikumura, Akemi, and Harry [H. L.] Kitano. "Interracial Marriage: A Picture of the Japanese Americans." *Journal of Social Issues* 29 (1973): 67–81.

Kitagawa, Daisuke. *Issei and Nisei: The Internment Years.* New York: Seabury Press, 1967.

Kitano, Harry H. L. *Japanese Americans: The Evolution of a Subculture.* Englewood Cliffs, N.J.: Prentice Hall, 1969.

Kitano, Kerrily J., and Harry H. L. Kitano. "The Japanese-American Family." In *Ethnic Families in America: Patterns and Variations,* ed. Charles Mindel, Robert Habenstein, and Roosevelt Wright Jr. 4th edition. Upper Saddle River, N.J.: Prentice Hall, 1998.

Kiyota, Minoru. *Beyond Loyalty: The Story of a Kibei.* Honolulu: University of Hawaii Press, 1997.

Langer, William L., and S. Everett Gleason. *The Challenge to Isolation 1937–1940*. New York: Harper and Row, 1952.
————. *The Undeclared War 1940–1941*. New York: Harper and Row, 1953.
Lee, Ulysses. *United States Army in World War II: Special Studies: The Employment of Negro Troops*. Washington, D.C.: U.S. Government Printing Office, 1966.
Lehr, Doreen D. "Military Wives: Breaking the Silence." In *Gender Camouflage: Women and the U.S. Military*, ed. Francine D'Amico and Laurie Weinstein, 117–131. New York: New York University Press, 1999
Lieberson, Stanley. *A Piece of the Pie: Blacks and White Immigrants since 1880*. Berkeley and Los Angeles: University of California Press, 1980.
Lind, Andrew W. *Hawaii's Japanese: An Experiment in Democracy*. Princeton, N.J.: Princeton University Press, 1946.
Litof, Judy Barrett, and David C. Smith. "The Wartime History of the WAVES, SPARS, Women Marines, Army and Navy Nurses, and Wasps." In *A Woman's War Too: U.S. Women in the Military in World War II*, ed. Paula Nassen Poulos, 47–67. Washington, D.C.: National Archives and Records Administration, 1996.
Littleton, Louise. "Worse than Slaves." *San Francisco Chronicle*, 1 October 1893.
Loewen, James W. *The Mississippi Chinese: Between Black and White*. Cambridge, Mass.: Harvard University Press, 1971.
Lopreato, Sally, and Dudley Poston. "Differences in Earnings and Earnings Ability between Black Veterans and Nonveterans in the United States." *Social Science Quarterly* 57 (1977): 750–766.
Lovejoy, Esther P. *Women Doctors of the World*. New York: Macmillan, 1957.
Luebke, Frederick C. *Bonds of Loyalty: German-Americans and World War I*. Dekalb: Northern Illinois University Press.
Lyons, Michael J. *World War II: A Short History*. 2nd edition. Englewood Cliffs, N.J.: Prentice Hall, 1994.
Manchester, William. *The Glory and the Dream: A Narrative History of America, 1932–1972*. New York: Bantam Books, 1973.
Marshall, T. H. *Class, Citizenship, and Social Development*. Chicago: University of Chicago Press, 1963.
Matsumoto, Valerie. "Japanese American Women during World War II." *Frontiers* 8 (1984): 1–14.
Maykovich, Minako K. *Japanese American Identity Dilemma*. Tokyo: Waseda University Press, 1972.
Meyer, Leisa D. *Creating GI Jane: Sexuality and Power in the Women's Army Corps during World War II*. New York: Columbia University Press, 1996.
Millis, H. A. *The Japanese Problem in the United States*. New York: Macmillan, 1915.
Modell, John. "Tradition and Opportunity: The Japanese Immigrant in America." *Pacific Historical Review* 40 (May 1971): 163–182.
Modell, John, Marc Goulden, and Sigurdur Magnusson. "World War II in the Lives of Black Americans: Some Findings and an Interpretation." *Journal of American History* 76 (1989): 830–848.
Modell, John, and Timothy Haggerty. "The Social Impact of War." *Annual Review of Sociology* 17 (1991): 205–224.
Moore, Brenda L. "Reflections of Society: The Intersection of Race and Gender in the U.S. Army in World War II." In *Beyond Zero Tolerance: Discrimination in Military Culture*, ed. Mary Fainsod Katzenstein and Judith Reppy, 125–142. Boulder, Colo., and Lanham, Md.: Rowman and Littlefield, 1999.
————. *To Serve My Country, To Serve My Race: The Story of the Only African-American WACs Stationed Overseas during World War II*. New York: New York University Press, 1996.

Morden, Bettie. *The Women's Army Corps, 1945–1978*. Washington, D.C.: Center of Military History, United States Army, 1990.

Morison, Samuel Eliot. *The Battle of the Atlantic*. Boston: Little, Brown, and Company, 1947.

Moskos, Charles C. "Black in the Army." *Atlantic Monthly*, May 1986, 62–72.

———. "From Citizens' Army to Social Laboratory." *Wilson Quarterly* 27 (1993): 83–94.

Moskos, Charles C., and John S. Butler. *All That We Can Be: Black Leadership and Racial Integration the Army Way*. New York: Basic Books, 1996.

Muller, Eric L. *Free to Die for Their Country: The Story of the Japanese American Draft Resisters in World War II*. Chicago: University of Chicago Press, 2001.

Nakano, Mei T. *Japanese American Women: Three Generations, 1840–1990*. Berkeley, Calif.: Mina Press Publishing, 1990.

National Archives. Washington, D.C., and College Park, Md.

Neverton-Morton, Cynthia. "Securing the 'Double V': African-American and Japanese-American Women in the Military during World War II." In *A Woman's War Too: U.S. Women in the Military in World War II*, ed. Paula Nassen Poulos, 327–354. Washington, D.C.: National Archives and Record Administration, 1996.

Nishimoto, Richard S. *Inside an American Concentration Camp: Japanese American Resistance at Poston Arizona*. Ed. Lane Ryo Hirabayashi. Tucson: University of Arizona Press, 1995.

Noel, Donald L. "A Theory of the Origin of Ethnic Stratification." *Social Problems* 16 (fall 1968): 157–172.

Ogawa, Dennis M. *From Japs to Japanese*. Berkeley, Calif.: McCutchan, 1971.

Okada, John. *No-No Boy*. Seattle: University of Washington Press, 1976.

Okihiro, Gary Y. *Margins and Mainstreams: Asians in American History and Culture*. Seattle: University of Washington Press, 1994.

Olson, Keith W. *The G.I. Bill, the Veterans, and the Colleges*. Lexington: University Press of Kentucky, 1974.

Omi, Michael, and Howard Winant. *Racial Formation in the United States: From the 1960s to the 1990s*. New York: Routledge, 1994.

———. *Racial Formation in the United States: From the 1960s to the 1980s*. New York: Routledge, 1986.

Perea, Juan. "The Black/White Binary Paradigm of Race: The Normal Science of American Racial Thought." *California Law Review* 85 (1997): 1213.

Pozzetta, George E. "My Children Are My Jewels: Italian-American Generations during World War II." In *The Home-Front War: World War II and American Society*, ed. Kenneth Paul O'Brien and Lynn Hudson Parsons. Westport, Conn.: Greenwood Press, 1995.

Putney, Martha. *When the Nation Was in Need: Blacks in the Women's Army Corps during World War II*. Metuchen, N.J.: Scarecrow Press, 1992.

Sarnecky, Mary T. *A History of the U.S. Army Nurse Corps*. Philadelphia: University of Pennsylvania Press, 1999.

———. "Women, Medicine, and War." In *A Woman's War Too: U.S. Women in the Military in World War II*, ed. Paula Nassen Poulos. Washington, D.C.: National Archives and Records Administration, 1996.

Segal, David R. *Recruiting for Uncle Sam: Citizenship and Military Manpower Policy*. Lawrence: University Press of Kansas, 1989.

Segal, Mady Wechsler. "Women's Military Roles Cross-Nationally: Past, Present, and Future." *Gender and Society* 9 (1995): 757.

Shibutani, Tomotsu. *The Derelicts of Company K: A Sociological Study of Demoralization*. Berkeley and Los Angeles: University of California Press, 1978.

Spicer, Edward H., Aseal T. Hansen, Katherine Luomala, and Marvin K. Opler. *Impounded People*. Tucson: University of Arizona Press, 1969.

Strong, Edward K. *The Second-Generation Japanese Problem*. Stanford, Calif.: Stanford University Press, 1934.

Takaki, Ronald. *Iron Cages: Race and Culture in Nineteenth-Century America*. New York: Oxford University Press, 1990.

Tamura, Eileen H. *Americanization, Acculturation, and Ethnic Identity: The Nisei Generation in Hawaii*. Urbana and Chicago: University of Illinois Press, 1994.

Tamura, Linda. *The Hood River Issei: An Oral History of Japanese Settlers in Oregon's Hood River Valley*. Urbana and Chicago: University of Illinois Press, 1993.

tenBroek, Jacobus, Edward N. Barnhart, and Floyd W. Matson. *Prejudice, War, and the Constitution*. Berkeley and Los Angeles: University of California Press, 1954.

Thomas, Dorothy S., Charles Kikuchi, and James Sakoda. *The Salvage: Japanese American Evacuation and Resettlement*. Berkeley and Los Angeles: University of California Press, 1952.

Thomas, Dorothy S., and Richard S. Nishimoto. *The Spoilage: Japanese-American Evacuation and Resettlement during World War II*. Berkeley and Los Angeles: University of California Press, 1969.

Tinker, John N. "Intermarriage and Ethnic Boundaries: The Japanese American Case." *Journal of Social Issues* 29 (1973): 49–66.

Tomblin, Barbara B. *G.I. Nightingales: The Army Nurse Corps in World War II*. Lexington: University of Kentucky Press, 1996.

Treadwell, Mattie. *United States Army in World War II: Special Studies: The Women's Army Corps*. Washington, D.C.: U.S. Government Printing Office, 1954.

United Nations Relief and Rehabilitation Administration. *UNRRA: Organization Aims Progress*. Washington, D.C.: Government Printing Office, 1945.

United States Commission on Wartime Relocation and Internment of Civilians. *Personal Justice Denied*. Washington, D.C.: [Congressional] Committee on Interior and Insular Affairs, 1992.

United States Defense Equal Opportunity Management Institute. *Asian and Pacific Islander–American Heritage Month, 2000*. Patrick Air Force Base, Fla.: Defense Equal Opportunity Management Institute, 2000.

United States Department of Commerce. Bureau of the Census. *Statistical Abstract of the United States 1949*. Washington, D.C.: U.S. Government Printing Office, 1949.

United States Department of the Interior. *The Relocation Program*. New York: AMS Press, 1975.

United States War Agency Liquidation Unit. *People in Motion: The Postwar Adjustment of Evacuated Japanese Americans*. Washington, D.C.: U.S. Government Printing Office, 1947.

United States War Relocation Authority. Department of the Interior. *The Evacuated People: A Quantitative Description*. Washington, D.C.: U.S. Government Printing Office, 1946.

———. *Japanese Americans Educated in Japan*. Community Analysis Section Report, No. 8. Washington, D.C.: Government Printing Office, 1944.

University of Hawaii. Romanzo Adams Social Research Laboratory. [Confidential files.]

Uyeda, Clifford, and Barry Saiki, eds. *The Pacific War and Peace: Americans of Japanese Ancestry in Military Intelligence, 1941 to 1952*. San Francisco: National Japanese Historical Society, 1991.

Wagley, Charles, and Marvin Harris. *Minorities in the New World*. New York: Columbia University Press, 1958.

Wilson, Robert A., and Bill Hosokawa. *East to America: A History of the Japanese in the United States*. New York: William Morrow and Co., 1980.

Wu, Frank. "Neither Black nor White: Asian Americans and Affirmative Action." *Boston College Third World Law Journal* 15 (summer 1995): 225–284.

Yung, Judy. *Chinese Women of America: A Pictorial History.* Seattle: University of Washington Press, 1986.

———. *Unbound Voices: A Documentary History of Chinese Women in San Francisco.* Berkeley and Los Angeles: University of California Press, 1999.

Index

acculturation, 48, 70. *See also* assimilation
Africa, 5, 140
African Americans, 3, 38, 77, 86; civilian, 114–115; discrimination against, 5, 8, 62, 65, 84–85; and the military, 1–2, 4, 44, 78, 90, 94, 106, 107–108, 128, 140; segregation of, 4, 13, 21, 59, 94, 106, 107–108, 139
African American women, 32, 149; and the military, 12, 44, 94, 106, 107–108, 131–134, 139–140
aliens, enemy, 4–5, 63, 65, 69, 83
Ambrose, Stephen, 61–62
Ancheta, Angelo, 3
anti-African American sentiment, 84–85
anti-Asian sentiment, 38, 86, 171n18
anti-immigration movement, 6, 62, 171n18
anti-Japanese sentiment, 5–6, 62–68, 86, 153
Arakawa, Mary, 97–98
Arizona, 10, 72–73, 74, 84, 139
Arkansas, 73, 91
Army, U.S., 12, 15, 60, 74, 90, 98, 126, 144, 146, 157; Air Forces (AAF), 104–105, 133; Service Forces, 104, 141–142
Army Medical Corps, 13–14, 134–139
Army Nurse Corps (ANC), 3, 6, 11, 18, 19, 29–30, 78, 93, 139–144
arrests, 25, 133
Asakura, Mimi, 101

Asian Americans, 3, 63, 65–66, 133–134. *See also* Japanese Americans
assimilation, 59, 93, 162–164. *See also* acculturation
Australia, 118, 139–140

Barringer, Emily Dunning, 137
basic training, 102, 106–111, 142, 184n57
Beekman, Allan, 5
Bell, Richard, 51
Benedict, Ruth, 36
Biddle, Francis, 72
birth rates, 37–38
Blaisdell, Allen C., 20, 21
Blaisdell, Henry C., 90
Blaisdell, James, 102
Blanchfield, Florence A., 139, 140
Bolton, Frances Payne, 143
Bonacich, Edna, 57, 58, 62
Buddhism, Buddhists, 33, 39, 76, 91
Burrell, Prudence Burns, 139–140
Burton, Joyce, 93

California, 6, 9–10, 45, 48, 52, 67, 71, 81; economy of, 40, 84; evacuation from, 72–73; immigration to, 35, 37; jobs in, 152, 153; resettlement in, 85–86. *See also* Los Angeles; San Francisco
Campbell, D'Ann, 154
Camp Breckenridge, 131–132
Camp Hood, 115–116
Camp Ritchie, 117, 123

Caucasians. *See* whites
Celler, Emanuel, 132, 136, 137
Chan, Sucheng, 55
children, 35, 38, 64, 96, 129, 154, 155–156, 176n41; adult, 156, 157, 160–161; caring for, 43, 49–50, 149–150; labor of, 41, 42
Chin, Bertha, 124
China, 61–62, 65, 116–117, 145
Chinese Americans, 41, 44, 63, 155, 179n34; in the ANC, 140, 144; in the military, 65, 134, 186n46; in the WAC, 119, 122, 124, 133
Christianity, Christians, 34–35, 44, 47, 85, 125, 163
citizenship, 2, 3, 30, 65, 70, 82, 96, 98; denial of, 5, 69, 78, 179n34; dual, 38, 59, 81; renunciation of, 25, 80–81; rights of, 1, 20, 68, 79, 92, 141, 149, 159–160, 162, 165. *See also* Japanese American Citizenship League
civilians, 114–115, 118, 135, 148–150, 165
civil liberties, 2, 64
civil servants, 126–131, 151, 154, 155
class, 31, 36, 40, 41, 58, 75
Coggins, Cecil, 68
college education, 92, 99, 135, 148, 151–152, 156. *See also* education
Collins, Donald, 81–82, 83
Collins, Wayne M., 82
Commission on Wartime Relocation and Internment of Civilians, 10, 63, 77
community, 44, 63, 84; Japanese American, 22, 34, 43–44, 57, 59, 75–76
competition, 58, 83
Congress, U.S., 11, 12, 13–14, 79, 131, 136–138, 139, 160
court cases, 38, 81–82, 84, 126, 132, 160, 179n34
Craighill, Margaret, 138
culture, 162; Euro-American, 48, 49, 59, 70, 82, 93; Japanese, 40–41, 45, 47–51, 59, 82, 93, 117, 119, 123, 163–

164; norms of, 30, 39, 43, 162. *See also* values

Daniels, Roger, 5–6, 10, 51, 55–56, 58, 62, 82, 171n18
Deane, Margaret E., 92
democracy, 1, 2, 22, 27, 88, 93, 96–97, 125, 165
Denson Tribune, 25, 26
DeWitt, John L., 7–8, 9, 72
discrimination, 6, 59, 67, 84, 153, 171n18; citizenship, 1–2, 5, 69; employment, 29, 54–55, 57, 62, 66, 115–116, 122, 131–132; against Issei, 7, 8, 62–65, 69, 75–76; racial and ethnic, 17, 27, 31, 38, 44, 45, 70, 93, 139, 162; sex, 13, 36, 38, 122, 135–137, 139, 147, 174n64; wage, 68, 75, 136, 139, 150. *See also* African Americans: discrimination against; prejudice; racism; segregation; stereotypes
disloyalty, 79–81, 84
doctors, 13–14, 28, 52, 135–139, 145, 147
Dugway Proving Ground, 113–114

East Coast, 9, 124
economics, 6, 31, 50, 62, 66–67, 77, 150–151, 159, 164–165; in California, 40, 84, 152, 153
education, 45, 50–55, 101; higher, 2, 29, 34, 36, 42, 46, 52–53, 151–152, 163, 165. *See also* college education; GI Bill; schools; students
Elder, Glen Jr., 149, 165
elite, the, 33, 40, 41
Emmons, Delos, 76–77
employment, 14–15, 56–58, 82, 85, 86; discrimination in, 29, 54–55, 57, 62, 66, 115–116, 122, 131–132. *See also* jobs; labor; workers
Enloe, Cynthia, 148
Etow, Toshiko Nancy, 98–99
Europe, 33, 145, 146
European Americans, 49, 58, 69, 71, 75, 132. *See also* culture: Euro-American

evacuation, 9–10, 25, 58, 64, 72–75, 79, 86–87, 118, 171n26; results of, 49, 75, 150, 160. *See also* internment; internment camps

evacuees, 15, 118, 160; resettlement of, 14–15, 16, 80, 83–87, 130; in the WAC, 95, 96, 98

Falck, Lilliebell, 15, 89–90

family, 39–51, 79, 91, 95, 100–101, 154–158; businesses, 37, 40–41, 42, 56–58, 62–63, 86, 150; collective labor of, 41–43, 46, 150; and culture, 40–41, 45, 47, 50; extended, 49–50, 125, 129–130, 158; grandparents, 39, 49, 50; parents, 23–24, 32–38, 83, 92, 130–131, 159, 163; patriarchy of, 39, 48–49, 176nn41–42; siblings, 43, 54, 158. *See also* children; Sansei

farming, 33, 35, 41, 46, 47, 55–58, 62, 82, 150

FBI (Federal Bureau of Investigation), 8, 10, 19, 76, 173n47

fear, 5, 6, 22, 61, 67, 160

Filipino Americans, 63, 65, 133–134

Finch, Florence (Ebersole) Smith, 133–134

Floore, Frances Berkeley, 145–146

Fort Des Moines, 107–108, 112, 115, 117, 131, 136

Fort Oglethorpe, 102, 103, 104, 109–110

Frederick, E. D., 104

friends, 77, 95, 114, 122, 161, 162, 163

Fuchida, Ellen, 7, 29; family of, 28, 36–37, 47–48, 57–58, 68–69, 157, 160–161; in Japan, 127, 128, 129, 130; and the military, 24, 28, 107, 113–114, 123, 155, 161–162

Fujii, Ruth, 21, 67–68, 76, 77, 152; family of, 26–27, 38, 42–43, 48–49, 158; in the WAC, 108, 115–116, 132, 161

Fukagawa, May, 101

Fukuoka, Private, 95

Fumi, Neba, 97

Furutani, Brownie, 100

Furutani, Yaye, 99, 100

gender inequality, 30, 31, 36, 39, 123, 125, 157

gender relations, 148, 149, 165

German Americans, 63–64, 69, 88

German nationals, 63–64, 65, 87

Germany, 61, 63, 86, 117

Geurrero, Josefina V., 134

GI Bill, 2, 151–152, 153, 161

Gila River Relocation Center, 95, 97, 98, 101

Gimbel, Cynthia, 149, 165

Glenn, Evelyn Nakano, 40, 49

Gordon, Milton, 162–163

Gorman, Kathy, 125

Granada (Amache) Relocation Center, 73, 95, 99

Great Britain, 7, 33, 137, 140

Gunderson, Evelina, 110

Haggerty, Timothy, 148–149

Harada, Grace, 7, 23, 29, 47, 66, 150, 157; in Japan, 126, 127, 128–130, 155, 156; in the WAC, 108, 114, 121, 125, 155, 162

Harris, Marvin, 67

Hauck, C. J., 136

Hawaii, 5, 26–28, 29, 38, 48, 155, 158, 159; education in, 53–54; Honolulu, 36, 43, 67, 148, 152; immigration to, 32, 35; politics in, 59, 67–68, 76–77, 84; work in, 41–43, 56. *See also* Pearl Harbor, attack on

Hawaii, military personnel from, 90, 119, 123, 143, 152; in Japan, 124, 125, 127; in the WAC, 101–104, 107, 108–110, 115, 117

health, public, 138–139, 143, 145, 146, 153

health care, 44, 45–46, 47, 50, 92, 138. *See also* Army Medical Corps; Army Nurse Corps; doctors; hospitals; nurses

Heart Mountain Relocation Center, 73, 74, 93, 97

Higashi, Lillian, 111

Hildring, John H., 12
Hill, Manice M., 17, 91
Hirabayashi, Gordon, 160
Hirabayashi, Lane Ryo, 54, 74, 75–76
Hirakowa, Harriett, 124
Hirata, Toshito, 143
Hirose, Stacey, 2, 132–133
Hobby, Oveta Culp, 12, 13, 17–18, 20, 89, 90, 93–94, 131
Holian, Timothy, 63, 65
Honey, Maureen, 149
Hong Kong, 6–7
Honolulu Advertiser, 101, 109, 111, 125
Honolulu Star Bulletin, 103, 154–155
Horak, Henrietta, 22, 30, 91–92
hospitals, 44, 53, 112, 136, 138, 139–140, 141, 142, 143, 144
Hotta, Yoshio, 118
Houchi, Mitsue, 112
housing, 43–44, 45–46, 47, 56, 62, 69, 84–85, 86, 116–117
Hughes, Joseph D., 94
Hunt (Minidoka) Relocation Center, 73, 93, 97, 100
Hurt, Haruko Sugi, 62

Ichioka, Yuji, 34
Idaho, 7, 47, 73, 93
identity, 5, 49, 51, 63, 69, 128, 162–163, 164
immigrants, 1, 7, 32–38, 51, 69, 72, 125
integration, 48, 67, 163; in the military, 18–21, 65, 90, 93–94, 96, 108, 132–133, 139, 144. *See also* segregation
internment, 9, 49, 64, 72, 87
internment camps, 9, 73–80, 83, 86–87, 100; leaving, 14, 82; and military service, 17, 21, 89–93, 118, 119; violence in, 22, 30. *See also names of individual camps*
interpreters, 17, 44, 117, 119
Iritani, Frances, 95, 98
Irvine, W. W., 103
Iseri, Kathleen, 97
Isonaga, Chito, 123, 124
Issei, 50, 159, 163, 172–173n46; in camps, 83, 87, 91; discrimination

against, 7, 8, 62–65, 69, 75, 76; in Japan, 81–82; and loyalty, 16, 77–79; and opposition to serving, 22–24, 79, 92; women, 32–37, 39–41, 125
Issei, The (Ichioka), 34
Italian Americans, 63, 65, 69, 87, 88
Italy, 61, 98, 146
Ito, Leslie, 87
Ivie, Rachel, 149, 165
Izumi, Tamako Irene, 105

Janowitz, Morris, 1, 156
Japan, 36, 80–82, 119, 127, 164; government of, 32, 61–62, 67, 76, 133; Wacs in, 124–131, 155, 185n32. *See also* Tokyo
Japanese American Citizenship League (JACL), 15, 23, 47, 70, 71, 80, 83, 96
Japanese Americans, 4, 89–90, 123, 144, 154; expatriation and repatriation of, 79, 81, 92, 146; registration of, 16, 65, 77–79, 172–173n46. *See also* aliens, enemy; community: Japanese American; culture: Japanese; evacuation; family; internment; internment camps; Issei; Kibei; newspapers: Japanese American; Nisei; Nisei women; Sansei; Wacs/Waacs, Japanese American
Jerome Relocation Center, 91, 100
jobs, 7, 93, 104–105, 149–150, 152, 153, 184n58, 188n10. *See also* employment; labor; occupations; workers
Johnson, Emily B., 104
Judaism, Jews, 45, 86, 146–147, 158, 163

Kaneshiro, Florence Toshiko, 119
Kato, Florence Y., 95
Kato, Sue Ogata, 43, 132
Kibei (Kebei), 22, 49–51, 82, 92, 117, 123, 126
Kido, Matsuko, 124
Kim, Anna, 104

Kitagawa, Daisuke, 87
Kitano, Harry, 36, 39, 51, 75
Knudsen, Rhoda, 124, 185n30
Kodama, Edith, 124
Koloa, Chito, 125
Kono, Alice, 26, 27, 42, 109–110, 117, 123, 148, 152, 161
Konoye, Fumimaro, 61
Korean Americans, 63, 66, 134
Kurihara, Joseph Yoshisuke, 80
Kusanoki, Takako Taxie, 99
Kushida, Shige, 34
Kutaka, Fujiko (Grace), 27, 41, 101, 109, 111, 115, 155, 162

labor, 6, 52, 56, 62, 68, 75, 102, 131, 188n10; collective, 41–43, 46, 48, 54, 57–58, 150; domestic, 2, 9, 27, 29, 40–41, 43, 47, 55, 85, 131, 150; skilled, 150–151; unpaid, 40–41, 150, 157; unskilled, 33, 41; and the War Department, 11, 15, 20, 112, 118, 137. *See also* employment; jobs; occupations; workers
Lahey, Frank Howard, 137–138
language, 69, 92, 107, 128, 133, 145; English, 50, 87, 116, 126, 163, 164; Japanese, 66, 100, 112, 126–127, 129, 164, 181n2, 185n21. *See also* interpreters; linguists; Military Intelligence Service Language School; schools: Japanese-language; translators
lawsuits. *See* court cases
Lee, Ulysses, 131
Lehr, Doreen Drewry, 157
Lind, Andrew, 41, 42, 76
linguists, 16–17, 21, 82, 89, 117, 118, 120
Littleton, Louise, 40
Los Angeles, 6, 9, 43–44, 45–46, 52, 54, 56, 70, 74, 154
Lovejoy, Esther, 138
loyalty: of Japanese Americans, 16, 22, 68–71, 77–80, 134, 140; of Nisei Wacs, 30, 89, 93–94, 96–97, 101, 104; questionnaires about, 14, 15, 30, 76, 89

Luebke, Frederick, 64

MacArthur, Douglas, 106, 126
Mahler, Bobbie, 103
Manzanar Relocation Center, 90, 92, 95, 100, 143
Marcantonio, Vito, 132
marriage, 40, 91, 92, 154–158, 162–164, 165; arranged, 36–37, 39, 87, 163
married couples, 121, 125, 129, 130, 151
Marshall, George C., 11–12, 13
Marshall, T. H., 159
Matson, Floyd, 6–7
Matsumoto, Valerie, 87
Matsusaki, Kumi, 99, 112, 113
Maykovich, Minako, 39
media, 22, 62, 83; African American, 21, 131; Japanese American, 22, 70, 96. *See also* newspapers
men: African American, 4, 90, 140; Japanese American, 4, 16, 89, 90, 123; Korean American, 66; in the military, 94, 104, 128, 130, 149; minority, 159, 170n5; in the MISLS, 117–118, 121, 122–123. *See also* family; officers: male
men, Nisei, 25, 26, 75, 81, 90, 172–173n46; in the military, 3, 15–17, 94, 105, 110
Mexican Americans, 32, 44, 45, 65
military, U.S., 66; and African Americans, 1–2, 4, 44, 78, 90, 94, 106, 107–108, 128, 140; and African American women, 12, 44, 94, 106, 107–108, 131–134, 139–140; and benefits, 2, 11, 21, 29, 96, 137; discharge from, 4–5, 124, 126, 132; and the draft, 4, 15, 16, 24, 79, 91, 94, 98; effects of service in, 149–158; and integration, 18–21, 65, 90, 93–94, 96, 108, 132–133, 139, 144; intelligence service, 112, 120, 123, 133, 155, 156; and internment camps, 17, 21, 89–93, 118, 119; and men, 94, 104, 128, 130, 149; and military camps, 4, 137; morale in, 122, 124, 131, 132, 162; and Nisei

military (*continued*)
men, 3, 15–17, 94, 105, 110; Nisei women in, 6, 10, 14, 16–17, 19, 38; opposition to service in, 79, 92; promotions in, 114, 120, 143, 148, 155; rank in, 11, 12, 137, 138, 147, 174n64; recruitment for, 1, 16–17, 19, 51, 55, 78, 88, 90–94, 139, 148; segregation in, 4, 13, 17, 20, 21, 106, 107–108, 128, 131–134, 139; whites in, 4, 10, 17, 94, 103, 110, 115, 144. *See also* Army, U.S.; Army Medical Corps; Army Nurse Corps; GI Bill; Hawaii, military personnel from; Navy, U.S.; WAAC; WAC; Wacs/Waacs; *names of individual camps and forts*
Military Intelligence Service Language School (MISLS), 4, 27, 51, 92, 108, 113, 114, 117–124, 185n21
Miller, Emily, 91
Minata, Michkey (Marie), 124, 125
Mitchell, Noel Campbell, 44
Miyashiro, Atsumi, 102
Miyoko, Alice, 97
Mizusawa, Tsuruko, 99
Modell, John, 57, 58, 148–149
morality, 28, 34, 49
Morden, Bettie, 12, 13
Moriguchi, Diane, 95
Morimitsu, George, 163, 164
Moriuchi, Atsuko, 124
Moriya, Masako, 95
Mott-Smith, Lillian, 103–104, 109
Mukai, Michiyo, 25, 95
Murakami, Toyome, 95–96

Nakagawara, Cherry, 105
Nakamura, Mary, 124
Nakanishi, Toyome, 124
Nakasato, Dorothy, 111
nationalism, 69, 76
National Japanese American Historical Society, 144, 154
Native Americans, 65, 133
Navy, U.S., 10, 11, 76, 126, 136, 137, 138, 140

Nazis, 10, 63
Nestor, Marion, 122–123
newspapers, 17, 40, 68, 85, 104, 124–125, 132; internment camp, 25, 26, 99; Japanese American, 7, 35, 70, 91, 97, 98–99, 100, 163. *See also* *Honolulu Advertiser; Honolulu Star Bulletin; Pacific Citizen; Rafu Shimpo*
New York City, 14, 53, 71, 84
Nisei (Nikkei), 5, 16; in Japan, 81–82, 124
Nisei women, 18, 78, 172–173n46; exclusion of, 139–141; interviews with, 92–93, 97, 109; in the military, 2–3, 6, 10, 14, 16–17, 19, 25, 38, 115–116; surveys of, 91–93. *See also* Army Nurse Corps; WAAC; WAC; Wacs/Waacs
Nishiguchi, Kay Keiko, 95
Nishikaichi, Irene, 6, 14–15, 43–44, 82, 151–152, 153–154; family of, 23, 47, 53, 83, 159; internment of, 9–10, 74, 75; in Japan, 128, 129, 130; at the MISLS, 27, 119–120, 124; in the WAC, 94–95, 108, 124–126, 161
Nishimoto, Richard S., 23, 54–55, 57, 80, 83, 87
Nishimura, Bette, 95
Noguchi, Kisa, 99
Nouichi, Misue, 155
nurses, 2, 14, 28, 100, 135, 136, 139–140, 145, 147, 153. *See also* Army Nurse Corps

occupations, 18, 42, 55–59, 89, 97–100, 111, 151–154. *See also* civil servants; doctors; farming; nurses; shops; teachers
Oda, Elaine, 102
officers, 22, 89, 102, 107, 135, 154; female, 29–30, 126, 134, 136, 138, 141; male, 4, 7–8, 10, 17, 21, 69, 72, 76, 117, 127; WAAC, 91–94, 118; WAC, 103, 108–109
Ogata, Sue, 95
Ogawa, Chidori, 105
Ogura, Kay Keiko, 112

Okada, Amy, 99, 100
Onyett, Helen Pon, 140
Oregon, 10, 34, 36, 72–73, 84

Pacific Citizen (newspaper), 22, 25–26, 83–84, 85, 96, 99, 105
patriotism, 27–28, 69–71, 78–79, 87, 99, 111, 163
pay, 59, 93; discrimination in, 68, 75, 136, 139, 150; higher, 14, 21, 87, 149, 151–152; lower, 13, 15, 57, 150
Pearl Harbor, attack on, 4, 6, 7, 28, 51, 59, 67–68, 87, 98
Peattle, Donald Culcross, 71
Petty, Mary L., 140
Philippines, the, 106, 116, 133
plantations, 35, 41, 42, 43
politics, politicians, 6, 8, 35, 60, 62, 131, 133, 139, 150, 159–160, 164–165
Poston (Colorado River) Relocation Center, 73, 74, 75, 82, 83, 95, 98–99, 100, 105
poverty, 33, 41, 42, 83, 129
Powell, Adam Clayton, 78, 132
Pozzetta, George, 65, 69
prejudice, 83, 151, 160. *See also* discrimination; racism; stereotypes
Pulley, Marie Harlow, 84–85

quotas, 18–19, 29, 113

race, 5, 69, 75–76, 92, 149, 150, 158, 164, 165, 173n59
racism, 7–8, 44, 54, 58, 62, 65–66, 68, 131–132, 134, 151; verbal, 107, 128; and violence, 8, 83, 133. *See also* discrimination; prejudice; segregation
Rafu Shimpo (newspaper), 62, 69, 70, 72
Rasmussen, Kai, 92, 118, 120
Red Cross, 66, 128, 130, 141–142, 155, 156
refugees, 135, 144–145, 146–147
resistance movement, 133–134
Ringle, Kenneth D., 10
Rogers, Edith Nourse, 12, 13

Rohwer Relocation Center, 73, 91
Roosevelt, Franklin D., 9, 10, 12, 13, 61, 90, 95, 143
Rosenthal, Miwako, 9, 122, 160, 163–164; and education, 45, 52, 151; family of, 33, 35–36, 50, 157; in the WAC, 24, 106–107, 108, 114–115

Sadahiro, Miyoko, 112
Saiki, Barry, 4, 118
Sailor, Vance L., 103
San Francisco, 32, 34, 35, 37, 44, 58, 72, 93, 152
Sansei, 10, 163–164
Sarnecky, Mary, 29–30, 142
Sasuga, Aiko Nelly, 99
schools, 96, 112, 124, 143, 152; Japanese-language, 35, 44, 47, 48, 49, 76, 123. *See also* education
Segawa, Funiko (Florence), 123, 124, 125
segregation, 30, 76, 100; of African Americans, 4, 13, 21, 59, 94, 106, 107–108, 139; in housing, 43–44, 84–85; in the military, 4, 13, 17, 20, 21, 106, 107–108, 128, 131–134, 139; opposition to, 21, 91, 93. *See also* integration
sexuality, 19, 34, 174n64
Shibutani, Tomotsu, 25
Shinagawa, Chizuko (Shizuko), 88, 96–97, 124
Shinagawa, Shizue Sue, 105
Shiozawa, Cherry, 48, 73–74, 98, 152, 154
shops, 42, 45–46, 63, 150
social change, 149, 150, 160
social events, 110, 121, 122, 130, 155
Sparkman, John J., 136
status, 31, 46, 150, 153, 165; social, 40, 46, 133, 165
Steele, Margaret, 103
stereotypes, 6, 11, 62, 68, 102, 151, 165
Stimson, Barbara, 137
Stimson, Henry L., 9, 15, 20, 89–90
students, 32–33, 82, 85, 89, 97, 143. *See also* education; schools

Sugi, Haruko, 99, 100

Tagami, Ken, 4–5
Tajiri, Larry, 83–84, 85
Takano, Anna, 98
Takeuchi, Ryoichi Yamaguchi, 81
Taliaferro, Nymphia (Yok), 133
Tamashiro, Mildred, 154
Tamura, Eileen, 36, 41, 54, 84
Tamura, Linda, 34, 36, 39–40
Tanaka, Julie, 100
Tanaka, Katherine (Kathryn), 98, 112
Tanaka, Ruth, 143
Tanigaki, Irene, 95
Tarvin, Harry, 21–22
teachers, 113, 118, 120–121, 123, 124,
    137, 143, 152, 153
tenBroek, Jacobus, 6–7
Terauchi, Robert, 110
Thomas, Dorothy Swaine, 23, 37, 55–
    56, 80, 83, 87
Thompson, O. N., 102
Togasaki, Yae, 143
Togasaki, Yoshiye, 9, 44, 50, 51–52, 54,
    153; family of, 32–33, 34, 37, 44, 50,
    52; and the military, 28, 144–145,
    146–147
Tokeuchi, Nasumi, 81
Tokuyama, Peggy, 100
Tokyo, 34, 37, 50, 125, 126, 128–129,
    130, 155, 157
Topaz Relocation Center, 73, 74, 78, 93
translators, 5, 27, 113, 117, 119, 123–
    124, 126–127, 133
Treadwell, Mattie, 19, 105, 113, 133
Tsuchiyama, Tamie, 99
Tsuneishi, Warren, 70
Tule Lake Relocation Center, 22, 73,
    79, 83, 92

Uemura, Margaret, 99–100
Uni, Kenneth, 90
United Nations, 144–146
United States: government departments
    and agencies of, 65, 66, 72, 74, 77,
    85; and relations with Japan, 35, 60–
    61, 70, 175n24, 178n6; security of, 8,

10, 17, 72, 155, 160; Surgeon
    General of, 17–18, 94, 138, 139,
    140–141, 157. *See also* Congress,
    U.S.; FBI; military, U.S.; War
    Department, U.S.
upward mobility, 1, 152, 160
USOs (United Service Organizations),
    104, 183n53
Utah, 7, 24, 28, 47, 73, 78, 113
Uyeda, Clifford, 4, 118
Uyesaki, Mary Ryuko, 96

values, 39, 48, 49, 162
violence, 8, 22, 30, 34, 83, 133
Voss, Ernest E., 70

WAAC (Women's Army Auxiliary
    Corps), 12, 22, 24, 88, 135–136;
    recruitment for, 16–17, 78, 90–94,
    118, 182n8; segregation in, 13, 20,
    94
WAC (Women's Army Corps), 11, 21,
    23, 29, 108, 115, 132, 159; creation
    of, 14, 182n14; desire to join, 24,
    27–28; induction into, 25–26, 88,
    90, 94–103, 105, 109; integration in,
    18–19; in Japan, 124–131, 155,
    185n32; and loyalty, 30, 89, 93–94,
    96–97, 101, 104; recruitment for,
    88–91, 96, 102–103, 105; surveys for,
    91–93
Wacs/Waacs: African American, 12, 90,
    131–133; basic training of, 102, 106–
    111, 142, 184n57; Chinese
    American, 119, 122, 124, 133;
    evacuees, 95, 96, 98; at the MISLS,
    118–124; white, 103, 108–109, 133,
    134
Wacs/Waacs, Japanese American, 24,
    94–95, 106–107, 108–111, 114–117,
    121, 124–126, 155, 159, 161–162;
    Hawaiian, 27–28, 101–104, 107,
    108–111, 115–117, 132, 159, 161
Wagley, Charles, 67
War Department, U.S., 4, 13, 62, 117,
    136; and the ANC, 140–141; and
    evacuation, 72–73; and integration,

20–21; and labor, 11, 15, 20, 112,
118, 137; and loyalty, 79, 81, 93; and
racism, 131, 134; and recruitment,
17, 78, 87, 89–91, 96, 102–103, 139;
and registration, 16, 78–79
War Relocation Authority (WRA), 25,
50, 83, 97, 100; and internment, 9,
72–73, 74–75, 80; and loyalty, 16,
77–79; and resettlement, 14–15, 84
Washington State, 10, 72, 73, 84
Watanabe, Iris, 21–22, 25–26, 95
West Coast, 8, 9, 35, 38, 55–57, 72, 77,
83–84, 86, 94
whites, 37–38, 40, 71, 91, 128, 149,
150, 156; discrimination by, 8, 59,
62–63, 68–69, 84; dominance of, 3,
5, 41–42, 56, 58, 163–164; in the
military, 4, 10, 17, 94, 103, 110, 115,
126, 144; in the MISLS, 117–118,
119, 121, 122, 185n21;
neighborhoods of, 45, 47, 69, 84, 85;
and Nisei children, 42–43; in the
WAC, 103, 108–109, 133, 134
women, 42, 46, 66, 150, 159, 188n10;
Chinese American, 119, 122, 133,
134, 140, 144, 186n46; of color, 133,
150, 159; housewives, 39, 149, 154,
155–157, 160; during internment,
75, 78, 87, 118; Issei, 32–37, 39–41,
125; married, 91, 96, 121, 125, 129,
130, 149, 151, 154–158; Nisei, 2–3,
18, 25, 78, 172–173n46; pregnant,

37, 92, 156; roles of, 148, 149; single,
34, 91, 96; violence against, 22, 34;
white, 10, 17, 40, 94, 103, 122, 126,
149, 150. *See also* African American
women; discrimination: sex; family;
marriage; officers: female
Woodrum, Eric, 163
workers, 57, 59, 178n90, 188n10;
agricultural, 35, 41, 55, 58, 82;
clerical, 111, 112–113, 114, 115,
118, 124, 126, 127; domestic, 2, 9,
33, 43, 52, 55, 131; medical, 44, 53,
112, 153; menial, 131–132;
secretarial, 106, 108, 115, 124, 148,
151–152, 161. *See also* employment;
jobs; labor; occupations
World War I, 2, 11, 64, 69, 78, 139
Wyoming, 73, 93, 97

Yagami, Michic, 101
Yagi, Shizuo, 98
Yajiima, Kaji, 34
Yamada, Mary, 6, 28, 45–46, 52–53, 74,
140–144, 153, 164
Yamagiwa, Mary, 98
Yamashita, Hisako, 67, 76, 152; family
of, 26, 41, 46, 53, 80–81; at the
MISLS, 123–124; and the WAC,
27–28, 110–111, 117, 159
Yanamoto, Miwako, 62, 100–101, 124
Yang, Margaret K. C., 104
Yasuda, Priscilla, 95

About the Author

Brenda L. Moore is an associate professor of sociology at the State University of New York at Buffalo. She specializes in race and ethnic relations and in military sociology. She is the author of *To Serve My Country, To Serve My Race: The Story of the Only African American WACs Stationed Overseas during World War II*. She has published a number of scholarly articles in refereed journals, chapters in anthologies, and conference papers on the subject of minorities and women in the military.

She served six years on active duty, 1973–1979, and was a presidential appointee to the American Battle Monuments Commission during the Clinton administration. In 1995 she served as a subject expert with the Women in International Securities delegation at the World's Women's Conference in Beijing.

CPSIA information can be obtained
at www.ICGtesting.com
Printed in the USA
LVHW042044280219
609109LV00001B/12